THE WHITE ARMY

THE WHITE ARMY

BY

GENERAL A. DENIKINE

Translated from the Russian
by
CATHERINE ZVEGINTZOV

ACADEMIC INTERNATIONAL PRESS

1973

THE RUSSIAN SERIES / Volume 45

Anton I. Denikin *THE WHITE ARMY*

Reimpression of the London edition of 1930

Library of Congress Catalog Card Number: 72-97041
ISBN 0-87569-052-1
A Catalog Card follows the Epilogue

Printed in the United States of America

ACADEMIC INTERNATIONAL PRESS
Box 555   Gulf Breeze, Florida   32561

CONTENTS

THE WHITE ARMY

PART III

THE ENTENTE INTERVENTION. THE WHITE ARMIES ADVANCE ON MOSCOW

THE WHITE ARMY

PART IV

THE COLLAPSE OF THE WHITE ARMIES

LIST OF MAPS

AUTHOR'S FOREWORD

THIS book represents a short summary of my work on the Russian Revolution, published in Russian in five volumes.

Russia was swept by a tempest of unprecedented violence, which brought in its wake, and is still producing, terrible destruction. In the years of 1917–20 the *White Movement* arose as an elemental reaction against the Bolshevist enslavement. That movement grew and spread, embracing fresh territories and involving wider sections of the population. It rose and fell; more than once it brought Soviet rule to the brink of destruction, and finally itself collapsed. But it did not perish; the struggle still goes on, even after the collapse of all the 'White' fronts: actively and passively, openly and secretly it is still carried on by the Russian people languishing in their native land and in emigration.

The history of the White Movement and the struggle of the White Armies, though abounding in heroism and self-sacrifice, offers many instances of wrongdoing and mistakes on the part of the people, the army and its leaders. It also discloses a striking lack of political insight on the part of many statesmen of those countries which were drawn into the Russian vortex, either as our allies or adversaries.

For Russians all this belongs to the past, is a page of history that has been turned over. But to foreigners the 'Russian experiment' may serve as a warning. For the end of the Great War has brought no real peace to the world, rather an increase of bitter hatred. Neither has it brought social peace, having debased moral standards and deepened class and individual egotism.

There is much inflammable matter accumulated throughout the world, and incendiaries are on the alert. All the more so because, whereas criminal law punishes incendiarism by imprisonment, international law promises recognition and credits.

THE WHITE ARMY

PART ONE

CHAPTER 1

General Kornilov's Move – The Bolshevist Revolution

By the autumn of 1917 the disintegration of Russia's national life, particularly in the sphere of defence of the country, had reached its climax. The army was in process of complete disruption; industry declined in alarming proportions; a general railway strike seemed impending; whole provinces severed their connection with the centre of government and the Russian state was being transformed into a number of autonomous territories; social warfare was spreading everywhere and assuming a more and more grotesque and cruel shape. And against the background of all this turmoil there stood out a fresh disaster – the renewed and open preparations for a Bolshevist revolution.

The country was faced with two alternatives: either to surrender without struggle and within a very short time to Bolshevist rule or to raise some force capable and willing to put up a determined fight against Bolshevism. Herein lies the meaning of *Kornilov's move*. It was the natural and inevitable reaction of a national organism fighting for its life.[1]

The Commander-in-Chief, General Kornilov, despairing of the likelihood of moving the Provisional Government to definite action against the Bolsheviks, himself rose against the Government and the Bolshevist Soviet of Workers' and Soldiers' Delegates. Kornilov failed. The

---

[1] The first period of the Russian Revolution forms the contents of my book (in English), *The Russian Turmoil*.

causes of his failure were multiple: the determined opposition he met from a section of the Government, together with the Bolshevist Soviets and the Socialist parties; the absolutely opportunist attitude of the Liberal Democracy; the hurried, and therefore inadequate preparation of his own advance; various mistakes on the part of General Kornilov's political entourage; the unreliable state of the troops, who might be induced to fight the Bolsheviks but did not wish to go against the Government; and so on.

Kornilov's rising gave a fresh impetus to excesses and bloodshed against the unfortunate officers; these, however, were but paroxysms in the course of the general deadly disease. Generals Kornilov, Denikine,[1] Lukomsky,[2] Romanovsky,[3] Markov,[4] and others were flung into prison at Bykhov. The Government made wholesale changes in the commanding staff and dismissed another batch of ten thousand officers, thereby completely disabling the army.

The state of the Russian Army in the autumn of 1917 is best described by an officer newly arrived from the front, at a meeting of the Petrograd Soviet:

'The soldiers at present care neither for land nor liberty. All they want is to end the war. You here may say what you like, but the soldiers will not fight any more.'

The army was moving to its appointed end.

I nevertheless feel it my duty to draw my foreign readers' attention to the following most important fact: even at this, the last stage of its existence, and in spite of its disruption and collapse of discipline, the Russian Army continued to render invaluable service to the Allies. The

---

[1] Commander-in-Chief of the south-western front.
[2] Chief of the G.H.Q. Staff.
[3] Quartermaster-General, G.H.Q.
[4] Chief of the G.H.Q. Staff of the south-western front.

Russian front still held 127 enemy divisions, of which
80 were German, *i.e.* one-third of the German Army.

*

The Provisional Government, which had committed
the signal error of severing itself from the Officers' Staff
and from all patriotic elements within the army, now
found itself isolated. There existed no longer a single
class or party on which the Government could rely for
support. At the time of the Bolshevist rising on 7th
November no armed force rallied to the Government's
defence. Several military cadet contingents, moved by a
sense of the Bolshevist danger, opened fire. Other
ostensibly loyal units, called up from the environs of the
capital, were soon won over by the agents of Trotsky, then
President of the Petrograd Soviet, and refused to fight;
the Cossack regiments remained 'favourably' neutral to
the Bolsheviks. The rest of the garrison and the armed
factory workers sided with the Soviet; they were joined by
sailors from Cronstadt and by several warships.

The military youth alone – officers, cadets, and part
of the women's battalions formed under Kerensky –
strewed the streets of Petrograd, and especially Moscow,
with their corpses, dying without pose or pompous
phrases. . . .

For the Government? For the Revolution?

No, to save Russia!

What caused such a feeble resistance to Bolshevism?

Absolute war and turmoil weariness; widespread dissatisfaction with existing conditions; the not yet outlived
slavish mentality of the masses; the inertia of the majority
as opposed to the boundless and daring activity of an
organized, unprincipled, and strong-willed minority; alluring catchwords: 'power to the proletariat, land for the
peasants, factories for the workers, immediate peace,' and

'rob the robbers.' Such, roughly speaking, were the main causes of the Russian people's acceptance of, or rather *non-resistance* to the advent of Bolshevism.

Power dropped from the Provisional Government's feeble hands, and save for the Bolsheviks, not a single organization throughout the country proved itself capable of asserting its right to take up the burden of its heritage.

It was this fact which, in October 1917, pronounced the verdict upon the country, the people, and the Revolution.

*

The idea of bolstering up the decaying army by Volunteer formations had already arisen in the spring of 1917, but failed to materialize because the various Soviets and committees were afraid that the Volunteers would become 'the bulwark of counter-revolution.' The different 'revolutionary,' 'storm,' and women's battalions which sprang up everywhere, were unable to infuse their spirit into the army. They gradually dispersed. Only the Kornilov 'storm' regiment, a small cadre of the St. George's regiment and a band of women rescued from the October massacres, were later drafted into the Volunteer Army.

Nevertheless, the idea of Volunteer service was not abandoned. It was being propagated by the generals imprisoned at Bykhov[1] and by the former Commander-in-Chief, General Alexeyev, with whom we kept in touch. The vicinity of Mohilev enabled us also frequently to communicate with the Stavka (G.H.Q.), which, though loyal to Kerensky, recognized the authority of the Bykhov captives. Kerensky was nominally Commander-in-Chief, but the virtual commander was his Chief of the General Staff, General Dukhonin. After the Bolshevist Revolution

[1] Only generals and officers concerned in Kornilov's move were imprisoned at Bykhov.

General Kornilov addressed a letter to Dukhonin, bidding him either to 'dare or resign.' He proposed to concentrate around Mohilev a Polish (Poles drafted from Russian regiments), and a Czecho-Slovak (from Austrian Slav prisoners) army corps and several Cossack divisions, and to organize in Mohilev a munition depot for officers and Volunteers who, he was certain, would flock to the Stavka. Dukhonin took a hopeless view of the case. He considered the units mentioned to be unreliable, while preparations in Mohilev might create 'excesses.' Clearly, the Stavka was incapable of becoming a moral organizing centre for the struggle against Bolshevism.

If formerly, for political and moral reasons we did not avail ourselves of the opportunity to escape, now that the power had passed to the Bolsheviks, there was nothing to keep us at Bykhov. Most of the prisoners had already been set free by the Investigation Commission; the five senior generals alone remained. With Dukhonin's secret permission we produced forged documents to the warders and were released.

Where to go next? Undoubtedly, to the Don Cossack territory.

The Cossacks, with their strong traditional social order, their army which held out longest against disintegration – the Cossacks, with their prosperity and large land holdings won in the past by their defence of the Russian borders, and in the present by *universal* military service – the Cossacks, a freedom-loving community which had not bowed to the Bolsheviks, and was restoring its self-government – were looked upon as the mainstay of law and order, and by their very nature as opposed to Communism.

None of us suspected the bitter disappointments which awaited us in Don Cossack territory.

General Kornilov decided to march along with his own

loyal Tekinese regiment,[1] which fought under him at the front, sided with him during his uprising, and later formed the inner guard of the Bykhov prison, protecting the captives from the outer sentries, who were Bolshevized soldiers.

The way lay across fifteen hundred versts of a country aflame with Red Revolution. The frost was severe. The regiment advanced, tracked on all sides, falling into Bolshevist ambushes, fired upon at every river or railway crossing, suffering casualties. And at last there came a moment when even the Tekinese lost their nerve. These simple children of the steppes, worn out and bewildered, asked falteringly of their officers:

'What can we do, when all Russia has gone Bolshevist?'

They became obsessed by the absurd idea that they could surrender themselves to the Bolsheviks, but not allow the Bolsheviks to touch Kornilov. At one of the bivouacs the crowd of horsemen became restive and voices arose:

'Surrender, surrender!'

On hearing this General Kornilov walked quickly up to the riders and shouted:

'I give you five minutes to think it over. If you decide to surrender you're to shoot me first. Better to die by your hand than by that of the Bolsheviks.'

There was a dead silence. And when one of the officers gave the command: 'To horse!' the whole regiment obediently mounted and moved on.

However, after covering more than four hundred and fifty kilometres, Kornilov saw that the march would claim too many victims. Not wishing to endanger the men still more by his presence, he resolved to push on by himself. He bade the regiment farewell, and, disguised as a peasant,

---

[1] The Tekinese are a tribe of Turkestan. Kornilov spoke their language and was greatly loved by them.

boarded a train at a remote station. After this, the Bolsheviks, on learning of Kornilov's departure, ceased to
molest the regiment, which made its way to the Ukraine
free of them.

The other generals left Bykhov by train, under disguise
and with forged documents, travelling in trucks crowded
with boisterous, mutinous troops, passing stations at which
were posted the proclamations of revolutionary committees ordering the seizure and chastisement of 'the
fugitive Bykhov generals.' To trace us amid the general
chaos was difficult, and we all reached the Don territory
safely.

CHAPTER 2

The Creation of the Volunteer Army

GENERAL ALEXEYEV arrived in Novocherkassk, the capital of the Don territory on 15th November, before us, and immediately set about the formation of an armed force, which was destined to play such an important part in the history of the Russian Revolution. He intended to use as a base the south-eastern area, particularly the rich Don territory, possessing *its own armed force*, in order there to concentrate all the remaining loyalists – officers, cadets, 'storm' units, perhaps old soldiers – and to organize an army so urgently needed to restore order in Russia. The Cossacks, he saw, were unwilling to come to the fore in this matter, but hoped that 'they would defend their own territory and heritage.' Moreover, in those days there existed no safer territories in Russia. Conditions in the Don area, however, as in other Cossack lands, proved to be both unfavourable and extremely complicated.

Since the beginning of the Revolution, partly as a result of the weakened power of the Government, partly to safeguard their territory from the general dissolution, the Cossacks had begun to organize themselves. Cossack governments sprang up on all sides with elected *atamans* (chiefs) and representative bodies, whose sphere of competence increased in proportion as the Central Provisional Government grew weaker.

Neither these Cossack governments nor the *atamans*, however, held any authority whatever. General Kaledin, a prominent leader and staunch Russian patriot, elected as the Ataman of the Don, also had none.

Between the Cossacks proper and the peasants who leased small holdings on Cossack lands a fierce feud was raging,[1] in which an active part was taken by the local Soviets, supported by riotous soldier rabble which, as reserve Empire troops, had overrun the territory. The Cossacks were powerless to resist them, as their own contingents were still at the front. When, however, the Cossack divisions began to trek homeward, they brought bitter disappointment. From the front they imported actual Bolshevism, divested, of course, of all idealism, but conspicuous by a repudiation of all authority, by mutinies, aggression, and chiefly by a refusal to fight against the Soviet Government, which had falsely pledged itself 'to maintain the immunity of Cossack rights.'

The Volunteer rally in these circumstances roused open apprehension and discontent in Cossack circles. The opinion prevailed that the Soviet Government's preparations for a military expedition against the Don were caused by the presence of these 'uninvited guests,' and that the Soviet's favour and personal safety could be purchased by submission.

*

In spite of the total lack of funds, General Alexeyev, full of ardour, set about forming the Volunteer Army. Telegrams in cipher were sent everywhere summoning officers to Novocherkassk. One of the hospitals was converted into an officers' hostel, which became the cradle of the Volunteer Movement, and contributions for 'Alexeyev's organization' soon began to pour in. It was a touching – and to some, perhaps, a comic sight, to see

---

[1] The non-Cossack population, which formed about fifty per cent. of the inhabitants of the Don and Kuban regions was called *inogorodnie*, *i.e.* 'aliens from other towns.'

the former Commander-in-Chief, who had ruled over armies millions strong and wielded a war budget of milliards, now fussing around to procure a dozen beds, a few poods of sugar, and, if possible, a paltry sum of money to house, warm, and feed the homeless, persecuted warriors.

And they came in their numbers – officers, cadets, military schoolboys, and a very few old soldiers – at first one by one, then in groups. Those who could escaped from the prisons, others from disrupted army units. Some managed to get through the Bolshevist cordons easily, others were seized and flung into prison, held as hostages, or drafted into the Red Guard, often flung into the grave. . . . All trekked to the Don without the least knowledge of what awaited them there; they pushed blindly on through the close darkness of the Bolshevist night, to where the names of leaders whom popular legend linked with the Don shone as a beacon amid the surrounding gloom. Unfortunately these were but hundreds, while tens of thousands, at their wit's end what to do, compelled by circumstances to 'wait and see,' turned to peaceful occupations, became civilians or went submissively to register with the Bolshevist commissars, to be first tortured in the Tcheka and later drafted into the Red Army.

The earliest stages of the formation of the first White Army present a truly unparalleled spectacle.

Thus, for instance, the Kornilovsky regiment, which remained loyal to its chief after his imprisonment, and suffered many indignities from the turbulent troops of the south-western front. As the sole remaining disciplined unit it was used by the commissaries of the already non-existing Provisional Government to quell a revolt in Kiev. There perished, for no object whatever, the gallant youth of Kornilov's regiment, shot down in fighting, or simply in the streets and in the houses, both by the mutinied Bolsheviks and the Ukrainian indepen-

dents. Having with difficulty extricated the regiment from
Kiev, the commander, Lieut.-Col. Niezhintsev, requested
from General Dukhonin at the Stavka permission to take
the regiment to the Don, but was refused. Niezhintsev
then resorted to extreme measures. A detachment with
the baggage, and provided with a forged certificate as to
its forming part of a Caucasian division, was dispatched
under a small escort to the Don, the rest of the regiment
was disbanded, and a report sent to the Stavka that all
the men had deserted. . . .

After many and prolonged hardships, part of the
regiment, singly or in groups, dribbled to the Don Cossack
territory, and in January 1918 reassembled in Novocherkassk.

Still more picturesque was the history of the formation
of the Volunteer artillery. One battery (two guns) we
stole from the demoralized Thirty-ninth Division, which
had deserted from the Caucasian front and quartered
itself in our neighbourhood in the province of Stavropol.
A band of officers and cadets made a night raid on one
of the villages where the battery was billeted and wrested
the guns from the soldiers. We obtained two more guns
from the Don artillery depot by permission of the
Revolutionary Committee, ostensibly for the purpose of
firing a salute at the funeral of a slain Volunteer officer,
and then said we had lost them! One battery we *bought*
for five thousand roubles from some demoralized Cossack
artillerymen back from the front, whom we first treated
to vodka. . . .

Our quests, however, were not always so successful.
When a detachment of forty officers and cadets was
dispatched to Ekaterinodar to fetch guns promised by the
Kuban Ataman, they were stopped at one of the railway
stations by semi-Bolshevized Kuban Cossacks, who disarmed and sent them to Novorossisk, then held by a

Bolshevist Government. There the Volunteers were flung into prison, where they languished for eight months, escaping death by a miracle, for the Novorossisk Bolsheviks were renowned for their extreme cruelty. Rumours of their atrocities reached the prison. Our captives soon learnt of the tragedy of the Varnavinsk regiment, which was evacuated from the Caucasus via Novorossisk. The transport with the regiment had already left port, when it was overtaken by a torpedo boat with the municipal Bolshevist authorities on board. The officers were stripped, bound, mutilated, hacked, shot, and flung into the sea. . . . A few months later a diver working on the spot to raise a sunken ship met an appalling spectacle: livid, greenish, swollen, mangled corpses kept upright owing to the weights tied to their legs, stood in serried ranks, swaying to and fro, as if talking to one another. . . . The diver became insane.

Such were the difficulties which beset the formation of the contingent which later became known as the *Volunteer Army*. By common consent of the senior generals and public men who took part in the movement, its leadership was entrusted to General Kornilov, recently arrived from Bykhov. General Alexeyev, already suffering from a grave disease, took over the control of external relations and finance.

N.B. – Relations between the two generals were none too cordial, owing to a long-standing mutual antipathy. But both knew how to place the national cause above personal disagreements.

An Army G.H.Q. was attached to General Kornilov, with the same men at its head who were at the head of the Stavka at Mohilev: Generals Lukomsky (Chief of Staff) and Romanovsky (Quartermaster-General).

*

What in those days was the Volunteer Army?

At the beginning of February the 'army' consisted of two infantry regiments, three officers' battalions, one cadet battalion, the Rostov Volunteer regiment composed of raw schoolboys, two cavalry detachments, two batteries, and various small units. As a matter of fact all these regiments, battalions, and divisions were but skeleton cadres, and the total 'army' did not exceed *four thousand* fighters, dwindling at times, as during the hard fighting at Rostov, to absolutely insignificant proportions.

The army possessed no secure base. It was compelled simultaneously to organize itself and fight, suffering heavy casualties which often disseminated a unit newly formed by dint of strenuous effort.

The army exchequer was in a precarious condition. At first it was replenished solely by petty contributions, later the Moscow bourgeoisie sent eight hundred thousand roubles; the Rostov-on-Don plutocracy collected about two million roubles. Finally, we received part of the revenues of the local exchequer.

The army was organized on the voluntary basis, each Volunteer signing on for four months and pledging implicit obedience to the commanding staff. Owing to the scarcity of funds the Volunteers received beggarly wages. Thus, in November, both officers and men received only their upkeep; during the next three months the officers touched from one hundred to two hundred and seventy depreciated roubles, the men thirty to one hundred and fifty roubles. The officers' wages were equal to half the minimum living wage fixed for manual workers by the trade unions. In the officers' battalions and batteries, the officers serving as privates were virtually utterly unprovided for. Enormous supplies were stored in the Don military depots, but these we were unable to procure otherwise than by theft or bribery of the Cossack committees. So that our troops were short of absolutely everything: arms and munitions, baggage, field kitchens, warm clothing, boots. . . .

*

Just as the physical, so also was the spiritual physiognomy of the Volunteer Army composed of various elements.

We were joined by all those who sympathized with the idea of the struggle and were prepared to face its hardships. The bad came to us together with the good. But four years of war followed by the nightmare of revolution had left their aftermath. Men became divested of the outward trappings of civilization and all their higher and baser passions stood revealed. It would be hypocrisy on the part of a society which had touched the bottom of moral decay to demand from the Volunteers the practice of asceticism and the higher virtues. There were deeds of valour and base depravity; heroism and cruelty; compassion and hatred; social tolerance and class antagonism.

Yet in spite of all its defects the Volunteer Movement maintained its heroic image and national idea.

The Volunteers were alien to politics, true to the idea of saving the motherland, brave in battle, and obedient to their superiors. For them the future held in store mutilation, a roving life, often death. They fought on the approach to Rostov,[1] knowing that behind their backs hundreds of thousands of Cossacks and the Rostov bourgeoisie were sitting safe and snug. Cold, tattered, and hungry, they looked on at the merrymaking in opulent Rostov.

The civil war completed the psychological process which had been merely outlined by the war at the front.

It soon became known that the Bolsheviks *killed all Volunteers* taken prisoners, after *preliminarily subjecting*

[1] A large industrial town near Novocherkassk.

them to inhuman tortures. I well remember the terrible shock I felt when the eight bodies of the first tortured Volunteers were brought from Bataisk – slashed with sword-cuts, prodded with bayonets, disfigured so that their despairing relatives could scarcely recognize the familiar features. . . . And when the priest, glancing round fearfully in the flickering light of the wax candles, pronounced 'eternal memory to the slain,' how one's heart ached for them all and how impossible it was to find forgiveness for their torturers.

I well remember, too, my visit to the Taganrog front. On the platform of a station we recently occupied lay a corpse covered by matting. It was the body of the stationmaster killed by the Bolsheviks when they learnt that his sons served in the Volunteer Army. The father's abdomen was split open and he was buried alive. The unfortunate man's distorted limbs and lacerated fingers testified to the violent efforts he had made to climb out of the grave. His two officer sons were also here, come to fetch their father's body and bring it to Rostov. The truck with the coffin was attached to the train in which I travelled back. At some wayside station one of the sons, catching sight of a waggon with Bolshevist prisoners, was seized with frenzy, rushed into the waggon, and before the sentries knew what he was about, shot all the Bolsheviks. . . .

There were many such; men broken and mutilated in life's mangle, who had lost their nearest and dearest, or left their families to starve far away at the mercy of the Red frenzy. Such as these did not constitute the real image of the army, but their mentality had to be reckoned with by those inclined to see but the dark patches across the Volunteers' path to Golgotha.

From the very outset the Bolsheviks had summarized the nature of the civil war in a single word: Extermination!

This system of warfare introduced by the Bolsheviks admitted of no choice of methods by the other side, particularly under conditions of a continual tactical envelopment, in which the Volunteer Army found itself, deprived of territory, rear or base. In many instances life itself dictated the terrible method of 'war to extermination,' reminiscent of the gloomy annals of *la Vendée*. . . . On the other hand, when during the fighting near Rostov several railway waggons with wounded Volunteers and nurses became detached from the train and rolled down the slope towards the Bolshevist positions, many in a fit of frenzied despair committed suicide. They knew what awaited them, particularly the women.

Kornilov ordered sentries to be placed at the captured Bolshevist hospitals. Mercy to the wounded – it was all he could demand in those stern days. Long afterwards, after the Soviet Government by compulsory mobilization had drawn the civil population into the strife, and the Volunteer Army acquired the forms of a state institution with a territory of its own, it became possible to introduce more humane methods, in so far as this was generally possible in the demoralized atmosphere of civil war.

For it mutilated not only the body but the soul.

*

Lastly, the army's political outlook.

The rank and file were definitely conscious of one idea – to save the motherland. All the rest was of secondary importance, transient, and therefore unnecessary. Officially the aims pursued by the army were published in a proclamation by the General Staff. These were: to struggle, to fight against anarchy and the Germano-Bolshevist invasion, and to steer the country to the Constituent Assembly, the army pledging itself implicitly to submit to the Government legally elected by the former. The proclamation ended in an appeal to *all* who loved our long-suffering motherland to join the ranks of the Russian Army.

As I said before, those who responded were the officers, cadets, students, and schoolboys, and very few others. The 'All National' legion did not materialize.

How to explain this indifference of the Russian people and intelligentsia towards the struggle against Bolshevism? The true substance of Bolshevism was at the time realized by very few among the people, while the duration and extent of the terrible ravages of the Bolshevist regime were foreseen by none. Some trusted the alluring but false promises made by Bolshevist propaganda, others believed that a regime opposed to God, nature, the interests of the nation, and finally, to common sense could exist but a very short time and would collapse of itself.

Yet if none were found at this most tragic hour of our national life ready to rise against the frenzy and crimes of the Soviet Government and sacrifice their blood and life to save their perishing motherland, that would indeed be proof of the nation's deepest moral degradation.

CHAPTER 3

The Strategic Position of Russia in January 1918 – The Fighting against the Red Guard at Rostov

At Brest-Litovsk a bargain was struck between the Central Powers and the Soviet Government the mere remembrance of which brings pain and bitter humiliation to every true Russian. The Council of People's Commissars, financially tied to the German General Staff and concerned primarily with its own safety, surrendered to the will of the Germans. At a Council of War held at the Stavka on the 4th February, the Commander-in-Chief Krylenko,[1] with incomparable cynicism, declared as follows:

'Whether Germany does or does not intend to enlarge her territory is no business of ours. What do we care whether or not Russia will be shorn of territories. And finally, what is it to us whether Russia herself continues to exist in that form which alone is intelligible to bourgeois mentality. Damn territory! All this is on the bourgeois plane of thought and must be done away with once and for all. . . . The war must be ended at once – the old army disbanded, so that no trace shall remain of all those country bumpkins. . . . The new Socialist army must not wage war on the external front. . . . It will defend the Soviet Government and its chief aim will be to crush the bourgeoisie. . . .'

Taking this as a starting-point and having abolished the old army, the Soviet Government issued a decree at the

---

[1] A school-teacher by profession; was mobilized as an ensign during the war.

36

end of January 1918 announcing the organization of 'the army of workers and peasants' recruited from 'the most conscious and well-organized elements of the toiling classes.' The formation of this new 'class' army, however, did not proceed smoothly, and the Soviets were obliged to turn to the old organizations: units were selected from the front or from the reserve battalions, also detachments of Letts, sailors, etc.; alongside of which factory committees organized the *Red Guard* – the name soon becoming general for all the Soviet armed forces of the first 'guerilla' period of the struggle.

All these contingents were thrown against the Ukraine and Don Cossack territory.

What was the driving force which moved these men, mortally war weary, to face anew cruel hardships and sacrifices? Least of all – loyalty to the Soviet Government and its ideals. Hunger, unemployment, prospects of an idle life in plenty, of enrichment by plunder, the impossibility of the demobilized reaching their homesteads by any other means, habit acquired by many during four years of war of soldiering as a profession, and lastly, to a greater or lesser extent the feeling of class hatred and resentment nurtured through centuries and now fanned into flame by frenzied propaganda.

The exact strength of the troops advancing against us was unknown both to us and to the Soviet Government itself. Number and composition of the Red Guard detachments was a changing and unknown quantity; sometimes they dispersed, then came together again; advanced, or held meetings and refused to obey. Nevertheless, they were continually pushing south, thousands against hundreds. In spite of the apparent lack of system in the activities of the separate Bolshevist detachments, their general movements revealed the hand of the old Stavka and a definite strategical plan. It consisted in separating the Ukraine from the Don Cossack

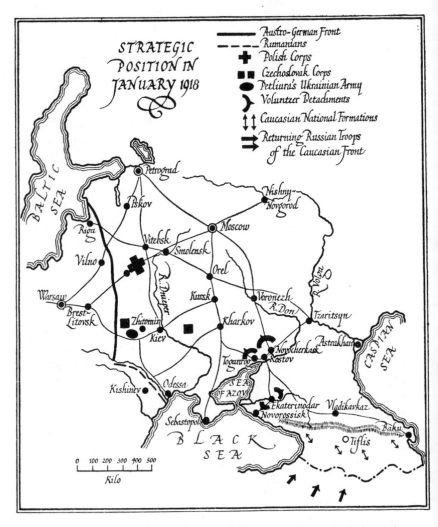

area and capturing Kiev and Rostov, the administrative centres of the newly formed territories.

The general command of the offensive was entrusted to the Commissar Antonov-Ovseyenko, while the forces advancing against Rostov were led by an ex-officer, Sievers.

THE WHITE ARMY

*

By the beginning of February 1918 the situation on the 'home front' was as follows:

In the Ukraine, which had seceded from Russia,[1] Petliura's troops were beating a hasty retreat from Kiev towards Berditchev, thus leaving the way clear for the Bolshevist advance on Don Cossack territory. In view of the Kuban Cossacks' refusal to fight, the Kuban Government had also formed Volunteer detachments, which were covering the approaches to Ekaterinodar, the principal town of the region from the direction of Tikhoretskaia and Novorossisk. In the Northern Caucasus the motley crowd of various tribes were settling their age-long feuds by bloodshed, and falling, one by one, under the rule of the Soviets. In Transcaucasia the national armies – Georgian, Armenian, Tartar, and so forth, were only in process of formation, and were preparing to resist both the Bolsheviks and the Turkish Army, which had already occupied Trebizond. Under pressure from the latter a mass of Russian soldiers left the Caucasian front and descended northward like a raging torrent, plundering and devastating everything that lay across their path. Unable to reach their homes owing to the blocked-up railways, they settled in the Caucasus and the Black Sea ports, where they spread Bolshevism and provided ready-made material for the Red Guard.

The anti-Bolshevist forces were like tiny, disconnected scarcely discernible islets scattered over the uniformly red map of Russia.

It is true that two strong and sufficiently organized army corps were still quartered in the west and south-west of Russia, and their co-operation in the early stages of the anti-Bolshevist movement might have played an historical

[1] Seven provinces of South-western Russia.

part. These were the Polish corps under General Dovborg-Musnitsky quartered in the region of Vitebsk-Minsk-Zhlobin, and the Czecho-Slovak, commanded by the Russian General Shokarev, in Volhynia and Podolia.

Both these corps had long since attracted our attention, and Generals Alexeyev and Kornilov were conducting protracted negotiations with their leaders in the hope of enlisting their assistance for a joint campaign against the Bolsheviks. The idea was to persuade them to act as cover to our territory and so enable us to organize the Volunteer Army. No greater sacrifice was asked of them.

Our plans found no favour either with the political leaders of the Polish and Czecho-Slovak contingents or with the French diplomats, whose views were the decisive factor, because both the corps since the end of 1917 had been placed under French jurisdiction and were maintained at the French Government's expense. Both the French Ambassador in Russia, M. Noulens, and the French Military Mission at Kiev continued their short-sighted policy of preserving the Russian front at first jointly with the Bolsheviks, who had already *demobilized the army*, and later with the Ukraine, *which had already opened secret peace negotiations with Germany*.

These mistakes were cruelly avenged by subsequent events. We shall see, as early as February, at the time of the German invasion of the Ukraine, the Czecho-Slovaks engaged in fierce fighting against the Germans and the Ukrainian allies foisted on them by the French, *on the Bolshevist side*. They afterwards started on the interminable trek across Siberia, in pursuance of the fantastic plan of the French G.H.Q. – the transference of a fifty-thousand army corps to the western front, separated from the eastern by a distance of seven thousand miles and several oceans. . . . In the spring they turned against their Bolshevist allies, who betrayed them to the Germans. . . .

The end of the Polish corps was sadder still. The beginning of February saw fierce fighting between the Poles and the Bolsheviks, in which luck turned against the former. By the end of the month – when the Czechs were fighting *with the Bolsheviks against the Germans*, the Polish divisions, having recognized the 'Regency Council' in Warsaw started *a joint offensive with the Germans against the Bolsheviks*, with no other result than that of being treacherously disarmed and disbanded by the Germans a few weeks later.

*

And so we were left alone.

In the middle of January the staff and all the Volunteer contingents crossed from Rostov to Novocherkassk in order to cover the important road to Kharkov, abandoned by the Don Cossacks. The officers' battalion under Colonel Kutepov and the cadet school were stationed at Taganrog; a small detachment at Bataisk acted as cover from the south. As the towns of Rostov and Taganrog had a large labour population hostile to us, the policing of these towns took up many men. The bourgeoisie, however, remained absolutely indifferent on that score; only children – pupils of the secondary schools who enlisted in the Rostov regiment – helped us to police the town.

The Bolshevist offensive against Rostov and Novocherkassk commenced about the 10th January, and this put a stop to all organization work. All the cadres were moved to the front. At the request of the Ataman General Kaledin, one officers' detachment was dispatched in the direction of Novocherkassk where, owing to the Cossacks' refusal to fight, a menacing situation had arisen. Colonel Kutepov, advancing from Taganrog, where his unit obtained reinforcements, defeated Sievers' Red Guards twice near Matveiev Kurgan. This was the first serious encounter in which the frenzied onslaught of the Bolsheviks was confronted with the efficiency and enthusiasm of the officers. The officers carried off an easy victory. . . . But they were only a handful against thousands. The defeated Bolsheviks fled, only to be replaced by others; meanwhile, fighting went on day after day, causing intense weariness among the Volunteers, who remained constantly on the alert in the front line.

Simultaneously a revolt broke out in the rear of the detachment at Taganrog. For two days armed workmen terrorized the town and attacked the feeble and sparsely distributed cadet pickets. The head of the Cadet Training College, badly wounded, gave orders that he was to be left behind, and committed suicide; the cadets suffered heavy casualties, and only a part managed to escape and join the Volunteers.

Heavy enemy pressure from the north and the loss of Taganrog compelled Kutepov to withdraw his unit to a day's march from Rostov. There, reinforced by all available troops, they continued to hold back the Bolsheviks. We succeeded eventually in raising a few hundred Cossacks to join us, but after their first reverse, this Don militia evaporated and was seen no more.

The winter was bitterly cold. The Volunteers, badly clothed, remained unrelieved at their posts and simply melted away day by day.

*

On the Novocherkassk section matters were still worse. Kaledin called a mobilization of officers and the four junior Cossack classes, and started organizing guerilla detachments.

But no response came from the Don Cossack territory. Novocherkassk depended for its defence solely upon a guerilla detachment under the Cossack Captain Tchernetsov, consisting almost entirely of students and schoolboys. It seemed as if the dying spirit of the Don Cossacks was embodied in that gallant officer. His name was a by-word of pride and hope. Tchernetsov's activities spread in all directions, and were everywhere crowned with success. Legends were woven round his name, and the Bolsheviks offered a high price for his head. In a combat against three regiments of his own fellow Cossacks Tchernetsov was taken prisoner, and after barbarous torture hacked to pieces.

It seemed as if with Tchernetsov's death the defence of the Don Cossack territory had lost its soul. Everything there went to pieces. The Don Government had already opened negotiations with the Bolshevist Revolutionary Committee, when Kaledin sounded a last call to the Don territory to rally in its own defence. In this proclamation he depicted the complete disruption of the Cossack contingents. The regiments which had committed their Cain-like deed towards Tchernetsov had abandoned their artillery, ransacked the regimental exchequer and property, and dispersed to their villages. Others had completely destroyed the railway, thereby cutting off the northern districts of the territory from all supplies. Others again *sold* their officers to the Bolsheviks for cash. . . .

In the beginning of February General Kornilov, despairing of the Volunteers being able to remain longer in the Don Cossack region where, in view of the total absence of help from the Cossacks, they were doomed soon to perish, determined to push on to the Kuban. With this object in view a plan for the capture of the Tikhoretskaia station was drawn up, and Ataman Kaledin was apprised by telegram of our intended departure.

On the 11th General Kaledin, stern and calm as usual, summoned the members of the Government, read out Kornilov's telegram, and announced that for the defence of the Don territory (with a two-million Cossack population and army numbering up to seventy regiments) only one hundred and forty-seven combatants had volunteered for the front. He laid down the insignia of his office, resigned his post, advised the Government to do likewise, and in leaving the room, added:

'Gentlemen, be brief! Time presses! Remember, Russia was lost by too much talk.'

That same day General Kaledin ended his life by a revolver shot through the heart.

That shot resounded throughout the Don Cossack region like a tocsin.

Hope revived that such a heavy expiatory sacrifice would bring the Cossacks to their senses. . . . News came from Novocherkassk of a general mobilization throughout the territory, of spreading enthusiasm; the 'Krug' (Cossack assembly) had elected General Nasarov ataman and called all Cossacks between the ages of seventeen and fifty to the colours. The new ataman and a delegation from the Krug begged us to stay.

We stayed. Soon, however, all our hopes dwindled away. The 'enthusiasm' lasted only a few days, and the newly enrolled Cossacks once more started holding riotous meetings and finally went home.

Meanwhile, conditions on the Rostov front became considerably worse. The Bolsheviks succeeded in persuading the garrison of Stavropol, numbering three thousand men with artillery, to declare against us. This detachment advanced along the railway line, and on the 14th February unexpectedly attacked our troops at Bataisk. Surrounded on all sides, they fought gallantly all day, and, suffering heavy casualties, finally broke through the enemy line in the night, and crossing the river over thin ice, managed to reach Rostov. From then onwards the Bolsheviks began to bombard the town from Bataisk with heavy guns, creating panic among the civil population.

Fighting continued in the direction of Taganrog. The

Volunteer contingents melted away each day, disseminated by fighting, disease, frost-bite, and desertion on the part of the weaker elements, who had lost their moral balance under conditions seemingly well-nigh desperate. The Bolshevist forces under Sievers were advancing, and on the 22nd February our troops, badly mauled, were retreating towards Rostov under fire from front and rear – opened on the latter by Cossacks from a suburban village. In the Rostov suburb workmen raised a revolt and opened fire on the railway station. The position of the little 'army,' swamped as it were in the midst of a dense Bolshevist sea, was becoming critical.

That day Kornilov gave the order to abandon Rostov and withdraw beyond the Don to the Olginskaia stanitsa (a stanitsa is a large Cossack village). Where to go next was still unsettled; the alternatives were either the Kuban or the southern steppes of the Don Cossack territory. The main thing was to escape from Rostov, the defence of which was beyond our strength.

Taciturn and oppressed, the members of the staff, armed with rifles, stood in formation, and preceded by Kornilov, marched off along the deserted, deadly silent streets towards the suburbs, there to join the troops. Lights twinkled in the windows of the inhospitable town we were abandoning. Random shots rang out. Silently we trudged on, each intent upon his own gloomy thoughts.

Whither were we going, what future lay in store for us? The lines written that day by one of our leaders, General Alexeyev, to one dear to him – lines which were preserved – seemed to contain an answer to that torturing question:

'. . . We are plunging into the steppes. We can return only by God's mercy. *But a torch must be lit, so that at least one speck of light will shine amid the darkness which has enveloped Russia.*'

CHAPTER 4

General Kornilov's First Kuban Campaign, in the beginning of 1918

WE were retreating.

Madness followed in our wake. It filled the forsaken towns with turbulent debauchery, plunder, and murder. There remained our wounded, who were pulled out of the hospitals into the streets and murdered. There remained our families, doomed to a life of perpetual fear of Bolshevist reprisals, should their identity chance to be discovered. . . .

We started our campaign under exceptional conditions: a mere handful of men lost in the wide Don steppes, in the midst of the raging sea which had submerged our native land. Among these men were two Commanders-in-Chief of the Russian Army, a Commander-in-Chief of a front, senior staff-officers, corps commanders, veteran colonels. . . . With a rifle slung over their shoulder, a soldier's haversack on their back, carrying the whole of their shabby kit, they trudged through the deep snow in a winding column. . . . Leaving behind darkness and moral enslavement to wander into the unknown. . . .

In quest of the Blue-bird!

While there remains life and strength – all is not yet lost. Those who have not yet awakened will discern the faint glimmer of the torch, hearken to the voice bidding them to rise and fight. Herein lay the profound significance of the *first Kuban campaign*. Across the free steppes of the Don Cossack and the Kuban area moved the Volunteer Army – small in number, tattered and torn, surrounded and tracked from pillar to post – a symbol of persecuted Russia.

Throughout the length and breadth of the vast country there remained but one spot where the national tricolour flag soared freely – and that spot was General Kornilov's headquarters.

*

We halted at our rallying-place, the barracks of the Rostov regiment. The colonel in command had that morning offered to allow the Rostov youths to go home; the campaign would be full of hardships and the future quite uncertain. A few went off, but some of them returned by nightfall. 'All the neighbours knew that we were in the army, somebody'll report and then . . .' As a matter of fact the campaign from which many never returned was not the worst alternative, for those who remained in Rostov were for many days tracked, tortured and finally killed by the Bolsheviks.

'Powerless to avert these continuous murders, we declare our willingness at any moment to be shot in place of the children sentenced to death!' Such was the despairing and powerless appeal of the Rostov Social-Democratic leaders to the fiends, for whose advent they were in a great measure responsible.

We moved on at last along the outskirts of the town at dead of night through the deep snow. At the Aksaiskaia stanitsa, where we halted, the Cossacks only allowed us to stay the night under threat of being shot. . . . Next morning, after laying boards and straw on the thawing ice we crossed the River Don. A spectacle never to be forgotten! A dark ribbon winding along the interminable snow-fields; a motley crowd like a gipsy caravan; carts; nondescript civilians plodding along; women in town costumes and thin shoes stumbling through the snow; and as if lost among them – marching military columns in the midst of the 'caravan' – all that remained of the erstwhile great Russian army. They advanced with measured rhythmic tread. But their clothes! Officers' overcoats, mufti, schoolboy caps; some wore leather boots, others felt snow-boots, rag puttees. . . . What matter – beneath the beggar's garb there burned a living soul!

General Alexeyev drove past in a cart; he carried a small suitcase; in it and in the breast pockets of several officers of his convoy all our meagre fortune lay hidden – about six million depreciated roubles.

Kornilov salutes the passing troops. They answer back joyously. And a few paces further on break out in their crude but hearty marching song:

> 'Keep step, Kornilov's men,
> Kornilov is with us here,
> He'll save our motherland
> And ne'er betray her people.'

Youth, enthusiasm, faith in the future and this strong healthy link with their leader will carry them through every trial.

*

On reaching the Olginskaia stanitsa, Kornilov proceeded to 'reorganize' the army, which numbered in all about four thousand combatants and about five thousand mouths to feed.[1]

By joining together various small units, the army was finally reduced to the following:

1st Officers' regiment under General Markov,
The Cadet battalion – General Borovsky,

---

[1] The Bolshevist general staff reckoned us as having fifty thousand.

Kornilovsky regiment – Lieut.-Col. Niezhintsev,
Guerilla regiment (Don Cossacks) – General Bogaievsky,
Artillery division (4 2-gun batteries),
Czecho-Slovak Engineer battalion – Captain Niemetchik,
3 separate cavalry detachments (2 Cossack and one regular).

I was appointed Assistant Army Commander.

We had barely six hundred or seven hundred shells, and only about two hundred rounds of ammunition per rifle. There was only one way of meeting the shortage – by wresting ammunition from the Bolsheviks at the price of blood. We were hastily equipping our cavalry, buying horses with great difficulty and at fabulous prices from the Cossacks. We looked upon the Cossacks as on our mainstay, if not at present, at least for the future. Therefore, Kornilov demanded that we should treat the stanitsas with special consideration and forbade requisitions. It was an amazing feature – this passion of the principal anti-Bolshevist leaders for 'lawful proceedings,' and one which in the midst of the ruins of the legal and social order and the prevailing anarchic tendencies often placed us at great disadvantage. Thus, on leaving Rostov we did not tap the safes of the State Bank, and all their contents were appropriated by the Bolsheviks. . . . We *asked* for shelter, *asked* for victuals, at a high price; we were unable to obtain either boots or clothing at any price for the barefooted and half-clad Volunteers, though they were still plentiful. Conditions were unequal: to-morrow the Bolsheviks will come and seize hold of everything – and everything will be handed over to them to the last item without murmur, with bowing and scraping and inward cursing.

Later circumstances compelled us to resort to orders and requisitions for cash.

Meanwhile, Novocherkassk fell on the 25th February. The Krug was dispersed by the Bolsheviks, the Ataman, the President of the Krug and many other Cossacks were shot. The day before a guerilla Don Cossack detachment under General Popov, who refused to submit to the Bolsheviks, left the town. It numbered one thousand five hundred combatants, mainly cavalry, five guns and forty machine guns.

The question was, what to do next?

We were faced with two alternatives. Either to plunge into Don Cossack steppes, there to await the re-awakening of the Cossacks. . . . Once there, however, pressed on one side by the approaching spring flood of the River Don and on the other by the Tsaritsyn-Tikhoretskaia-Rostov railway line held by the Bolsheviks, we would be absolutely cut off from the outside world. The steppe region with its scattered *zimovniky* [1] convenient for small guerilla bands possessed neither habitation, fuel, nor food supplies sufficient for an army. Finally, we could not expect to be left unmolested by the Bolsheviks, who would undoubtedly try to destroy our scattered units.

The next alternative was to move to the Kuban. There we not only expected to find a rich and prosperous country, but kindred spirits, a fighting government and Volunteer forces considerably exaggerated by rumour. And lastly, the fact that Ekaterinodar, the principal town of the region, was free from Bolshevist rule, seemed to offer a possibility of starting serious organization work.

After prolonged arguments and vacillation we decided to head for the Kuban. A message was dispatched to General Popov inviting him to join us. He refused on the pretext that the temper of his troops would not allow him to leave the Don Cossack territory. . . . It was said, however, that

[1] Small wintering hamlets belonging to the horse-breeders whose horses grazed in the steppes.

ambition prevented him from becoming Kornilov's subordinate. Whatever the reason, his defection deprived us
of much-needed reinforcement, particularly as we were
very short of cavalry, and so rendering our position still
more difficult, lessened our already slender chances of
success.

*

And so, to the Kuban.

We advanced slowly at first, knocking the newly formed
units into shape and collecting baggage. It took us six
days to cover the eighty-eight versts between Olginskaia
and Egorlytskaia. After deciding to go to the Kuban, however, we advanced more rapidly, avoiding fighting in order
the quicker to reach Ekaterinodar.

The first serious encounter took place on the 6th March
at the village of Lezhanka. The fighting was short and
sharp. The Officers' regiment was in front. The old and
the young; colonels in command of platoons. General
Markov galloped to the foremost line. . . . A shot rang out,
somewhere high up a shrapnel burst. . . . It had begun.

The Officers' regiment deploy and move to the attack,
calmly, without pausing, heading straight for the village.
It is encircled by trenches; a battery posted by the church
is pouring shrapnel along the road. Rifle and machine-gun
fire increases. Our formations halt and lie down; a little
marshy river, not frozen over, is in front. We shall have to
sidetrack it.

The Kornilov regiment is ordered a right flank movement. A group of horsemen is seen galloping after it, a
tricolour standard waving in the wind. . . .

Kornilov!

There is commotion in the ranks, all eyes are turned to
the figure of the commander. . . . While along the road
cadets are openly drawing up guns, right under enemy
fire. . . .

51

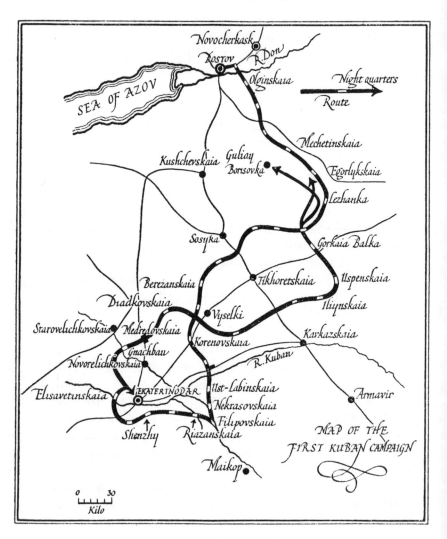

MAP OF THE
FIRST KUBAN CAMPAIGN

The Officers' regiment cannot bear the delay; one of the
companies rushes into the ice-cold, sticky, clamming mud
of the river and wades across. Commotion ensues. Soon
the whole field is covered by panic-stricken fugitives,

stampeding cart-horses, batteries advancing full speed. The Officers' and Kornilovsky regiments, the latter having crossed by the dam to the left of the village, are in hot pursuit.

We enter the village which seems dead. The streets are strewn with corpses. The silence is uncanny. For a long time it is broken by the dry crackling of rifle shots: 'settling' the Bolsheviks. Corpses and bloodshed. . . .

Who were they? Why should they, 'mortally weary of a four years' massacre,' again go to fight and face death? A regiment and battery, deserters from the Turkish front, turbulent country roughs, stranger workmen together with some soldier rabble had long ago seized power in the committees and terrorized the whole province. Perhaps, also, peaceful peasants forcibly mobilized by the Soviets. . . . None of them understand the meaning of this struggle. And their conception of the Volunteers as enemies is also none too clear:

'Cadets,[1] officers . . . they want things to be as before. . . .'

The peasants' minds were in a state of complete chaos. The ground had shifted from under their feet. They cared neither for 'politics,' 'Constituent Assembly,' 'Republic' nor 'Tsar'; even the land question here in the wide spaces beyond the Don, and especially in the fertile steppes of Stavropol, had lost its specific acuteness. Unwillingly, we found ourselves drawn into the vicious circle of the general social struggle: one section of the population, the more well-to-do, who stood for law and order, sympathized either openly or secretly with the army; the other which, deservedly or not built their welfare on the absence of government and chaos, were hostile. There was no way of escape out of this circle, no means to make clear to them the army's

---

[1] A play of words. 'Cadets' was the nickname of the constitutional democratic party, and cadets were the pupils of the military colleges.

true aims. By words? Of what avail are words which beat against an impenetrable wall of mistrust, fear and servility.

Beside the house occupied by the staff, artillery officer prisoners belonging to the Bolshevist division quartered in Lezhanka were lined up in a row with a sentry at each end.

Here was a fresh tragedy for the Russian officer staff. One after another Volunteer detachments marched past in front of the prisoners. Hate and contempt were in their eyes. Threats and curses were flung at the prisoners. The faces of the latter were deadly pale. The proximity of headquarters alone saved them from being lynched. General Alexeyev walked past. Greatly moved he indignantly rebuked the captive officers, and a heavy curse escaped his lips. . . . Kornilov settled their fate:

'Court martial!'

They produced the usual justifications: – 'Knew nothing of the Volunteer Army's existence' . . . 'was detained, forced to serve' . . . 'family were held as hostages.' . . . The court martial decided the charge to be not proven. As a matter of fact this was not acquittal, but free *pardon*. The officers joined our army.

Another time, the captain in command of a battery which had kept up a magnificently accurate fire against us was taken prisoner. When questioned as to the motive of such behaviour, his reply, probably sincere, was:

'Professional training!'

Thus, inertia, lack of will power, impossible family conditions and 'professional training' were gradually building up for the Red Army solid officer cadres which raised their arms against the Volunteers in fratricidal war.

*

On the 9th March we crossed into the Kuban territory. What a contrast. Everywhere the army was warmly welcomed with 'bread and salt.'[1] Coming from the north, we were struck by the wealth of the Kuban territory, its vast corn-fields, bulging corn-stacks, huge droves of cattle and horses. We were won over by the open-hearted, cheery demeanour of the Kuban Cossacks and their women – so remote they seemed, and alien to the Bolshevist infatuation. The Cossacks began to enlist as Volunteers. Still, all was not quite as we had expected.

At first the Kuban Cossacks, with no resistance whatever, calmly surrendered to the Bolsheviks all the guns and ammunition brought from the front by their own men, then looked on anxiously for months, but without stirring a finger while groups of the Red Guard, consisting of regular soldiers, non-Cossack riffraff and their own young men demoralized at the front, sprang up in every village. Under pressure from these Red Guards Bolshevist Soviets were established with, as a result, the wholesale plunder of all well-to-do Cossacks. . . . Their eyes were opened at last, but fear and irresolution kept them inactive.

It was yet too soon: here as elsewhere, we failed to meet with an active national response ready to develop into an open struggle.

Meanwhile the entire region was gradually passing under Bolshevist rule.

The Bolshevist government centre was at Armavir, where considerable Red forces were assembled, and which was holding its own fairly successfully against Ekaterinodar. We had to cross the Vladicaucasian railway, all the junctions of which, including those nearest to us—Tikhoretskaia and Sosyka – were occupied by strong Red detachments, while their armoured trains circulated along the line. To avoid an encounter with them Kornilov, after a number of false demonstrations, ordered the permanent

[1] An ancient Russian custom of presenting bread and salt in token of hospitality.

way to be blown up in both directions, and after a forced march of sixty versts in one day, broke through the line between the two junctions. Only a solitary Bolshevist armoured train, unable to proceed along the torn-up way, sent harmless shells in our wake.

After only once encountering resistance from a band of young Kuban Cossacks at the Berezanskaia station, of which we made short work, we emerged at last into territory occupied by Avtonomov's troops, which were advancing on Ekaterinodar. Somewhere quite near, we did not know exactly where, between Korenevskaia and Ust-Labinskaia lay the front line of the Kuban Volunteer troops (with which we were not yet in touch). To avoid combat now would be inexpedient. Kornilov determined to approach the main line and attack the Bolsheviks in the *rear*. This was the more necessary as already we were experiencing an acute shortage of munitions and we expected to find supplies at the railway stations.

On the 15th March our main forces crossed to Zhuravskaia, while the Kornilovsky regiment, which formed a flank vanguard, captured the Vyselky station and advanced further. Owing to the negligence of our cavalry detachment which had been left at Vyselky and which had abandoned the station without fighting, it was reoccupied by a strong group of Bolsheviks. We only managed to retake it on the 16th after a severe skirmish.

That day we heard most unpleasant news: a short time ago some fighting occurred between the Bolsheviks and Kuban Volunteers under Pokrovsky. The latter were routed and beat a hasty retreat towards Ekaterinodar. Ominous rumours were afloat concerning the capital itself. . . . So far, these were only rumours. . . . Therefore, next day we were ordered to continue the advance on Korenevskaia, where a Bolshevist force, no less than ten thousand men, was concentrated with armoured trains and numerous artillery. They were under the command of a Kuban Cossack named Sorokin, a medical assistant by profession.

We were now confronted, not, as we had thought, by the *rear*, but by the *front* of the group of Ekaterinodar Bolsheviks.

Heavy fighting again on the 17th.

We are advancing in the van with Borovsky's detachment, which had already deployed opposite the northern outskirts of the stanitsa. There is heavy firing. We advance in extended order, no one lies down. Soon the thin lines of the cadets, all upright, are seen moving towards the stanitsa, encircled by a long line of trenches, in which the naked eye could distinguish the massed Bolsheviks. It was a touching and stirring sight, this offensive of striplings, almost children, outwardly so ineffective, yet so beautiful in its gallantry and simplicity.

The main blow against the Stanichnaia station is struck from the left by the Officers' and Kornilovsky regiments. Yet there is a hitch: the Kornilovsky are retreating all along the front. Kornilov and his staff gallop hither under heavy rifle fire. The Bolsheviks are coming on thick and fast. They swarm like black flies against the grey background of the field. A veritable tornado of gun-fire. . . . Shrapnel bullets are raining down on our retreating lines. . . . And the report comes from our baggage:

'We're short of ammunition and shells; shall we deal out the last?'

'Yes; we'll find plenty at the station,' replies Kornilov. Now the Kornilovsky regiment has halted, shuffles, and again advances. The fighting is being drawn out, but here the crisis is over.

Kornilov dispatches the Partisan regiment and the Czecho-Slovak battalion under Bogaevsky – all his reserves

– to outflank the position from the west. No sooner had Bogaevsky left than a report arrives from the baggage column: 'Bolshevist cavalry has appeared close to us in the rear, we are without any cover.' . . . Things are becoming complicated. . . . 'Tell the baggage commander,' replies Kornilov, 'that they have two machine guns and plenty of healthy men. I can give them nothing.'

We rejoin Bogaevsky. His men are slowly deploying, followed by the battery, advancing together with the lines. Borovsky's battalion, which had already twice captured the outskirts of the stanitsa and twice been evicted, rose again and joined in the attack. Half an hour later we were entering Korenevskaia. The battery, having outdistanced the infantry lines, was tearing at a gallop along the wide street towards the bridge across the river, where it charged the crowded mass of Bolsheviks with grape-shot. . . .

At the same time, too, the Officers' and Kornilovsky regiments came up from the east, having overcome the armoured trains and hurricane firing, and forded the river, strewing their course with enemy corpses. The capture of the bridge by the Officers' regiment settled the issue of the battle.

The defeated enemy retired towards the Platnizovskaia stanitsa.

At Korenevskaia the army replenished its supplies, particularly the ammunition. But, alas, at too high a price: in those last few days of fighting our little army lost four hundred men in killed and wounded. True, the loss was somewhat made good by newly recruited Kuban Cossacks.

*

At Korenevskaia the ominous rumours were confirmed. On the night of the 14th March the Kuban Volunteers, the Ataman and 'Rada' (national assembly), abandoned Ekaterinodar and made for the mountains beyond the

River Kuban. This was a heavy blow for the army. The object of the whole operation was lost on the eve of its fulfilment! We were only within two or three marches of Ekaterinodar. The spell of 'Ekaterinodar' had great hold on the Volunteers, and their morale could not but suffer from the disappointment. We were entirely surrounded. Enemy bands met us at nearly every inhabited point; we were compelled to fight almost daily. What were we to do next?

Opinions were divided. Supported by the Chief of Staff, General Romanovsky, I considered it necessary to pursue our original plan, more especially as our break through the enemy circle enveloping us would be determined not so much by this or that direction, as by the destruction of the enemy's live forces, which would entail their political collapse. And then the Kuban would declare for us. Kornilov thought otherwise:

'Would Ekaterinodar but still hold out,' he said, 'there could be no other alternative. But now we cannot afford to run risks. The men must be given a rest from fighting and the nightmare of a field hospital. We shall retire across the Kuban River and there rest in the mountain stanitsas and Tcherkess villages, organize ourselves, and await more favourable conditions.'

Both of us were guided solely by intuition, because beyond our own army circle we knew absolutely nothing. Only rumours crept up from all sides. . . . All around was complete anarchy. . . . Our small cavalry prevented our making any serious distant reconnaissance. Those of our secret scouts, whom we could trust, usually never came back: they were caught, tortured, murdered, at best languished in prisons. . . . We did not know then that beyond the Kuban, too, the army would find itself in a compact Bolshevist environment, and that continuous fighting day after day would be our lot for a long time to come. Nor that by an irony of fate, on the very morning when our army was to turn southward from the Ekaterinodar road, the Kuban Volunteer detachment, believing at last in Kornilov's arrival, would start an advance from the south – towards Ekaterinodar.

On the 18th March an army order was given: At nightfall, and in complete silence, to turn about and make for the Ust-Labinskaia crossing on the Kuban River.

CHAPTER 5

Within the Bolshevist Ring

WE started at dead of night. No sooner had we left Korenevskaia than it was occupied by Sorokin's Bolsheviks, who began to press on our rear. We continued our advance, but two versts from Ust-Labinskaia our vanguard halted, faced with enemy fire. . . .

Our manœuvre was rash almost to folly. It could only be attempted with such an army as the Volunteer Army. It could only be attempted because Kornilov knew his men, and they placed implicit trust in him.

Sorokin's fairly strong detachment was pressing on from the rear, threatening to crush our feeble rearguard under Bogaevsky. Before us lay the stanitsa occupied by forces unknown: a narrow dam two to three versts long; a big bridge which for all we knew might have been blown up; and finally, the railway between Kavkazskaia and Ekaterinodar – two Bolshevist military centres whence reinforcements and armoured trains could be sent to Ust-Labinskaia. . . .

Fighting began both from north and south, the circle closing in nearer and nearer our huge baggage transport, stationed in the middle of the open field, and already under fire of Sorokin's artillery.

That transport held our very life, and, with all our suffering and the terrible chains which clogged our every movement, was the cause of many extra casualties, which in their turn increased and burdened it. It contained all our material supplies, particularly the precious munitions of the nomad army, which possessed neither base nor depots. It numbered already at that time nearly five hundred sick and wounded, whose total by the end of the campaign exceeded fifteen hundred. Lastly, there were many fugitives. The transport shared the life of the army, remaining for hours in the field under fire. Shelter there was none: fighting in front, fighting in the rear, enemy patrols to right and left. . . . The transport patiently awaited the issue of the fighting, listening intently to the firing.

If all suffered, the position of the wounded, particularly of the critical cases, was truly desperate. Nearly every day a long weary journey in a jolting cart through deep mud, ruts, without roads, often at a trot. . . . Three-quarters of the day spent in the open, under pelting rain or in intense cold. Night in a stanitsa just captured from the Bolsheviks, and where often no proper shelter could be found at such short notice for the troops crowding it to overflowing. At times there would be no unloading for two days and nights, with only one halt for reharnessing the horses. And always – on the march or at bivouac – the perpetual boom of firing.

We had no proper sanitary service and were almost entirely deprived of surgical instruments, medicines and bandages. Operations were performed without anæsthetics. . . . The wounded suffered agonies, and even the light cases died from blood-poisoning. The army knew what was going on in the hospital and what was to be found there. Groans and cries for help came from there. But none could remedy the general conditions of the army or heal its gaping wounds, before we broke through the Bolshevist circle.

Death hovered over the hospital, and those young lives fought against it often solely by the strength of their spirit. Many of the wounded kept revolvers under their pillows. . . . No one dared take away their firearms: to dispose of his life at the last was the inalienable right of every Volunteer.

*

Speed was necessary at Ust-Laba on account of the pressure on Bogaevsky's rearguard. Kornilov ordered the Kornilovsky regiment to make a frontal attack on the stanitsa, and sent the Cadet battalion to the right towards the embankment of the Ekaterinodar railway. The cadets advanced rapidly without firing a shot. Met just in front of the railway line by concentrated fire, they charged with a 'Hurrah!' and disappeared over the embankment. The Kornilovsky regiment moved cautiously forward, waiting for the results of the left flank movement. . . .

Suddenly a horseman appeared from the stanitsa, waving frantically – a delegate. The Ust-Labinskaia Bolsheviks have decided to let the army through without fighting. . . . The men rose and moved on, followed by the staff. They had not advanced half a verst, however, when suddenly machine-gun and rifle fire was opened on them from another quarter of the stanitsa, while shrapnel bullets rained from a newly arrived armoured train. These, it appeared, were fresh reinforcements from Kavkazskaia station.

General Kornilov was again exposed to terrific fire, and General Markov, in command of the column, bitterly upbraided the staff:

'Take him away, for goodness' sake! I can't direct the fighting when I'm morally responsible for his life.'

'Will you try yourself, your Excellency?'

A short distance away stood General Alexeyev with his son and aide-de-camp. To an elderly and sick man all these vicissitudes were hard to bear, but none ever heard him complain. While avoiding anything that might appear to General Kornilov as interference in the management of the army, he nevertheless could be seen everywhere, in the hospital, among the transport, in the middle of the fighting. He took everything to heart and helped the Volunteers wherever he could – by advice, cheering words, and his own meagre means.

The flank movement of the Kornilovsky regiment became apparent. The frontal attack was resumed, and soon the whole regiment rushed into the stanitsa and railway station, precipitated the Bolsheviks from the perpendicular cliff which crowned the entrance on the dam, captured the bridge, and crossed the River Kuban. In the heat of the skirmish Colonel Niezhintsev forgot to cover the approaches from Kavkazskaia, so that when the staff entered the stanitsa in the wake of the regiment, a Bolshevist armoured train rolled up, from which fresh infantry alighted. Soon six-inch shells began to explode over the station and stanitsa. . . . And there were the staff and their escort, and no one else!

General Kornilov ordered the Officers' regiment to be called up and a battalion of the Kornilovsky to be brought back from across the river; he also stopped a passing battery of the famous Colonel Mionchinsky. It took almost an hour for the units to assemble, and the Bolshevist attack was kept at bay by the battery alone. . . . We were surrounded on all sides. . . .

Soon, however, General Markov's officers passed the station at a brisk trot and together with Kornilovsky men routed the Bolsheviks, who by now had almost reached the station. The running noose round the army's neck was loosened.

The way lay clear!

As if by telepathy this news immediately spread to the members of our three-verst-long transport. There was general rejoicing. It reached Bogaevsky's rearguard and Borovsky's cadets. They both had carried out their task of holding back the enemy, pressing on us from north and west.

The stanitsa Nekrasovskaia, where we were to halt for the night, was still ten versts away. All night long continued the endless trek of baggage carts and marching columns. The streets of Nekrasovskaia were congested. In twenty-four hours we had made forty-six versts, with continuous fighting to the four points of the compass, besides crossing a river! Utterly exhausted, the men dropped asleep in the street while waiting for their billets, to sleep and dream of the longed-for rest.

They little knew that they would be awakened in the morning by the malicious patter of Bolshevist shrapnel upon the roofs.

*

Nekrasovskaia was situated on the River Laba. Several Bolshevist bands and a battery occupied its reed-grown left bank and the adjacent homesteads, and on the morning of the 7th opened gun and machine-gun fire on the stanitsa perched on the hilly opposite bank. Our troops were worn out, and to build a pontoon bridge and cross the deep river in daylight under enemy fire would bring heavy casualties. General Kornilov ordered the vanguard to start crossing in the night.

In the daytime we discussed our further plans. Fate was cruelly mocking: the trans-Kuban region where the army had expected to rest was seething with Bolsheviks. In this particular district, with a dense non-Cossack population, Soviet rule had been introduced long since, alongside a military organization consisting of undisciplined but well-armed savage bands with headquarters in the village of Philipovskoe. Following the general itinerary of our army's movements, the Bolsheviks intended to intercept us at Maikop, whither the Kuban Revolutionary Committee was concentrating troops, guns and munitions. We decided to confirm the supposition of the Bolsheviks by making a demonstration march to the south; then after crossing the River Bielaia to veer sharply westward. This would bring us into the region of the Tcherkess *aouls*,[1] friendly disposed to our army, and without diverting us from our main objective – Ekaterinodar – would enable us to join the Kuban Volunteer unit which, it was rumoured, had retreated towards the Hot Springs.

All day long shells flying from the south exploded over the stanitsa; all day could be heard the roar of the cannon from the north, in the direction of Ust-Laba, against which the Kornilovsky formed a cover. A tall stone church stood in the middle of the village green; its belfry towered far above the low-lying opposite bank and could be seen miles away. Now it served as a target. The green was deserted; now and again some terrified inhabitant would dart across to the church. A service was going on. The church was filled with worshippers, both villagers and Volunteers; wounded stood leaning on crutches or swathed in bandages. Whenever a sharp report echoed behind the wall, or bullets pattered against the cupola like hail, the voice from the altar grew more muffled, and the heads of the congregation bowed lower.

The church – the sole refuge as yet uninvaded by the bestial hordes. . . . To-morrow 'they' would come, kill the priest and profane the church.

*

In the night of the 21st March our advance units crossed, fighting, to the left bank of the Laba, and having

[1] A small mountain people inhabiting the southern district of the Kuban territory. Aoul – village, hamlet.

repulsed the Bolsheviks, enabled the army to follow. The first to do so was the Cadet battalion, which forded the river, the water being often above the head of many a lad. After crossing our troops found themselves immediately surrounded by compact Bolshevist masses. Every farmstead, every copse and separate building was bristling with hundreds of rifles, and greeted the advancing Volunteers with volleys. Any platoon swerving from the road fell into an ambush and disappeared. . . . Soon the broad river valley, as far as the eye could reach, was lit up by conflagrations; the fires sprang up from exploded shells or were the work of the avenging hand of a Cossack or Volunteer, or simply the result of some smouldering torch left carelessly near the huts deserted by the population.

The Markovsky, Partisans, and Cadets were advancing south fanwise, ousting the enemy, who sprang up everywhere, unexpected and elusive. Niezhintsev's rearguard, which had covered us from Ust-Laba, had now shifted to the northern outskirts of Nekrasovskaia. Down below, beneath the steep bank, the baggage transport was still feverishly crossing the river. The slender bridge was overcrowded, and some of the vans laden with fugitives and the heavily wounded descended to the deep fords. Sometimes the vans would overturn, or carried downstream to some deep spot would sink almost completely into the icy water with their contents of helplessly writhing human cargo. On the further bank the transport halted in a widely spread bivouac, waiting for the way to be 'opened up.'

It was only at sunset that the army succeeded somewhat in distending the ring which encompassed it and reached the cramped Kiselevsky farms for the night. We were actually masters of only those two small farms, guarded by outposts a short distance off. Beyond them, during the night, the ring round us was again drawn closer. In the early morning of the 22nd the army, surrounded on all sides, began to push onwards towards Philipovskoe. To widen our zone of action, the columns advanced in extending radius, stubbornly fighting for every verst of ground. The transport halted within a verst of the village. Already fighting was going on at the outskirts, and shells were bursting over the transport in front, behind, and from somewhere else besides, apparently from Nekrasovskaia.

We rode up to the Officers' regiment and watched their splendid advance and attack. Attacked by the Officers, the Bolsheviks fell back. The ring had expanded. The way was clear. Immediately the main forces and transport, under cover of part of the Officers' regiment, which continued the pursuit, pushed on towards Philipovskoe, but after advancing three versts halted again: fighting was still going on to the right of them, distant firing could be heard in front, and no news came from Niezhintsev, who had been dispatched to Philipovskoe.

We stood for a long time in the field. Night came on, calm and starless. Men lay down by the roadside, talking softly to one another.

What were they thinking of?

Of their perishing mother country. . . . Of the past – so far off, never to return. . . . Of fame and feats of valour, of the joy of life. . . . Of the morrow, when we should again be surrounded. . . . Of the grave-mounds that have sprung everywhere in our wake . . . perhaps to-day or to-morrow more will be added to them. . . . And lastly, simply of a warm shelter and a plentiful supper.

Straight to the west, in the direction of Ekaterinodar, the dark sky was suddenly crossed as by pale lightning, and from afar came the rumble as of distant thunder.

Look, look; that's Pokrovsky!

It was as though an electric tremor shook the column.

All strained their eyes, trying to solve the mysterious meaning of these far-off lightning flashes; they saw the invisible, listened to the soundless. . . .

One thing was certain: somewhere, some scores of versts away, there was an artillery duel. Two forces opposed each other, of which one was not unfriendly to us. We were not alone.

Soon there came other good news: after a short skirmish the Kornilovsky had entered Philipovskoe, abandoned by the Bolsheviks, and completely deserted by all its inhabitants.

*

In Philipovskoe itself stores were being looted, packing-cases smashed open. . . . That was the reverse side of the medal. The hard conditions of civil war were in direct opposition to social morality. Our commissariat was unable to organize a regular local service of supplies from the villages occupied in fighting overnight and abandoned next morning. The number of our field kitchens and cauldrons was insignificant. The troops depended on the inmates of every house. Towards the middle of the campaign we had scarcely any money left and organized barter was handicapped by the insurmountable mistrust of the population. The non-Cossack populace often concealed their supplies and drove the cattle away to distant fields. Hunger, cold, and ragged clothing are bad counsellors – especially when a village is deserted by its inhabitants. How great was our need may be gauged by the fact that even officers, with their almost bare feet lacerated and bleeding, did not scruple to pull the boots off dead Bolsheviks! This painful question was further complicated by a purely psychological factor. It was extremely difficult to inspire a Cossack or Tcherkess, whose cottage had just been burnt down or homestead plundered by the Bolsheviks, with respect for the 'private property' of the Bolsheviks, which they sincerely thought all the non-Cossacks to be. The elusiveness, and consequently the impunity of most crimes, provided wide scope for unprincipled men, temptation to the morally unbalanced, and caused much suffering to the upright.

War and revolution were too bad a school for the moral training of the nation and army.

General Kornilov fought these abuses with stern measures. He was unable completely to eradicate lawlessness, but succeeded in keeping it within certain bounds.

*

On the 23rd March the fighting was particularly severe and sanguinary.

At dawn a battalion of the Kornilovsky regiment, which moved in the van, crossed the River Bielaia and veering sharp to the left, pushed on towards the Riazanskaia stanitsa. The road lay along a low valley, gradually drawing away from the river and approaching a ridge of hillocks running parallel to it. No sooner did the bulk of the regiment commence crossing, than thick lines of Bolsheviks appeared over the ridge and opened a heavy fire on the bridges. There was a momentary confusion. The men hurled themselves from the bridge; many fell in the water. There were some casualties, but soon the regiment rallied and, aided by artillery fire, repulsed the Bolshevist front. Merely repulsed it, because we were confronted by forces considerably superior to our army, and assembled from all parts to defend the approaches to Maikop. Their successful deployment along the heights parallel to the river placed the Volunteer Army in a critical position, confined as it was in the narrow valley of of a marshy, unfordable river.

Scarcely had our main forces time to rally than the

Bolsheviks renewed their offensive on a wide front. And in spite of this, our unfortunate baggage transport had to cross the river and move forward to meet their fire, because our enemies of yesterday were already pressing on to Philipovskoe from the north; their batteries were shelling the village and the crossing from the rear, and Borovsky and his cadets had great difficulty to keep them at bay.

The crossing by one bridge seemed interminable; should we be able to hold the ridge?

Already the Czecho-Slovaks were beginning to retreat, having spent all their cartridges; their separate figures could be seen coming down from the hill. General Kornilov's escort galloped towards them. The Kornilovsky regiment was well-nigh exhausted; already one battalion, whose commander was killed, vacillated. . . . The Bolsheviks were coming on incessantly in serried lines, like a compact wall; one could hear their shouting and cursing. Our losses were growing. . . . Niezhintsev sent to ask for reinforcements. Where to find them?

General Kornilov with his staff stood at the bridge watching a column march past. His look was stern and calm. By his order officers and men attached to the transport who looked fit to fight were taken aside. Rifles and cartridges were distributed to them, and two companies of fifty to sixty men each marched towards the heights.

'Moral reinforcements!'

Their fighting value was not great, but the mere sight of any fresh 'force' on the field of battle produced an impression on friend and foe alike.

All day fighting went on with alternating success, the forces were too unequal. All day enemy shells dropped on the ridge, the village, the crossing, and the valley where stood the transport, as if rooted to earth. Our guns replied but seldom, by solitary shots – shells and cartridges had almost completely run short. There were many wounded.

. . . Several vans in the transport were smashed by shells. General Alexeyev's cart was overturned and his driver mortally wounded; he himself was watching the fighting from a neighbouring promontory. Already rifles were distributed to the lightly wounded in the hospital. . . . And when the dry crackling of machine guns became painfully clear and close, there was commotion in the waggons laden with helpless, quivering bodies. A muffled voice was heard asking: 'Sister, is it time to shoot oneself?'

The distance between the river and the black advancing lines was lessening visibly. . . .

In all heavy battles there are moments, sometimes long hours, of a strange, unstable equilibrium. A mere impulse, insignificant and imperceptible, suffices to upset it and break the will power of the side which *psychologically* acknowledges itself to be defeated. So it was that day. With and without command our troops suddenly charged all along the front of the left bank, and the enemy was thrown back. In the westward direction a wide breach was cleared, and the column, winding in and out among the foothills of the Caucasian range, was pushing rapidly westward, speeded from right and left by harmless artillery fire.

This soon ceased. We advanced sometimes along the steppe, sometimes through thin brushwood in the silent, soundless calm of the dying day. Peace and joy were in our hearts. All the weariness and strain of battle had disappeared. Laughter, jokes. . . . Suddenly a song burst out:

'So to Kornilov, Russia, and our Faith
We'll raise a loud "Hurrah"!'

*

We halted at Riazanskaia. For the first time a Cossack stanitsa felt unhomely, almost oppressive. Fear and servility! Only next day in a Tcherkess village did we learn the cause of this. It appeared that this stanitsa was the first to embrace Bolshevism, Cossacks and 'strangers' uniting. Together they attacked and looted the peaceful neighbouring aouls, and in Gabunai, the nearest, murdered nearly all (three hundred and twenty) the male population. Murdered savagely! In the empty Tcherkess huts the Volunteers discovered heaped-up human intestines. . . . For several days afterwards the Cossacks and peasants of Riazanskaia with their women and children drove to the aoul and carried away the plunder. . . . The aoul was like a cemetery.

The Tcherkess were overwhelmed and crushed by the revolution, which to them appeared as wholesale banditism. We were welcomed as liberators, made much of, and seen off with apprehension.

Here, in the aoul, the staff at last obtained correct information concerning the Kuban Volunteers under Pokrovsky: he was lately known to be fighting in the neighbourhood of the aoul Shendzhy, about fifty versts from where we were. It was necessary to hurry to prevent the Bolsheviks from defeating the Kuban Volunteers before they joined us. General Kornilov therefore led the army by heavy roads at as rapid a pace as was compatible with our transport, now swollen to enormous proportions. We marched forty versts from Philipovskoe to Panazhukai in two days without unloading. Thence, similarly, after a day's rest, another forty versts to Shendzhy. The army well understood the significance of these forced marches. Those who, with festering wounds and broken bones, were jolted night and day in carts along ruts and bumps, also understood, bore it patiently and looked on . . . how death carried them away one by one. . . .

On the 26th March we entered Shendzhy, and next day, accompanied by a motley escort, Pokrovsky rode into the aoul.

CHAPTER 6

The Kuban Detachment Joins the Volunteer Army

THE abandonment of Ekaterinodar by the Kuban troops was not so much a matter of necessity as of psychology.

Already, in the beginning of October, the regional Kuban 'Rada' (assembly) proclaimed the Kuban region's transformation into an independent 'Kuban Republic.' This, for some, represented a temporary issue out of the chaos into which Russia had been plunged at the end of the Provisional Government; for others it meant the realization of unfounded separatist tendencies and petty local ambitions. The resolution was passed by a considerable majority, composed of the somewhat original combination of the votes of the 'elders' – a conservative element alien to all politics, and those of the Cossack intelligentsia. This latter sported the party names of Social Revolutionaries and Social Democrats, but used socialist theories merely 'for export,' while preserving at home all the traditional caste barriers. Thus neither the Conservatives nor Socialists recognized the equal rights of the non-Cossack population, nor were willing to share the Cossack land fund with the peasants who constituted nearly one-half of the population. The 'Rada' and the Socialist Government were flatly opposed by the young Cossacks from the front and the non-Cossack population, both of whom, as I said, strongly inclined to Bolshevism.

When, therefore, militant Bolshevism hurled itself on the region and defence became imminent, the Kuban

Government had no one to turn to, and was obliged to resort to a universal panacea – the formation of a Volunteer detachment of officers and cadets whom chance had brought to the Kuban.

Being alike intolerant in its attitude both towards the Cossacks and non-Cossacks, the Kuban Government found itself compelled to hand over the command of these troops, not to a Cossack, but to a captain of the air force, Pokrovsky.

Pokrovsky was a young man whom no one knew anything about. He was, however, boiling over with energy, was daring, cruel, and ambitious. He accomplished what others failed to do: mustered a detachment which alone presented an active force. But the aims held out to him were vague and uncertain: to defend the 'Kuban Republic' and its socialistic and somewhat pro-Ukrainian Government? . . . Such aims were alien to a Russian officer. So the Kuban Volunteers fought in the dark and lived on rumours of Kornilov, of the Czecho-Slovaks, the Allied fleet – of all those actual and yet irrealizable phantoms which, they thought, *must appear*, sweep away the Bolsheviks, and save the country and themselves.

Pokrovsky defeated the Bolsheviks advancing from Novorossisk and covered Ekaterinodar from the direction of Tikhoretskaia. But in the beginning of February, after an unsuccessful encounter near Vysselky, he was forced to withdraw his troops towards Ekaterinodar and encamp on the nearest approaches to the town.

The Don Cossack territory succumbed in February and the Bolshevist forces approached Ekaterinodar. The 'Rada' and the Government went on with their endless political debates, and the elaboration of a 'most perfect' Constitution, but were both unable and incapable of strengthening their army. In these circumstances the decision to

abandon Ekaterinodar was quite correct. But on the
10th March the situation completely changed. That day,
as though by a miracle, an officer, dispatched by the
staff of the Volunteer Army, appeared in the town, having
managed to pass through the Bolshevist cordon. For a
long time he earnestly and in vain tried to persuade the
Kuban authorities to delay their departure in view of
Kornilov's speedy arrival in Ekaterinodar. He was, he
affirmed, quite close. They disbelieved him. . . . They
decided to go to the mountains.

In the evening of the 13th March the Volunteers, and
the ataman, followed by all the Kuban authorities, the
municipal 'notables' and numerous fugitives, crossed the
River Kuban and headed southward. Among them was
the late President of the Russian Imperial Duma,
Rodsianko.

On the 14th March Sorokin's Bolshevist troops entered
the town. This marked the beginning of unheard-of
atrocities, plunder, and murder.

*

The Kuban troops, drawn into larger units, represented
a force of three thousand men, foot and horse, with
artillery. Advancing southward into the mountains they
reached the Penzenskaia stanitsa. The absence, however,
of a definite political and strategic objective capable of
welding together this heterogeneous mass made itself so
acutely felt already during these few days of campaign, that
the Kuban authorities decided to make the junction with
General Kornilov their first aim. It should be noted that
ever since January General Erdeli and M. Fedorov, the
emissaries of the Volunteer Army, had endeavoured to
persuade the Kuban Government of the necessity for
entrusting united command to General Kornilov and to
render material assistance to the Volunteer Army. Their

76

mission had met with resistance. Now, day and night, the Kuban wireless rent the air with the alarm call:

'Kornilov! Kornilov!'

We never heard them – we had no wireless station. But by intuition we felt it. . . .

Meanwhile, authentic information was received at Kuban headquarters of the Volunteer Army's advance on Ekaterinodar and of the fighting which took place east of the town on the 15th to 17th March. Pokrovsky turned back. On the 20th, by a surprise attack, he captured the river-crossing at Pashkovskaia, and for two days kept up an artillery duel near Ekaterinodar without, however, engaging himself in a serious affair. But on the night of the 23rd, despairing of Kornilov's coming, he turned eastward where, at the aoul of Vochepshy, he encountered serious Bolshevist resistance. The fighting lasted till nightfall. The failure to rejoin Kornilov and the apparently aimless movements of the unit had a disastrous effect on the morale of the troops. The village was not taken. The detachment, in confusion, abandoning the baggage, struck out at dead of night, and without roads, for the mountains, towards the Kaluzhskaia stanitsa. But already considerable Bolshevist forces were advancing from Kaluzhskaia. Sharp fighting lasted all the next day, during which the Kuban troops, their backs to the wall, succeeded in driving off the Bolsheviks with great loss.

Worn out and deadly cold, the troops spent the night in an open field in pouring rain. Behind them lay Vochepshy, occupied by Bolsheviks; in front – Kaluzhskaia, where fighting was still going on with their advance parties.

Suddenly, amid those despairing moments, the news ran like wildfire across the field to the transport camp, among the troops:

'Kornilov's patrol has arrived! Kornilov's army is near!'

'We were mad with joy,' one of the Kuban men told me afterwards. 'It was as if a lid which pressed down on us had suddenly flown open, and we again saw the light of day.'

Kaluzhskaia was taken next day and the Kuban detachment was billeted in the village.

On the 27th a meeting took place between Pokrovsky and the senior generals of the Volunteer Army at the aoul of Shendzhy. We insisted that the Kuban Volunteers should be in complete subordination to General Kornilov and drafted into our army. Pokrovsky, with all due modesty but with insistence, held the opposite view. 'The Kuban Government,' he said, 'wished to have an army of its own, as conforming to the country's Constitution. Any change might provoke unrest in the ranks.' He proposed merely 'working subordination.' Such arguing among the scant forces completely surrounded by the Bolsheviks produced an incongruous and painful impression. General Kornilov wound it up tersely and sharply:

'A single army under one commander! I admit of nothing else! Kindly inform your Government.'

Although the question still remained open, the strategic position admitted of no procrastination. It was therefore decided to launch next day a concentric advance on the Novo-Dmitrovskaia stanitsa held by a strong Bolshevist force, and there to effect a junction.

This move in a south-westerly direction, instead of to Kaluzhskaia and the mountains, where we should be doomed to starvation and dispersion, embodied the impression of willingness for an active struggle, testified to confidence in our own strength and foreshadowed the trend of subsequent developments.

*

28th March – the *Ice Campaign* – the glory of Markov and the Officers' regiment, the pride of the Volunteer Army. Vivid are the memories of every campaigner of those days which appear more like a legend than reality!

It rained heavily all the previous night, and continued to rain in the morning. The army moved across spaces completely covered with water and liquid mud, along roads and without them, in dense fog which enveloped the whole country round. Cold moisture permeated the clothes. The men advanced slowly, shivering with cold, dragging their feet in their heavy water-clogged boots. By noon it started snowing heavily and a wind sprang up. Eyes, nose, ears were choked, sharp needles stung the face.

Shots were heard in front. About two or three versts from Novo-Dmitrovskaia ran a river on the opposite bank of which was a Bolshevist outpost. They were thrown back by our vanguard, but the bridge had been carried away by the swollen, rushing river. Horsemen were sent in search of a ford. They searched for a long time, missing their footing and sometimes plunging man and horse deep into the water. At last the Markovsky mounted scouts discovered a deep ford near by. At that moment the men caught a glimpse of General Markov's white *papakha* (tall fur cap), and his sonorous voice sounded from across the river:

'All horses to the bridge! The regiment to cross on horseback and pillion!'

The crossing, tedious and wearying, began: the depth was half the height of a horse, and not more than two at a time could move abreast. They tried to drag a gun. The horses shied, got entangled in the harness, and overturned both the gun and outriders into the water. Simultaneously, the ford began to be shelled by enemy artillery. Shell after shell struck the bank and splashed into the river.

One fell into a bonfire round which Volunteers were warming themselves, scattering, bruising and wounding the men.

Once more the weather changed: it began to freeze hard,
the wind increased, and a blizzard set in. Men and horses
were covered with an ice crust; everything seemed frozen
to the very core, clothes became hard as though wooden,
and hampered every movement; it was difficult to turn
one's head.

Evening was drawing in. The sound of rifle shots was
drowned by the howling of the snowstorm. In the field
by the side of the road leading to Novo-Dmitrovskaia
were abandoned guns and waggons stuck in the deep
mud, now covered with a crust of ice. A long file of men
was plodding along the road. Moving like shadows, they
took no notice of the bullets whistling by. They plodded
along and dropped by the wayside, half frozen and
exhausted. . . . General Kornilov with his staff rode past;
his escort was assisting the infantry to cross. Complete
darkness set in.

General Markov, having crossed the river with the
Officers' regiment, which he deployed against the stanitsa,
now found himself completely isolated. The cavalry, sent
to carry out a right-flank movement, failed to discover a
ford and returned to where the bulk were crossing; the
artillery had stuck in the mud; the next regiment – the
Partisans, had by 5 p.m. barely started crossing.
Pokrovsky, who was to have attacked the stanitsa from
the south, did not appear, deeming it impossible to move
his men in such weather and along such roads.

General Markov decided:

'See here, boys! There's no one to wait for. Without
shelter on such a night as this we'll all perish. Forward,
then, to the stanitsa!'

And at the head of his regiment hurled himself against
a hailstorm of rifle and machine-gun fire.

Half frozen, clutching their rifles in their numbed fingers, tripping and falling in the morass of mud, snow, and ice, the officers ran towards the stanitsa, rushed in, and joined in a hand-to-hand fight with the Bolsheviks. They pursued the Bolsheviks right across the village, met by volleys from nearly every cottage, in which Red reserve troops, not expecting such an impetuous attack, sat warming themselves.

Without waiting for the stanitsa to be cleared, General Kornilov with several members of his staff rode up to the customary rallying-point, the administrative headquarters of the stanitsa. The General entered the building by one door just as a crowd of Bolsheviks was trying to escape by another, but were fired at point-blank.

Firing went on all night. All night the army continued crossing the river, and all the next day was taken up with hauling the vans and artillery out of the mud. In the morning the Bolsheviks attacked Novo-Dmitrovskaia but were repulsed with heavy loss. Since then our stanitsa was shelled daily by their artillery stationed at Grigorievskaia.

That same day, the 28th, our transport pushed on to Kaluzhskaia, which it reached late at night. The sick and wounded had lain all day in icy cold water. . . . Death hovered over them.

*

The Kuban delegates arrived at Novo-Dmitrovskaia on the 30th. Before that the military section of the Kuban group sent word that they recognized General Kornilov as their sole authority, and should their own superiors and the Kuban Government refuse to submit to him, they would all cross over to us. In order not to create dangerous precedents, and not to undermine discipline, we decided to try and persuade the Kuban authorities to accept a peaceful settlement.

F

Long and tedious discussions ensued. One side was compelled to prove the elementary principles of military discipline, while the other brought forth such arguments as 'the Constitution of the sovereign Kuban republic,' the need of maintaining an autonomous army as the mainstay of the Government, and so forth. To us, all this rhetoric, following on the stern and cruel experiences of war, was reminiscent of something long past and seemingly dead and buried: the long-winded harangues of 1917 which ruined the army, the disputes with the Don Government, the assemblies and committees, all of which had paved the way to the Don territory for Sievers and his Red troops.

General Kornilov definitely announced that he refused to command 'autonomous' armies.

The ridiculous quibble went on, but the conference was soon brought back to a sense of reality: the walls shook and windows rattled; several shells dropped near our house; one splashed the window panes with mud, another smashed the gate. . . .

Finally an agreement was reached. The protocol stated that:

'Par. 1. – The absolute subordination of the Kuban Government's detachment to General Kornilov is recognized as being necessary. Par. 2. – That the Kuban Government continued their activities.' And 'Par. 3. – That Pokrovsky was appointed a member of the Government, to proceed further with the formation of the Kuban Army.' This clause which the Kuban delegates insisted on including, on the alleged motive of giving moral satisfaction to the deposed commander, was the cause of many future complications in our relations with the Kuban.

Within the next few days the Kuban troops joined us from Kaluzhskaia and were drafted into the Volunteer Army, which, after some shifting, was organized as follows:

1st Brigade (*General Markov*): Officers' regiment; 1st Kuban snipers' regiment; 1st Engineer company; 1st and 4th Batteries.

2nd Brigade (*General Bogaevsky*): Kornilovsky 'shock' regiment; Partisan regiment; Plastunsky regiment; 2nd Engineer company; 2nd, 3rd, and 5th Batteries.

Cavalry Brigade (*General Erdeli*):[1] 1st Cavalry regiment; Kuban regiment; Tcherkess regiment; Mounted Battery.

The Czecho-Slovak Engineer battalion was not included in the brigades.

The total strength of the army had now risen to six thousand fighters. But our baggage transport had also doubled. . . .

*

The attack on Ekaterinodar was decided upon. Some were doubtful, but none disagreed, since so far the army had suffered no reverses, and in the face of stupendous difficulties had carried out every manœuvre undertaken by the commander.

The plan was as follows: (1) To disperse the enemy bands operating round Ekaterinodar in order to guarantee the crossing of the River Kuban and replenish munitions from the Bolsheviks; (2) by a sudden attack to seize Elisavetinskaia stanitsa, twenty kilometres west of Ekaterinodar, where there was only a ferry-crossing and where we were least expected; (3) there to cross the Kuban River and attack Ekaterinodar.

In pursuance of this plan the Volunteers in the beginning of April cleared, by fighting, a wide sector south of Ekaterinodar, then on the 7th the army moved further west, and on the 8th concentrated at the crossing at Elisavetinskaia already occupied by our cavalry.

*

[1] Was army commander in the Great War.

The way the crossing of the River Kuban was carried out is extremely interesting, not only on technical grounds, but by its extremely daring idea.

The river at Elisavetinskaia was crossed by a ferry carrying normally either fifteen horsemen or four waggons or fifty foot-passengers. Later, a second smaller ferry was towed up from somewhere downstream, with hawser out of order and working by fits and starts. There were also a dozen or so fishing smacks. These were all the means at our disposal for transporting an army with baggage and fugitives, amounting to not less than nine thousand men, about four thousand horses, and six hundred waggons, guns, caissons, etc. The operation was being carried out under menace from the left bank on the part of the Bolsheviks holding the railway bridge, and under certain pressure from the right on the part of the vanguard of the Ekaterinodar group.

The crossing, carried out in perfect order, lasted three days under almost peaceful conditions, being under fire only for several hours. A retreat with fighting would have taken much longer, or rather, would have been impossible, and, in the event of a reverse, would have meant destruction. Once brought across to the right bank, the huge transport – the army's movable rear, with its back to the river, would be at the mercy of any chance issue of the fighting. . . .

To resolve on such an operation needed the *firm* faith of the leader in his army and his war luck.

General Kornilov had no doubts. We talked on the 9th of the seizure of Ekaterinodar as of something inevitable and absolutely certain. That same day General Kornilov for the first time issued an *order* to the neighbouring stanitsas to present a fixed number of Cossacks fully armed to the Volunteer Army.

Neither had the army any doubts.

The Kornilovsky and Partisans, following the cavalry, crowded joyfully at the ferry, in a hurry to cross. Markov's officers chafed, jealous of those who had gone forward to fight, while their general grumbled at being left with his brigade in the rearguard on the left bank till the whole transport should have crossed. Good spirits reigned, too, in the transport's little nomad town, which by a freak of fate had suddenly sprung up on the bank of the Kuban. There stood hundreds of waggons; fettered horses grazed; multicoloured tatters were spread out to dry in the still cold spring sunshine; bonfires smoked and crackled; groups of people were scattered all over the field, impatiently awaiting their turn to cross and thirsting for news from across the river. . . .

As in the days of yore – a camp of crusaders – lunatics or saints, arrived from beyond the seas and mountains, beneath the walls of the holy city. . . .

Our army, too, had its little 'Jerusalem.' Not yet *the* one, the sacred heart of Russia – Moscow – but one nearer.

Ekaterinodar! It drew us on as by a magic force. Even men of a cool brain, clearly apprising the whole military and political situation, fell under its hypnotic spell. While to the masses it meant an end to all their sufferings and the beginning of a new life.

Why this should be so no one exactly knew, but all believed that so it would be.

CHAPTER 7

The Assault of Ekaterinodar and Death of General Kornilov

By 9th April Erdeli's cavalry and the 2nd brigade under Bogaevsky had already crossed to the right bank of the River Kuban. General Markov's brigade covered the transport. The bold plan which had struck the Bolsheviks and upset all their own calculations was not carried to its logical conclusion.

Sentiment triumphed over the principles of tactics – the great moral force of the leader drew towards him the hearts of his men, and at the same time narrowed the scope of strategy and tactics.

In view of the difficulties presented by the marshes of the left bank, General Kornilov could have left only a small party to protect the transport and so concentrate Markov's brigade at Elisavetinskaia by the 9th. But the wounded had spent three nights in the open, and should a serious attack supervene, the whole body of the transport would fall into the hands of the Bolsheviks.

So General Kornilov left on the left bank one-third of his troops with such a moral force as Markov. The 1st brigade entered the firing line in sections from noon on the 10th to the evening of the 11th.

The fight for Ekaterinodar had begun.

On the morning of the 9th a Bolshevist detachment from Ekaterinodar launched an offensive against Elisavetinskaia and opened artillery fire, trying to locate the place of crossing. They were thrown back by the men of Bogaev-sky's brigade, however. Unable to stand this counter-attack crowds of the Bolsheviks ran in complete disorder, and halted only on the line of the 'farm,' some three versts from the town.

This easily won success, together with the news of a panic in Ekaterinodar, evacuation of which was alleged to have begun, as well as reports of advancing Bolshevist reinforcements, prompted General Kornilov to deal a decisive blow without waiting for the final concentration of all our forces. Late at night came the order to the Sniper regiment of the Markov brigade to speed up the crossing of the Kuban while Bogaevsky and Erdeli were to launch the attack on Ekaterinodar on the 10th.

That morning Bogaevsky began the march on Ekateri-nodar. The Partisan regiment was ordered to attack the western suburb of the town, and the Kornilovsky the Black Sea railway station to the north. The cavalry advanced still further to the left in an encircling flank movement from north and north-east, to cut off com-munication along the Black Sea and Vladikavkaz railways, and raise the Cossacks of the Pashkovskaia stanitsa.

After a twofold attack and some severe fighting General Kasanovitch with his Partisans and reinforced by Kuban Cossacks under Colonel Ulagai, succeeded at last in capturing the farm. Many brave men fell that day, and many others were wounded, including Kasanovitch him-self, the Kuban Chief, Colonel Ulagai and a prominent Partisan, Lasarev. We arrived at the farm soon after it had been taken. From the hill-top on which it was situated, spread the panorama of Ekaterinodar with rows of Bol-shevist trenches in the foreground. Next to the farm stood our battery. Each instalment on a new position spelt tragedy: ten rounds of ammunition against a range needing hundreds; compulsory silence when the infantry was unable to rise under a hailstorm of enemy bullets. . . . The Kornilovsky regiment, with Colonel Niezhintsev leading, was advancing across an open field to the north of the railway, towards the ancient burial mound. To the right, the Partisan and Scouts' regiments crept stealthily towards the river-bank and disappeared in the wood in the direction of the tanneries. Just before nightfall the news was received that after severe fighting they had captured the suburb and were pushing on. Among the staff spirits ran high. No one doubted now the fall of Ekaterinodar. The Red Guard had never been known, after losing a suburb, to accept a fight within the town itself.

*

General Kornilov and his staff were quartered at the farm. Perched on the high precipitous bank, standing alone in the midst of an open field surrounded by a line of tall, leafless poplars and with a big square at the back, the farm could be seen distinctly from any spot on the outskirts of the town. Its four small rooms were filled to overflowing; the whole staff were there and also the dressing-station, whence cries and groans resounded all night. General Kornilov with his two aides-de-camp lay down in one of the rooms on a heap of straw.

. On the morning of the 11th we were roused by the bursting of the enemy shells; from then onwards, day after day, from sunrise to sunset, the Bolshevist batteries never ceased to bombard the farm and wood with a cross fire. The danger of choosing such a spot for Staff Headquarters was often pointed out to General Kornilov, but he refused to listen.

As it turned out we failed to move our lines during the night. Kasanovitch met with stubborn resistance at the artillery barracks surrounded by an earthen rampart. His repeated attacks, while resulting in serious casualties were unsuccessful. He was now undertaking 'a more thorough artillery preparation,' which in our jargon signified fifteen to twenty extra shells! The Kornilovsky regiment, greatly weakened by previous fighting, was melting away. The newly drafted contingents of raw, almost untrained Kuban Cossacks, when launched into the thick of the fighting, lost their heads and became unnerved. And Niezhintsev placed the last weight in the balance – the fascination of his personality, and remained for two days on end on the summit of the mound, round which bullets rained and human bodies were torn to atoms by bursting shells. General Erdeli alone appeared to be successful: his cavalry occupied the northern suburb of 'Sady' and pushed further towards Pashkovskaia.

Meanwhile, companies of the Officers' regiment from the other bank of the river filed past us along the tow-path; Markov also appeared with his men. Now that the entire brigade was concentrated in one place, it was decided to disentangle the mixed-up units and at five o'clock to renew the attack all along the front.

Markov's regiments seemed stationary before the artillery barracks. The men lay as if rooted to the ground; one could not raise one's head without being grazed by a bullet. . . . Markov himself, with two officers and scouts, sat in a deep ditch impatiently waiting for the attack to begin: the command has been given, yet the men hesitate.

'Well, it seems without us there's nothing doing!' Markov ran up the rampart and on towards the lines.

'Forward, friends, attack!'

The field came to life; the Volunteers sprang up and all the living hurled themselves against the death-bearing rampart, leaving behind on the cobbled pavement or the turned-up field convulsively writhing or deadly still bodies.

The artillery barracks were captured.

When news of this reached the left flank, Niezhintsev

commanded the attack. From the top of the mound he could see how the line got up and lay down again; he felt that the limit of human daring had been reached and the time came to draw on the 'last reserve.' . . . He ran down the mound, crossed into the ravine and raised the lines.

'Kornilov's men, forward!'

His voice choked in his throat! A bullet struck his head. He fell! Rose again, tottered a few steps and dropped again, struck dead by a second bullet.

Staggered by the death of their commander and having lost many officers in dead and wounded, the confused lines of the Kornilovsky, Partisans and Kuban Cossacks rolled back into the ravine and the trenches.

The last reserve battalion was meantime advancing to the fatal mound, and General Kasanovitch, overcoming the pain of his fractured shoulder, was leading it to the attack. By his enthusiasm, under terrific fire, he carried the Elisavetinskis, overthrew the advance Bolshevist lines, and in hot pursuit in the darkness pushed on towards the town. . . .

That same evening General Bogaevsky, making a round of the position, visited Niezhintsev's mound, with its gallant little garrison, of whom only three were alive, all the rest lying dead. Bullets whizzed round them, burying themselves in the bodies of the slain. Lying alongside the fallen commander of the Kornilovsky, General Bogaevsky calmly heard the whispered report of his successor. . . .

When Niezhentsev's death was reported to Kornilov, he buried his face in his hands and for a long time remained silent. He became stern and moody. After that not a joke ever left his lips, nor did anyone ever see him smile.

*

By nightfall the army's position was as follows: General Markov's brigade was consolidating its position round the artillery barracks. With the Partisans all connection was severed and nothing known of their fate. The Kornilovsky regiment, much depleted, was occupying its old positions. General Erdeli was retiring towards Sady.

Yet we learnt next day that success had been almost guaranteed, and that it had been snatched from our hands by a series of fatal misadventures.

In the evening of the 11th, General Kasanovitch, in pursuit of the Bolsheviks, rushed into the town and, meeting with no resistance, advanced further down the streets. Firing had ceased completely, and Kasanovitch was convinced that his right-hand neighbours were likewise advancing down the adjoining streets. They thus reached the Haymarket. Loaded baggage waggons were moving from the opposite direction, and these Kasanovitch seized, thus renewing his supplies of precious rifle and artillery cartridges.

'Meantime the night wore away,' General Kasanovitch told us afterwards. 'I was beginning to feel anxious at the absence of news from our other units and dispatched patrols, on horses seized from the Bolsheviks, to explore the streets through which we had passed. On their return the patrols reported that none of our troops were in sight, but that the suburb which we had broken was now occupied by Bolsheviks, who apparently did not suspect the enemy's presence in their rear. Having lost hope of the arrival of reinforcements, I decided that to remain till daybreak in the middle of a thickly populated town in the centre of the enemy's position, and with only 250 men, would be to doom them all to certain death. I turned back, ordering the reply to be given to Bolshevik questions that we were a "Caucasian detachment" going to occupy the trenches outside the town. We first butted against the Bolshevist reserves, then came to their front line. I had meant, on reaching the Bolsheviks, to rush at them in a bayonet

attack and so break through. But my own men and the
Bolsheviks, who engaged them in peaceful conversation,
became so mixed up together that this became impossible.
All went well, till our baggage waggons began to crawl
through the Bolshevist lines. They then came to their
senses and opened fire in our backs, cutting off some of
the vans.'

Day broke, and all was over. The impetus, unsupported,
fizzled out.

*

It was the fourth day of incessant fighting. The enemy
was exhibiting a tenacity so far unsurpassed. His forces
were markedly superior to ours. Their actual numbers
were unknown both to us and probably to the Bolshevist
commanders themselves. Our intelligence service estimated them at eighteen thousand men in the front line
with two to three armoured trains, two to four howitzers
and eight to ten light field guns. But the units were reinforced, re-shuffled and supplemented by new arrivals
from every side. We read later in the Ekaterinodar
Izvestia, that the defence of the town had cost the Bolsheviks fifteen thousand men, of whom ten thousand were
wounded, and crowded all the hospitals and trains.

Our numbers did not exceed two thousand five hundred
to three thousand fighting men. Howbeit, it was clearly
felt that the impetus of our attack had greatly weakened.

That day General Kornilov summoned a council of war,
the first since the one held at Olginskaia which had decided
the direction of our army's advance. Generals Alexeyev,
Romanovsky, Markov, Bogaevsky, myself and the Kuban
ataman, Colonel Filimonov, assembled in General Kornilov's narrow little room.

The debate revealed the army's plight:

The enemy was many times our superior and, moreover, possessed unlimited quantities of munitions and supplies.

Our troops had suffered heavy casualties. The units were mixed up and utterly worn out. The Officers' regiment was more or less intact, the Kuban badly mauled; of the Partisans only three hundred men remained, and still fewer of the Kornilovsky. The Cossacks were dispersing to their villages. The cavalry was unable to do anything really serious.

There were no shells and no cartridges.

The number of wounded exceeded fifteen hundred.

The state of mind of those present at the council was gloomy. They sat with downcast eyes. But General Markov fell asleep, snoring gently. Someone nudged him.

' Excuse me, Your Excellency, I've been up forty-eight hours, I'm dead beat.'

General Kornilov did not attempt to strike a note of confidence. He seemed to have grown haggard in a single night, a deep furrow lined his brow, giving his face an expression of grim suffering. In a hollow voice, he spoke sharply and distinctly:

'The position undoubtedly is very bad, and I see no issue but to take Ekaterinodar. Therefore I am resolved to launch a general attack to-morrow at daybreak. What have you to say, gentlemen?'

All the generals except Alexeyev replied in the negative.

We felt that the first impetus had oozed out, and that we should be broken against Ekaterinodar; the failure of the assault would spell catastrophe; even were Ekaterinodar taken, it would bring heavy casualties and would result in those few left in the field who were capable of fighting being completely dispersed in garrisoning and guarding a large town. Yet we knew all the time that General Kornilov's decision to storm the town was unalterable.

A heavy silence followed. It was broken by General Alexeyev.

'It seems to me it would be better to postpone the assault until after to-morrow. The troops will have a day's rest, would be re-grouped, and Cossacks might turn up to reinforce us.'

Such a half-and-half decision, actually concealing vacillation, boded no good. It merely smoothed over the acute tension of the moment. But General Kornilov immediately acquiesced:

'So we shall storm Ekaterinodar at daybreak on the 14th April,' he concluded.

The council closed in an atmosphere of gloom.

After it was over I remained alone with General Kornilov.

'Lavr Georgievitch,' I asked, 'why are you so inflexible on this question?'

'There is no other way, Anton Ivanovitch. If we do not take Ekaterinodar, nothing is left me but to blow my brains out.'

'This you cannot do! How many thousands of lives would then be sacrificed! Why should we not give up Ekaterinodar in order to recuperate, reorganize ourselves and work out a fresh operation? Because if the assault fails, a retreat is hardly possible.'

'You will lead them out. . . .'

I rose, greatly agitated, and said:

'Excellency, if General Kornilov commits suicide, no one can bring the army out – it will all perish.'

Someone here entered the room and the conversation remained unfinished. That same evening General Kornilov appeared to take it up again when he remarked to Kasanovitch, just arrived from the position:

'Of course we may all be killed. But to my mind to die with honours is best. A retreat now would also be equal to

94

disaster: without ammunition it would merely mean a long-drawn-out agony. . . .'

On the 13th the bombardment of the farmstead re-commenced, as usual soon after daybreak. General Kornilov was again asked to move the staff headquarters, but he replied:

'It really isn't worth while now, to-morrow we attack.'

To have a look at the battlefield I walked to the eastern border of the farmstead: everything was quiet, no shots were heard, no movement in the lines discerned. I sat down on the bank near the farm-house. Down below, the River Kuban wound its quiet and lazy course; every moment shells struck its smooth surface, raising jets of rainbow spray. My heart felt heavy with foreboding after yesterday's conversation with General Kornilov. The irreparable should not be allowed to happen. To-morrow Romanovsky and I would not leave the commander's side. . . .

It was past seven o'clock. From behind the copse there came a heavy thud: horses stampeded, people were astir. A second crash, quite near, hard and sharp!

A few moments elapsed. . . .

'Your Excellency! General Kornilov. . . .'

In front of me, with distorted face, stood the com-mander's aide-de-camp, choking and unable to utter another word.

It was unnecessary. I understood everything.

*

General Kornilov was alone in his room when the enemy shell burst through the wall by the window and struck the floor beneath his chair. He was apparently blown upwards by the force of the explosion and flung against the stove. When people entered the smoke-filled room, General Kornilov lay on the floor covered with debris of plaster and dust. He was still breathing. Blood oozed from a small wound in the temple and flowed from the fractured thigh.

*

The aide-de-camp had barely uttered his broken warning before General Romanovsky and several officers approached the precipice; they bore a stretcher which they put down beside me. General Kornilov lay motionless; his rigid features bore the stamp of his last thoughts and anguish. His breath grew more and more feeble and ceased altogether. Controlling my sobs, I bowed over the hand, already growing cold, of our departed leader.

*

Destiny, ruthless and implacable, had long spared the life of this man who had faced death hundreds of times. He was struck down, and with him the heart of the army, at the hour of our bitterest trial.

Only a single shell had struck the house, hitting General Kornilov's room while he occupied it, and he alone was killed. The mysterious pall of a pre-ordained design covers the workings and fulfilment of an unknown Will. . . .

At first we thought it best to keep the commander's death from the army until the evening. No use – the news spread like wildfire! The blow was overwhelming. Men sobbed aloud, or spoke to each other in whispers, as though he who ruled their thoughts and hearts was present, invisibly, in their midst. In him everything had been focussed: faith in victory, hopes of salvation. And when he was no more, the hearts of brave men grew faint and anxious, doubts and fears got hold of them. Rumours, each more alarming than the last, crept from all sides: we were surrounded, would all be taken prisoners, murdered. . . .

The ship seemed to be sinking; and down below in the moral 'hold' grew ominous whispers of desertion.

THE WHITE ARMY

*

The waggon bearing General Kornilov's body covered with his *burka*,[1] was slowly moving along the road to Elisavetinskaia under escort of his own Tekinsky regiment. General Alexeyev, who was driving to the farm, crossed it on the way. He descended from his carriage, prostrated himself to the ground, kissed the cold forehead and stood gazing long at the calm and now dispassionate face. . . . It was the last parting between the two leaders who, bound together by a common idea, yet divided by some inexplicable feeling of mutual personal discord, would a year hence be united once more in death.

At Elisavetinskaia the body was placed in a pinewood coffin adorned with the first spring flowers. In the evening the coffin, secretly lifted on to a waggon and covered with a load of hay, was borne away with the baggage of the retreating army. . . . On the 15th April during the halt at the German colony of Gnatchbau the coffin was secretly interred, the grave made smooth and a plan of the spot drawn up.

Yet fate, pitiless to the leader in his lifetime, showed no mercy to him in death. When exactly four months later the victorious Volunteer Army entered Ekaterinodar, delegates were sent to Gnatchbau to exhume the beloved remains. They found nothing in the opened grave but a piece of the pinewood coffin!

The following passage is to be found in the records of the Special Commission of Inquiry: 'That same day, 15th April, the Volunteer Army left Gnatchbau colony, which next morning was occupied by the Bolsheviks. Their first act was to begin to search for the money and valuables alleged to have been buried by the cadets. . . . They came across newly filled-in graves. . . . On one of the

---

[1] Goat-skin cloak.

bodies they noticed full general's shoulder-straps and decided it must be that of General Kornilov. The body was stripped and clad only in a shirt and covered with tarpaulin brought to Ekaterinodar. . . .'

All day long it was dragged about the town, flung on to the pavement, hung on a tree, amid the drunken shouts and guffaws of the Red Guards. After having had their fill of insulting the corpse, now turned into a shapeless mass, they took it to the slaughter-house, where in the presence of the Bolshevist authorities the remains were burnt for two days. Trampled on and burnt!

The madmen! The name of dishonoured Russia's champion is inscribed in her chronicles in letters of fire. No filthy hand can tear it out of the nation's memory.

CHAPTER 8

General Denikine Assumes the Command – The Army Breaks through the Bolshevist Ring

L IFE followed its course, leaving no time for morbid regrets and from painful memories of our loss turned our thoughts to stern reality. In my official capacity of 'Assistant Army Commander,' it behoved me to take up the duties of the deceased. I had no moral right to shirk the heavy burden which fell to my lot at a moment when the army was threatened with annihilation. This, however, could be but a temporary measure on the field of battle because, though the Volunteer Army had no written status, I acknowledged General Alexeyev's natural right as head of the organization to nominate a permanent successor to our fallen Commander.

I reported the commander's death to General Alexeyev and that I had temporarily assumed his duties. General Alexeyev arrived at the farm, and turning to me said: 'Well, Anton Ivanovitch, shoulder this heavy inheritance and God help you!' He then signed an Army Order announcing the death of the commander and my appointment.

On outspread *burkas* down by the roadside, General Alexeyev, Romanovsky, Filimonov, and myself sat in a circle. I outlined the army's general position. It had become somewhat worse since 12th April. On General Erdeli's section the enemy had begun an enveloping movement against our left flank, which he kept in check by gallant cavalry attacks; nevertheless he had been forced under pressure to abandon Sady. Our last reserve, all that remained after the hard fighting borne by Kasanovitch's regiment (three hundred men!), had been sent hither. But the main factor lay elsewhere. The death of our leader had dealt the final blow to the army, already exhausted both physically and mentally by five days of continuous fighting, and despair gripped its heart. To save the army was my foremost concern, and I therefore proposed to raise the siege of Ekaterinodar to-day at sundown, and by forced marches to lead the army at all costs beyond the reach of attacks from the Bolshevist forces at Ekaterinodar.

There was no opposition and I issued an order for the army to proceed northward after nightfall along a comparatively safe route to the Starovelichkovskaia stanitsa.

*

At dead of night the army turned back from Ekaterinodar.

Men tramped in gloomy silence, crushed, but maintaining absolute order. It was essential to gain time, to let the men recover their balance and avoid fighting. This, however, we failed to do. After about forty versts our vanguard encountered at a wayside stanitsa numerous but unorganised parties of Bolsheviks and engaged them. Our main column, swerving to the right by a field by-pass, continued its march towards the River Ponura. The vanguard soon rushed the stanitsa, and by remaining there till nightfall covered our advance. Both the Staro- and Novo-Velichkovskaia stanitsas, where we intended to cross the river, proved to be occupied by the enemy. I therefore ordered the army to cross between these two points by two bridges near the German colony of Gnatchbau, where we were also to spend the night. After a fifty versts' march every one was tired out and needed rest, but the colony was too small to house us all, and many had to spend the night in the open.

The plan of campaign consisted in pushing further eastward in order to extricate ourselves from the thick network of railway lines, which to the weaker side represented the main and most dangerous arteries of civil war, and by leaving the more organised centre of the struggle, 'the Kuban and Black Sea Republics,' to concentrate ourselves at the junction of three 'republics' and three Bolshevist military sectors – the Don territory, Kuban territory and Stavropol.

Secrecy and rapidity were the essentials of success.

On 15th April we had to· cut across the Black Sea railway line near Medvedovskaia station. The baggage waggons were in readiness from early morning, and our advance was timed so as to reach the railway after dark. By noon, however, a surprise offensive by a strong Bolshevist detachment developed from the direction of Novo-Velichkovskaia, and soon our colony with its overcrowded Volunteer population was heavily shelled by about a dozen guns. Simultaneously the Bolshevist infantry began to envelop us from the east, thus threatening to trap and drown us in the bend of the river.

Secrecy under the circumstances was out of the question, and I decided on extreme measures: to remain at Gnatchbau till nightfall and then under cover of darkness to conceal our further movements both from the Gnatchbau and Medvedovskaia enemy groups. I ordered the baggage to be reduced to a minimum, all the surplus army waggons to be broken up; all surplus guns abandoned after putting them out of action by carrying off the locks and destroying the carriages, for four guns were amply sufficient for the remaining *thirty* shells. . . . The hospital waggons were to be placed in the vanguard.

The 2nd brigade, posted on the outskirts, held back the

advancing enemy, but their artillery bombarded the colony with great force.

That day will be for ever graven in the memory of the First Campaigners. For the first time in three wars I witnessed a panic. Men, with their backs to the river, lost all hope of salvation and sense of reality, and became the prey of the wildest and most incongruous rumours. The worst instincts—selfishness, mistrust, suspicion of one another, of the leaders, of one unit towards another – rose to the surface. This was particularly noticeable among the half-starved population of the baggage transport. Things were somewhat better in the fighting units, but there too the atmosphere was one of acute nervous tension. The faint-hearted probably indulged in loose talk because information received at headquarters was becoming increasingly alarming. One regiment was said to have resolved to cut adrift and attempt a separate break through . . . cavalry groups were alleged to be organizing in order to disperse themselves, etc.

I saw that many were losing self-control, and had to be saved in spite of themselves. Impatiently I waited for the all-concealing dusk. At last, just before sunset, I ordered a column to move off ostensibly in a northerly direction. The move was observed, and the valley through which the road lay began to be heavily shelled by the Bolsheviks. Night, however, was already coming on, the bombardment became disorderly. I then ordered a sharp turn about and we marched to the north-east along the road to Medvedovskaia. . . .

We were clear! A sigh of relief escaped from thousands of lips, thousands of hearts rendered fervent thanks to Providence, which had miraculously saved us from the jaws of death.

*

The column advanced in complete silence, without

pursuit from the enemy. General Markov's vanguard marched straight on to Medvedovskaia, with the cavalry skirting north and south as a demonstration.

After a march of twenty-four versts, sometime after 4 a.m. members of the staff accompanied me to the railway signal-box standing within a verst of the station. Everything was quite still and dark. The station as it proved was occupied by two marching companies of Red Guards and an armoured train. General Markov, marching in the van, rode noiselessly up to the signal-box, arrested the signalman, and in his name spoke by telephone with the Bolsheviks on duty at the station, whose suspicions, roused by unusual sounds, he succeeded in allaying. The bulk of the brigade had now come up, and was spreading in fighting formation along the railway line. A battalion of the Officers' regiment was placed facing the station buildings, the sappers stood to the south to damage the permanent way, while the mounted squads of the Army Staff were dispatched to seize the Medvedovskaia stanitsa. The troops moved off noiselessly. All were on the alert. . . . A deathlike stillness pervaded the field. . . .

Suddenly a rifle shot rang out, then a second. . . . Our patrol had incautiously startled enemy sentries at the station. A few minutes later a monster form was seen moving towards us from that direction.

'An armoured train!'

Slowly, all lights extinguished, it advanced upon us; only the light from the open furnace glided noiselessly along the way, forcing the Volunteers who were lying low against the bank to retreat precipitately. The train was already a few paces from the level-crossing. . . . At the signal-box were General Alexeyev, myself with the staff and General Markov. A single shell, several machine-gun rounds, and the whole command of the army would be done for. . . .

General Markov, brandishing his riding-whip, ran to the slowly crawling engine.

'Halt! You b — f — s, can't you see we're friends?'

The train stopped. Before the dumbfounded engine driver could realize what had happened, Markov seized a hand grenade from one of the snipers and hurled it right into the machine. There was an explosion, and immediately a heavy rifle and machine-gun fire opened against us from every carriage. The only guns not brought into play were those posted on open platforms.

Simultaneously Colonel Mionchinsky rapidly drew a gun up to the signal-box and in spite of bullets raining round him, managed to aim almost point-blank at the train.

'Move aside, lie down!' came General Markov's peremptory command.

The gun boomed, the shell struck the engine, which amid terrific uproar overturned on to the rails. A second and third shell crashed into the armoured carriages. Then from all sides rushed Markov's officers, with him at their head, hurling themselves against the train. They fired into the sides of the carriages, climbed on the roof, hacked apertures with axes and threw bombs through the holes; resinous tow was brought from the signal-box, and soon two carriages were ablaze. The Bolsheviks evinced fortitude and did not surrender; ceaseless firing went on from the carriages. Isolated Bolsheviks ran out on to the line, but were immediately bayoneted. . . .

Soon all was over. How fervently I embraced the perpetrator of this unheard-of exploit – an infantry attack on an armoured train!

There was no time to lose, however! I summoned the 2nd battery, and ordered the column to continue its march. Day was breaking. The spectacle of the fight lay before us: Borovsky with the Officers' regiment was attacking the station, whence the Bolsheviks were keeping up a heavy bombardment of the signal-box, the level-crossing and the road to the stanitsa. Smoke again appeared from the south, and another armoured train opened artillery fire on the column. In the midst of all this hell, an endless file of transport waggons laden with wounded and fugitives was passing over the level-crossing, sometimes at a quick canter through the ceaseless barrage, to dive as it were into the streets of the stanitsa. At the level-crossing itself there was feverish activity: carriages were being uncoupled, fires extinguished, precious ammunition unloaded. What luck! That day we seized over four hundred artillery and about one hundred thousand rifle cartridges. On our scale of reckoning, this meant several battles were provided for.

The second armoured train was soon sent back by our artillery. Colonel Borovsky captured the station and killed many of the Red Guards. Our cavalry, rather the worse for the encounter with the armoured train, crossed the railway line at a more northerly point. After a short rest the main column resumed its march unmolested towards Diadkovskaia situated some seventeen versts further on. Our casualties were absolutely insignificant.

That day as I overtook the marching sections, I could see by the faces of the men and by their remarks that the evil spell had been broken. Trudging across the wide steppe was the same Volunteer Army, strong of spirit, ready to fight and to conquer.

*

A day's halt at Diadkovskaia amid plenty of warmth and hospitality. The Cossacks welcomed us cordially and presented bread and salt. This to me was always a painful ordeal in view of possible reprisals of the Bolsheviks against those who thus welcomed us, after our departure. . . . But such ceremonies could not always be avoided.

The better to carry out my plan and confuse the

Bolsheviks' calculations, I decided to increase our days' marches by putting all the infantry in carts. This decision, however, meant extra hardship for the more than fifteen hundred population of the hospital transport. The case of the severely wounded became wellnigh desperate. As it was, they were being jolted along abominable roads for days on end. In the last three days the transport covered more than one hundred kilometres with only a short halt, and many waggons were not even unloaded. The death-rate, with the almost complete shortage of medicines and dressings, was appalling. But there was no choice: either forced and rapid marches, or the risk of having the whole army – wounded and all – surrounded and annihilated by the Bolsheviks.

In direct contradiction to the precepts of military science the Volunteer Army was obliged to advance not along but across the railway lines which were held by the Bolsheviks. These lines of communication and supplies in normal conditions became our worst enemies which it was necessary to damage and destroy; they held us as in a vice, surrounding us with pitfalls and dangers. The simple operation of crossing the line was complicated by the presence of our transport eight to ten kilometres long, which demanded passable roads, a level railway crossing, and took several hours to do it. Our asset lay in the absolute discipline and manœuvring capacity of our troops as opposed to the cumbrous 'mass-meeting' system of the Bolshevist military administration then in vogue. This saved us many a time.

On 18th April the army moved further eastward. We were faced with another crossing of the Vladikavkaz main-line – an extremely dangerous operation in view of the concentration of large Bolshevist forces and many armoured trains at the junctions of Ekaterinodar and Tikhoretskaia. After a forced march of seventy kilometres, having kept our movement secret, towards evening we seized the station of Visselky and the halt of it by a cavalry raid. Under cover of the darkness and in complete silence we crossed the railway and halted for the night at the Beisugskaia stanitsa.

Next day we had to tackle the still more difficult problem of breaking through the triangle of railways which obstructed our progress by crossing the Tikhoretskaia to Kavkazskaia line. Only sixty-six kilometres lay between these two points, making the intervening space liable to simultaneous attacks from both sides. Then another big demonstration to the south on our part in the direction of Tiflisskaia and Kazanskaia; a rapid north-easterly march; a halt at Vladimirskaia; a cavalry screen against the Tikhoretskaia and Kavkazskaia junctions; and for the third time a successful night crossing of the railway line between the Malorossiskaia and Mirskaia stations. By morning of 21st April, the army after a forced march of fifty kilometres was concentrated at the Khopersky settlement. A belated enemy armoured train only succeeded in harmlessly bombarding the tail end of our rearguard. That same night the army pushed forward to the Iliinskaia stanitsa, another twenty-five kilometres, where we camped for a longer rest.

The army's strategic conditions had altered considerably: in the nine days since leaving Ekaterinodar it had covered 245 kilometres, with scarcely any casualties, extricated itself from the thick network of railways, and obtained freedom of action. The Volunteers while physically exhausted had become morally recuperated and strengthened. After a three days' rest, I moved the army to Uspenskaia stanitsa under protection of cavalry screens.

Meantime, the Soviet Army command, completely baffled by all our movements, arrived at the most optimistic conclusions: the Soviet press in those days was full of the jubilant announcements – 'The complete rout and liquidation of the "White Guard" bands, which had dispersed all over Northern Caucasia.'

*

Nearly two months of campaigning in the Kuban region made friends of the population. The Volunteers were cordially and heartily welcomed in the stanitsas and they paid back in the same coin. The two thousand Kuban Cossacks who had enlisted in our army were a brave and trustworthy contingent. To assert that Bolshevism was played out in the Kuban would be a mistake. Still, time was in our favour: the Soviet regime with its inevitable system of murder, plunder and aggression was beginning to pall and to stir the will to *active* resistance, not only of the older and more conservative men but also among the Cossack youth. It usually took the form of sporadic, unorganized outbursts, cruelly suppressed by the Bolsheviks who brought all the resources of military technique into play against the almost unarmed Cossack militia.

Particularly cruel was the Soviet Government's persecution of the Cossack intelligentsia and clergy. Twenty-two priests were brutally murdered that spring in the Kuban province alone, for no greater guilt than 'sympathy for the cadets and "Bourzhouy"' or for celebrating services for the Volunteers. This persecution was directed not so much against individuals as against an idea. Thus, at the Nesamaevskaia stanitsa the Bolsheviks tortured the priest Ioann – a man, as stated at the inquiry, 'of extreme radical opinions.' On Easter night, during service, the Red Guards seized him in the middle of the church, pricked his eyes out, cut his ears and nose and smashed his skull. They displayed appalling cynicism in the profanation of churches. I recollect the painful impression left on me by the sight of the church at Korenevskaia stanitsa, after the Volunteers delivered it from the Bolsheviks in July: the walls were scribbled over with cynical inscriptions, the ikons smeared with obscene caricatures, and the altar had been used as a lavatory with the sacred vessels for utensils.

This moral savagery, coming as it were from outside, roused a pent-up resentment in the still uncorrupted masses of the people. The spark was being fanned into flame which sooner or later was bound to spread throughout the Kuban.

At Uspenskaia I was able for the first time to hold a review of some of our units.

Tattered clothes! Tanned, weather-beaten, but manly faces! The touching simplicity and modesty of men who had trod the way of blood, suffering and valour. Where are they now? They sleep the sleep that knows no waking, their bones scattered over the boundless spaces from Orel to Vladikavkaz, and from Tsaritsyin to Kiev.

'From that field but few returned . . .'

*

When resting at Iliinskaia we received good news from two directions.

Messengers arrived from the south of the Kuban region begging us to go hither. They told us of the existence of a secret organization spread over the entire south of the territory, which possessed ready cadres and hidden arms; preparations were afoot for seizing the town of Armavir, where there were large stores of munitions and other supplies. Briefly, southern Kuban was only waiting for the Volunteers to rise against the Bolsheviks.

Simultaneously, we heard persistent rumours of a mass rising of the Don Cossacks. Novocherkassk itself, the capital of the Don territory, was even reputed to be in the hands of the rebels.

The army's spirit revived completely.

It was necessary to ascertain how far these rumours were correct in order to make a decision on which depended the future destiny of the army and of the whole movement. I therefore sent out scouting parties towards Armavir and the Don. Colonel Baratsevitch's patrol left Iliinskaia and made a gallant few days' raid of 222 kilometres into the Don territory and returned to Uspenskaia full of enthusiasm and bringing a hundred Don Cossacks.

'The Don territory has risen! The stanitsas beyond the river have risen to a man, overthrown the Soviet rule, reinstated their officers and discipline and are desperately fighting the Bolsheviks. The Cossacks salute the Volunteer Army and beseech it to forget the past and to hasten to their aid!'

One thing was not clear in all this news: the Soviet troops along the whole of the northern Don Cossack front were exhibiting a strange nervousness, and Bolshevist marching columns were alleged to be hastily moving southward through Rostov as though driven by *some unknown force.*

*

However meagre was the information received, it was sufficient to determine our choice: by going to the Don territory, we again came into touch with the outer world; in the south were loneliness and isolation among the foothills of the Caucasian range; the Don territory offered a new military and political base and the possibility of organizing an operation towards the north; in the south was but the continuation of a guerilla warfare. . . .

Therefore, Don-ward ho!

General Alexeyev fully shared my views. The Kuban Cossacks accepted our decision sadly but without murmur. Their fears were finally allayed by my statement that I would not forsake the Kuban and in fulfilling our Pan-

Russian task, would come to their aid at the earliest opportunity.

For the fourth time we were obliged to cross the railway line at a point selected between the stations of Eiea and Bielaia Glina, which were strongly garrisoned and encircled by Bolshevist armoured trains.

We moved off in the afternoon. I purposely directed the column to the north-east, and while our vanguard engaged a defence post of Stavropol Red Guards, turned the main forces sharply to the left under cover of the darkness, and led them across country without roads till at dawn we reached a remote level-crossing.

Again the vanguard and cavalry deployed fan-wise to act as screen. They blew up the permanent way. The waggons, two abreast, thundered over the stone-paved crossing at a brisk canter. Again the men breathed freely, crossed themselves, and congratulated each other.

'Thank God, that's the last one!'

But as day broke the smoke of an armoured train appeared in the direction of Bielaia Glina. Enemy shells began to drop round the crossing. Dense formations could be seen deploying under cover of the train. . . . From behind, the enemy was pressing on the vanguard. In front, the head of the transport was fired on from the village of Gorkaia Balka. . . .

Our troops, already well seasoned, deployed and the batteries opened fire. The local rising at Gorkaia Balka – a hornet's nest of Bolshevism – was soon suppressed. After a long halt, during which fighting never ceased among our units to the east of the village, the army moved on and spent the night at a Kuban stanitsa, Plosskaia.

The army in the last twenty-four hours had covered seventy-seven kilometres while fighting.

The section of the Don Cossack territory beyond the river was passing through a critical stage. After a short reverse the Bolsheviks had reoccupied many stanitsas and started reprisals. The armed Cossacks had retreated south to Egorlykskaia whither the enemy was also advancing. . . . So in lieu of a respite we were faced with a new and serious operation for the liberation of the trans-Don region.

I dispatched one cavalry regiment direct to Egorlykskaia and the bulk of the army to Lazhanka. Next day, on clearing up the situation, General Bogaevsky's brigade was sent towards Guliai-Borisovka in the Bolshevist rear, while the cavalry regiment after delivering Egorlykskaia was ordered to advance north, taking command over the Don militia.

Bogaevsky left on 3rd May and immediately a strong Bolshevist offensive was started from the direction of Lopanka. . . . For two days enemy artillery bombarded the village, and their formations spread further and further west, cutting us off from Egorlykskaia. They were temporarily repulsed by Markov's frequent counter-attacks, but always returned in large masses. The enemy's immeasurable numerical superiority and the presence in the village of our defenceless transport greatly hampered the activities of Markov's brigade.

Those were the days of Holy Week – Good Friday and Saturday. Services were going on in the stanitsa's church; in fear and sorrow the people were praying amid the deafening crash of shells bursting round the church. From the altar sounded God's message of love and forgiveness, while in the village itself and beyond blood was poured and brother killed brother. . . .

On Saturday the firing was particularly heavy. Many of the wounded were killed. The transport had nowhere in which to take cover; they just had to await their fate and bear it. At last came the hoped-for news that Egorlykskaia was free and the long-suffering transport moved off thither by a roundabout road. Its departure left Markov free to act. He made a counter-attack all along the front: by a brilliant sally of the Officers' regiment, which before my very eyes advanced in silence without firing a single shot, the Bolsheviks were overthrown and fled, pursued by the cavalry. Meanwhile during these days Bogaevsky scattered the Bolshevist detachments which crossed his way, defeated their main forces at Guliai-Borisovka and encamped in that village. Simultaneously the cavalry regiment occupied first Metchetinskaia, then Kagalnitskaia. The trans-Don territory was liberated.

The fortunes of war were once more definitely favourable to the Volunteer Army.

Late on Easter night I was riding with my staff along the road to Egorlykskaia, hastening to the Easter midnight service. We were talking with my Chief of Staff, my faithful friend and confidential partner, General Romanovsky.

'There,' he cogitated, 'two months ago at the beginning of the campaign we passed through these very places. When were we stronger – then or now? I should say, now. Life pounded us in its devil's mortar, but failed to exterminate us; patience and will power were strengthened and that power to resist which defies all blows.'

'Well, what does your sub-consciousness say – shall we win?'

'Hard to say. . . . It seems to me that now we'll emerge on the highway. But we'll be embroiled in a fierce clash between two processes of disintegration and the rallying of the healthy national forces. In the nature of things there's bound to be war between them, while we, according to the progress of their struggle, are bound to win or be destroyed.'

We arrived at Egorlykskaia. The church was brilliantly lit. Crowds of people! Easter gladness to-day was joined to that of relief at the delivery from the invasion, with the

H   113

resurrection of hope. The faces of the worshippers seen through the mist of incense and the trembling light of innumerable candles looked radiant. The bells were pealing, and the whole church as one man joyously responded to the glad tidings:

– Christ is risen! –

CHAPTER 9

Concentration of the Volunteer and Don Armies and Colonel
Drozdovsky's Detachment in the Don Cossack Territory

In the Don Cossack territory, coming once more into
contact with the outside world, we were absolutely overwhelmed by the news which came pouring in from all sides.

The very first month of Soviet rule in the Don territory
proved to the Cossacks that under the new regime they lost
everything: land, freedom, and power. Local Cossack
'Communists' who at first placed themselves at the head of
the Government were soon superseded by a stranger proletariat. These newcomers seized power, plundered and
ran riot, absolutely ignoring the interests of the population.
Large consignments of grain and cattle were dispatched,
the peasants began to divide Cossack land, and severe
punishment was meted out to rebellious stanitsas by
punitive detachments. Contrary to what took place in the
Kuban region, the new Government turned out to be
equally insupportable both to the Cossacks whom it robbed
and to the peasants whom it patronized.

Already in March strong unrest began to stir among the
deceived Cossacks, who secretly started organizing themselves. On 14th April the Cossacks of the stanitsas round
Novocherkassk by a surprise raid seized the town. A
small number of Communists and Red Guards were
massacred, others fled, while the local Bolsheviks from
Golubev's Cossack division declared themselves 'neutral.'
This ill-organized affair ended badly: a few days later the

Bolsheviks recaptured the town and vented themselves on the population by wholesale plunder and fresh executions. Nevertheless the organization of an armed resistance continued openly, especially after the arrival from the steppes of a detachment under General Popov, who soon mustered nearly ten thousand territorials to his colours.

On 6th May Novocherkassk was again retaken by the Cossacks. But already on the 8th the Bolsheviks, reinforced from Rostov, started a counter-offensive and occupied the suburb, where great panic reigned for several hours. The Cossacks, unable to hold their own, fell back. The impetus seemed to be broken and the cause lost. The unfortunate inhabitants were again haunted with the prospective horrors of bloodshed and reprisals. But at the most critical moment a miracle occurred: suddenly, eight kilometres west of the town, appeared an unknown Officers' detachment a thousand strong and turned the scales.

Here was another heroic tale of adventure amid the darkness of Russia's time of trouble. For two months a band of officers commanded by Colonel Drozdovsky were fighting their way from the Rumanian front, more than one thousand kilometres away, across South Russia, aflame with civil war, to join the Volunteer Army, and who now appeared at Novocherkassk.

Great numbers of officers had been cast adrift by the abominable conditions of life in the army at the Rumanian front, as elsewhere. Some of them dispersed, but the majority congregated in the big towns near the front or at staff headquarters.

Conditions here were particularly favourable to the organization of Volunteer formations. All the more so that the turbulence of the demoralized bands of Russian soldiers was being somewhat held in check by the Rumanian army, where discipline was still maintained and because the Allied missions had still considerable influence over the Rumanian Government. General Stcherbachev, the Commander-in-Chief, however, lacked the determination to place himself at the head of the movement or at least to lend it a semblance of organization. Doubtless he was influenced by the attitude of the French Mission, then in favour of creating an 'independent Ukraine' and an 'allied Ukrainian Army' – an idea which would lead to Russia's dismemberment and which was in direct contradiction to the slogans of the Volunteer Army. Neither did General Stcherbatchev respond to General Alexeyev's request to organize the evacuation of officers to the Don Cossack territory.

The initiative came from below.

In the beginning of December Colonel Drozdovsky, former commander of the 14th Infantry Division, after repeated applications, obtained General Stcherbachev's permission to organize Volunteer formations. A gallant and determined officer and a great patriot, he fell to work near Jassy and soon began to recruit Volunteers and collect supplies. The methods employed for the latter were highly original. 'Volunteers were placed in ambush along the routes followed by regiments and batteries deserting from the front; by a surprise assault on the head of the column they kidnapped the commanders, rapidly disarmed the men, seized the baggage, and occasionally led away the officers who accompanied the units. No resistance was ever offered by the soldiers.'

Meanwhile the Ukrainian 'Rada' (Parliament), patronized by the Allies, started separate peace negotiations with the Central Powers. This fact at last opened the eyes of the Allied Missions, and they lent more attention to the idea of the Volunteer Movement. General Stcherbachev, acting under their influence, decided to extend the limits of the organization. But it was now too late. On 9th February the Ukraine concluded a separate peace with

Germany. Rumania, finding herself completely isolated, also started separate negotiations with the Central Powers. The position of the Volunteer organization, whose object was 'to fight the Bolsheviks and their satellites, the Germans,' became extremely difficult. German troops began an advance into Rumania, as yet unoccupied by them; the Allied Missions left Jassy; the Rumanian Government, to propitiate the Germans, presented a categorical demand for the disarming and disbanding of Russian Volunteer brigades. General Stcherbachev issued an order to that effect!

Colonel Drozdovsky, however, refused to submit. He resolutely declared:

'To disarm the Volunteers will not be as simple as the Government thinks. At the first hostile action the town (Jassy) and the royal palace might be heavily bombarded by artillery fire.'

Eventually, when on 8th March Rumanian troops began to surround the small town of Sokoly, occupied by the Volunteers, the latter at once deployed in fighting formation and registered their guns on the Jassy palace. The Rumanians hastily retreated, and next day trains arrived to transport the Volunteers to Kishinev, near the Rumanian frontier.

It was amid such difficulties, general depression, disorientation, and hopeless despondency that a handful of brave men (667 officers, 370 privates, 14 civil officials, and 12 nurses) found the heart to undertake a march of over one thousand kilometres. In front of them lay two serious water barriers – the rivers Bug and Dnieper, and spring floods, a country seething with turmoil, and in addition – the continuous advance right across their path of Austro-German units, moving at the invitation of the Ukrainian 'Rada' from Birsula towards Odessa, and eastward.

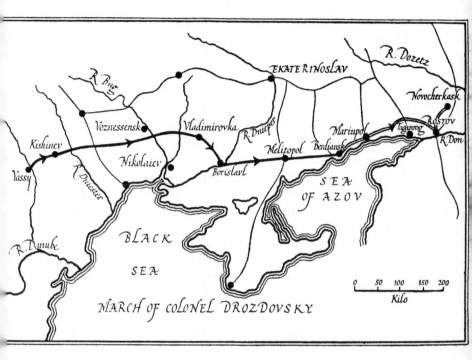

MARCH OF COLONEL DROZDOVSKY

The march of Colonel Drozdovsky's column from Sokoly to Novocherkassk lasted sixty-one days. On 21st March they left Dubossary; on the 28th crossed the Bug at Alexandrovka; on 10th April crossed the Dnieper at Borislavl; on the 16th occupied Melitopol; and on 4th May they appeared near Rostov.

The south of Russia was then passing through a confused period of anarchy, differing somewhat from conditions prevailing in the south-east. The land problem had already been settled by arbitrary seizure, there was no clash of interests between two separate social groups as existed between the Cossacks and aliens, nor were there, as in the Caucasus, any troops deserting from the

119

front and settling down. The country merely swarmed with small robber bands. Drozdovsky, therefore, encountered no serious resistance. Only near Kakhovka and Melitopol he came across some Bolshevist detachments which he easily defeated, undertaking two or three punitive expeditions.

Having neither the strength nor the means to prevent Russia's invasion by the Austro-Germans, Drozdovsky announced that he was fighting only the Bolsheviks, and remained neutral towards the Austro-Germans. The Volunteers advanced in close proximity to their erstwhile foreign enemies, trying to avoid them. But anxiety preyed heavily on their minds. They marched in silence, brooding gloomily.

Once, as Drozdovsky's column was crossing the railway between Birsula and Zhmerinka, they were intercepted by a marching Austrian unit. To the Volunteers' amazement the Austrian officers saluted, and shouted:

'Good luck!'

The first meeting with the Germans occurred when crossing the Dnieper at Borislavl. Notwithstanding his forced marches, Drozdovsky had not succeeded in forestalling the Germans, and found the crossing occupied by two of their battalions. After a short parley the German major agreed not to prevent the Volunteers from crossing. Both parties, however, took up positions convenient for immediate fighting if necessary.

It was a tragic freak of destiny.

There at the bridge at Borislavl stood the enemy – the Germans. Across the river at Kakhovka was posted another enemy – the Bolsheviks; they were shelling the Germans to *prevent* their crossing the river. And the Volunteers, by attacking the Bolsheviks, made as though *clearing* the way for the Germans to invade the wide steppes beyond the Dnieper. . . . None of those who took part in this will ever forget the heavy oppression which preyed on them on that dark, cold night, when reason and sentiment were rent asunder, and the mind strove painfully to solve the riddle of life's hopelessly paradoxical tangle.

Beyond the Dnieper things became harder still. News arrived that the Don territory was overrun with Bolsheviks, Kornilov killed, and the Volunteer Army dispersed. The goal lost, all the effort and hardships of the thousand kilometres march seemed wasted. The faint-hearted despaired. But Drozdovsky pushed forward against all odds, guided not so much by actual happenings as by faith and intuition. They did not fail him: on passing Berdiansk came the joyful message:

'The Don has risen!
'The Volunteer Army lives!'

*

On Easter night Drozdovsky, having outdistanced the Germans, dashed into Rostov after an affray with the Bolsheviks. His forces were inadequate, and the enterprise foolhardy. But Drozdovsky was determined to forestall the Germans, in order to render early assistance to the Don territory and profit by the profusion of war supplies stored within the town. The facility with which they occupied Rostov bred contempt of the enemy. No precautions were taken, so that when early next morning several Bolshevist columns arrived from Novocherkassk heavy fighting ensued, and Drozdovsky was forced to abandon the town, having lost one hundred men. Bitterly disappointed, they concentrated north of the town. A day later, however, everything brightened up: the Don Cossacks had captured Novocherkassk. That same day, Drozdovsky set out thither, and as I said before, arriving on 8th May in the nick of time, turned the battle in our favour.

Towards evening Colonel Drozdovsky's column, in perfect marching order, entered Novocherkassk. The spring flowers with which the thousands of people who lined the streets of the liberated town pelted the Volunteers were tokens of the love and gratitude felt by the population towards their deliverers.

Reviewing their past hardships in an order to his troops, Drozdovsky said: '. . . Let us in the coming struggle ever put bold aims before ourselves, and endeavour to reach them with iron determination, preferring glory and death to a base refusal to fight; let the faint-hearted and self-seekers follow the other path!'

That same day he reported to the commander of the Volunteer Army:

'The detachment has arrived and is at your disposal. The troops are worn out after the continuous march. We are, however, ready for immediate action if necessary. I await your orders.'

*

On 8th May the terrified inhabitants of Rostov saw with amazement, and some with bitter disappointment, columns of helmet-clad men marching through the streets. The vanguard division of the 1st German Army Corps was entering Rostov! This event fell like a bolt from the blue, and struck every one with its unexpected and sinister significance. The small Volunteer Army was now simultaneously faced with two hostile factors: the Soviet regime and a German invasion; a numerous Red Guard and the corps of a first-class European army.

What fresh calamities boded this invasion?

The following conversation ensued between a delegation sent by the Don Cossacks to Rostov and the German commanding officer:

'What motive and considerations prompted the Germans to invade the Don territory?'

'The political motives are unknown, but for strategic considerations we received the order to occupy Rostov and Bataisk in order to defend the Ukraine from the Bolsheviks.'

This conversation threw no light on the immediate prospects. Would the Germans remain neutral towards the Volunteer Army, make war on us, or leave us to measure forces with the Bolsheviks, coldly and exactly weighing the chances to open a way for themselves to the sea, the corn soil, at the price of flesh and blood? It became obvious· to us that peace, the dishonourable peace of Brest-Litovsk, was concluded by the Germans, not with *Russia*, but with the Bolsheviks. The war could not end *thus*. Although the broader policy and actual motives of the German invasion were not clear to us at the time, the great majority of the Volunteers looked upon it as a continuation of the war and an *enemy* invasion of Russian territory.

My instructions to the army were therefore concise:

'Have no dealings whatsoever with the commanding staff of an enemy Power.'

*

We were emerging on to the highway. The first heroic period of the White struggle, the first Kuban campaign, that Anabasis of the Volunteer Army cut off from the outside world, was over.

The army had spent eighty days on the march, having covered 1166 kilometres.

Out of the eighty days on forty-four there had been fighting.

At the commencement we possessed six hundred to seven hundred shells and about one hundred and fifty to two hundred cartridges per rifle. The rest were obtained at the price of blood.

In the Kuban steppes were left the graves of the leader and four hundred officers and men. More than fifteen hundred wounded were brought out; many of them remained in the ranks; many were wounded several times.

They returned to resume at once a fresh war to the death against Bolshevism. And those few who came through, and whom a cruel fate cast adrift all over the world, have not laid down their arms; they stand, and trust, and . . . wait.

PART TWO

CHAPTER 10

The Stimulus of the Struggle against Bolshevism – The Austro-German Invasion and the Balkanization of Russia.

By the middle of 1918 all Russia was seething with unrest, discontent, and revolt.

The motives for fighting the Soviet Government were extremely varied, but all found an echo among the different strata of the Russian people and touched the most sensitive chords of the nation's psychology.

The fundamental failing of the Soviet Government lay in its not being a *national* government. Never since the Tartar yoke had Russia's representatives suffered such indignities as at Brest-Litovsk. Never had Russia's 'plenipotentiaries' exhibited such crass ignorance and brutal contempt of her vital interests. Russian public opinion, political parties, the press (except that of the Bolsheviks), were outraged at this open betrayal of Russia.

Besides national sentiment there existed other motives.

The proletariat, disorganized by the new Government, was also forsaking it.

The senseless demobilization in one month of all munition factories and works, the nationalization of industry, the dislocation of trade and transport, with its consequent disorganization of exchange between town and country, and other causes brought about an acute crisis in the towns accompanied by unemployment, hunger, and disease. The more restive, ambitious, and withal unmoral elements among the proletariat had enrolled themselves into the Soviet bureaucracy or the Red Guard. There they either severed all ties with their own class or perished. Life daily became more cheerless. In the spring of 1918 strikes and even armed revolts broke out in the big factories. That of the Izhevsk factories in the Urals, which lasted three months, was suppressed with great bloodshed; on the very first day the Bolsheviks shot eight hundred workmen!

The peasants, too, forsook the Government.

Driven to despair by the 'pauper committees' and punitive detachments, ruined by continual requisitions of grain, cattle, and property, the peasants retaliated by rising in large numbers, often several thousand strong, armed with machine guns and artillery. In 1918 the whole of Russia was swept by a wave of peasant risings, accompanied by the destruction of Communist premises and stores and the murder of Soviet officials. As, however, the flow of supplies to the towns immediately ceased as a result of such risings, they roused the antagonism of the urban proletariat, and by the joint efforts of the latter and the Red Guard, were ruthlessly and cruelly suppressed.

As to the bourgeoisie, that is to say, the Russian intelligentsia, this was simply exterminated.

Lenin had set the task: 'To guarantee the Dictatorship of the Proletariat, overthrow the bourgeoisie and deprive it of all sources of power which impede the process of economic constructiveness.' The Tcheka solved that problem by practical means: 'We do not wage war against individuals,' wrote Latsis, one of the cruellest among the Bolshevist executioners; 'we exterminate the bourgeoisie as a class. In examining them do not search for material or evidence that the accused had opposed the Soviets by word or deed. The first question to be put is, what are his origin, upbringing, education, or profession? The answers to these questions must determine the fate of the accused.'

The extermination of the bourgeois class was carried out by various means: confiscation of property, expulsion from domicile, hunger rations, labour conscription, imprisonment; and lastly, by numberless executions. Sorrow and dread stalked the land; every family was in mourning; neither talent, nor strength, nor youth were spared; the institution of hostages was introduced in public life as a normal system; vendetta, untold suffering, and torrents of blood were the order of the day.

It seemed as if profound motives for the struggle against the unnational, unstatesmanlike, and unpopular Government could be found in every sphere of national life and among all sections of the population. . . .

Such actually were the feelings of the people. Unfortunately they lacked two most important factors: *activity and unity*. Between the three main strata into which the nation was divided – the bourgeoisie, the proletariat and the peasants – lay hardly reconcilable differences, the potential existence of which had been deepened by the Revolution and rendered acute by the disintegrating policy of the Bolsheviks.

These differences deprived us of our principal guarantee to success – *a united National front*.

*

While entirely original in its internal developments, the Russian Revolution was largely dependent on European policy and the active intervention of foreign Powers. Its entire first period, *i.e.* the year 1918, passed under *the sign of the German invasion and occupation*. The will of the German conquerors and fear of Bolshevism, no less than the nationalist chauvinism of her component peoples were responsible for the cutting up of Russia's political map.

Finland, on 9th December, declared its independence. Soon, however, the Government and the White troops under General Mannerheim were forced to retreat north, and with Soviet Russia's assistance Communist rule was established in the country. Fierce civil war broke out between the Red and White factions with alternating success, until the White Finnish Government sought the aid of Germany.

At the end of March a German division under General von der Holtz landed in Finland, and together with Mannerheim, cleared the country of the Reds within a month, but the German troops subsequently occupied all the most important strategic points. So strong was German influence in Finland that on 19th October, on the eve of Germany's collapse, the Finnish Seym (National Assembly) declared itself in favour of a monarchy with a Prince of Hesse as king.

The German G.H.Q., in occupying Finland, besides subjecting the country to Germany's political and economic influence, looked upon it, according to General Ludendorff, as a means to advance on Petrograd, when opportunity offered, to overthrow the Bolshevist Government; also of holding under menace the Murmansk railway and preventing the British who were using it from establishing themselves in Petrograd.

The *Baltic territory* was gradually occupied by the German Army, the German command pursuing a fierce policy of Germanization, while the future of the territory was predetermined by a statement of Herr Bethmann-Hollweg in the Reichstag to the effect that 'Germany would never again cede to reactionary Russia the peoples she and her allies had liberated between the Baltic Sea and Volhynia.'

Poland and *Lithuania* shared a like fate, with the sole difference that although under German and Austrian occupation and military administration, they were nevertheless promised independence.

German advance-guard contingents were posted from Narva along the line Pskov-Orsha-Rogatchev-Klintsy, covering the occupied region, which comprised the main portion of the province of Pskov and the whole of White Russia. This vast territory, not included in the German annexation plan, was occupied by them solely with a view to its exploitation.

For similar reasons the Germans overran the fertile and wealthy regions of southern and south-western Russia – the Ukraine, Novorossia, the Crimea, and the whole of the Black Sea coast. As General Ludendorff wrote: 'It was necessary to suppress Bolshevism in the Ukraine in order to penetrate into the depths of that country and establish conditions which would both give certain military advantages and enable us to procure grain and raw materials.' The proceedings were camouflaged by a certain amount of window-dressing: the governments of the Central Powers signed a 'peace treaty' with the self-appointed 'Ukrainian Government' under Golussevitch, at a time when the Ukraine was already in the hands of the Bolsheviks. The German army corps under General Eichorn then advanced into the Ukraine. In two or three months they reached the Sea of Azov. A month later they overthrew the Rada (assembly) and the Government, and in perfectly farcical circumstances appointed General Skoropadsky 'Hetman' (ruler) of the Ukraine, having as a preliminary compelled him to sign a pledge that he would 'invariably follow the counsels of the German command.' (Agreement dated 13th April with Generals Eichorn and Mumm.)

As, however, the Ukrainian railways would cease to function without Donets coal, the German troops advanced further towards Rostov and occupied a portion of

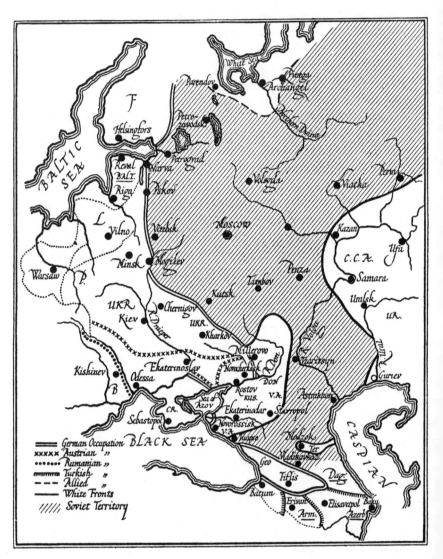

Don Cossack territory. The Don Cossack Ataman
Krasnov was favourably inclined towards them, thinking
they would preserve the territory from Bolshevism.

The line of the German invasion now ran through Pskov-Klintsy-Rylsk-Bielgorod and Millerovo.

*

Since the middle of March Turkey was negotiating with the Seym of Transcaucasia for the cession to Turkey of Kars, Ardagan, and Batum under the provisions of the Brest-Litovsk Peace Treaty. The negotiations having resulted in a stalemate, the Turkish Army started an offensive and occupied Batum. Meeting with no resistance, it pushed onward in the direction of Kutais and Tiflis, devastating the country and threatening the lives of the Georgian and Armenian inhabitants. Formerly the peoples of Transcaucasia had sought salvation in seceding from Russia and forming a joint 'Transcaucasian Republic.' Now, conscious of their impotency and mutual dissensions in the face of a Turkish invasion, they split up, and on 26th May the Government passed to the national councils of three newly formed states: Georgia, Armenia, and Azerbeijan. The Georgian social-democracy, without more ado, entrusted their country's destinies to the German Government. Germany willingly accepted the protectorate over Georgia, for motives thus explained by General Ludendorff: 'For us the protectorate meant access to raw materials and the exploitation of the railways of the Caucasus independently of Turkey. Turkey, in that respect, was not to be trusted. We could not depend on Baku oil unless we ourselves had access to it.' The *de facto* recognition of the 'Georgian Republic' was approved by the Reichstag on 24th June; a German Diplomatic Mission under military escort arrived in Tiflis, and the Turkish advance in Transcaucasia was checked.

Baku – that gold-bearing source of best naphtha, a splendid port, the centre of converging trade routes, the strategic and economic key to Central Asia, was a universal bait. Spring marked the beginning of acute competition, both political and military, for its possession. The British (Dunsterville) advanced from Enzeli; the Turks (Nuri-Pacha) across Azerbeijan; the Germans from Georgia. For that purpose General Hindenburg took from the Balkan front a cavalry brigade and seven battalions of infantry which were hastily shipped to Poti and Batum.

Events in Baku, meanwhile, were moving with the rapidity of a kaleidoscope. The town population, consisting mainly of Russians and Armenians, did not acknowledge the Tartar Azerbeijan Government. After the fall of the Russian Government and a period of chaos, power was seized jointly by Bolsheviks and Armenians, the latter having the most to fear from a Turkish invasion. Armenian administration was inaugurated by a massacre of nearly ten thousand Tartars. A small Armenian armed force, supported by Russians from the front, protected the town from the direction of Elisavetpol, the seat of the Azerbeijan Government, held by an equally small contingent of Turkish and Tartar troops. In the beginning of July a Russian detachment, fifteen hundred to two thousand strong, under General Bicherakhov, then in British service, arrived in Baku, shortly followed by General Dunsterville with a small British contingent. At first Bicherakhov supported the Armenian-Bolshevist combination. Fighting ceased at the front, but all around the country was seething with unrest. A *coup d'état* was brought off in July, and the Bolshevist Soviet replaced by a semi-Bolshevist organization of the Caspian fleet. Two months later (on 15th September) a Turkish army corps under Mursal-Pacha routed the feeble Baku troops, and in spite of German protests occupied Baku. The tragic scenes of April last were repeated inversely: for three days the Tartars massacred the Armenians, of whom twenty-five thousand were said to have perished.

Bicherakhov retired north to Petrovsk, and General Dunsterville south to Enzeli.

The Germans and Turks became masters of Transcaucasia.

*

The German cordon which separated nineteen provinces[1] from the Soviet territory, created a veritable blockade of Soviet Russia, and by cutting her off from the sea, her corn granaries and oil supplies, produced an acute political and economic crisis. The Bolshevist usurpers of power, however, stood to gain by the German occupation: the presence of the Germans, and the treaties with them, served as a guarantee against the invasion of some other power hostile to them, and at the same time prevented the formation of any really strong anti-Bolshevist organization within the sphere of the German occupation.

The Austro-German occupation rendered an inestimable service to the cause of Bolshevism, inasmuch as it guaranteed to the Soviets a much-needed period of *respite*.

[1] Not counting Poland and Finland.

CHAPTER 11

The Beginning of the Anti-Bolshevist Movement in the
Centre, on the Volga, and in Siberia – The Formation of
the Northern and Eastern Fronts.

WHEREAS the Soviets were protected from the west by
the Germans, storm-clouds were gathering against them
from north, south, and east.

After occupying Murmansk an Allied contingent under
the British General Poole landed in Archangel on 15th
August 1918, thereby laying the foundation of the *northern*
front. The Bolshevist authorities in Archangel were
overthrown and a new government established with
Tchaikovsky, the noted Russian revolutionary and a man
of honourable character and moderate views, as its head.

During the year 1918 the Allied contingent was added
to and reinforced by Russian formations. But on the whole
the sum total of the Allied, mainly British, forces in the
north did not exceed ten to fifteen thousand men, with
about seven to eight thousand ill-organized Russians.
The influx of Russians was greatly handicapped by the
natural conditions of that vast, cold, and deserted region.
To Russians the motive for the Allied landing in the
north was by no means intelligible. The Allied embassies
which had been evacuated to Archangel in July had issued
a proclamation which spoke of the necessity for preserving
the territory and its wealth from being seized by the
Finns and Germans,[1] for defending Russia from a further

---

[1] Enormous supplies of munitions and war material brought from
abroad for the Russian Army were dumped in the port of Archangel.

German occupation and for overthrowing Bolshevism. Whereas the two former clauses were treated seriously by the Allies, the third was in the nature of propaganda pure and simple.

So at least it could be inferred from General Poole's statement made immediately on his arrival in Archangel, that 'the Allies had come to defend their interests violated by the arrival of the Germans in Finland.' He therefore harassed the Russian command with requests to hasten with the organization of their own army.

Nevertheless the Allies, who occupied an enormous front from the Finnish frontier to Pinega, undertook in a half-hearted way an offensive in two directions: Petrosavodsk and Vologda. In the course of the year they advanced approximately to the line of Parandovo-Pliasetskaia-Pinega, and there carried on desultory fighting at long intervals and with alternating success.

Against them were two Soviet armies eighteen thousand strong with seventy guns, whose task was actively to defend the approaches to Moscow and Petrograd. These troops did not constitute any really serious obstacle.

It is noteworthy that the beginning of the Allied offensive caused great commotion in the Council of People's Commissars. Information as to the Allied strength and plan of action was grossly exaggerated.[1] Panic and confusion reigned in Moscow. The road to Petrograd was almost completely denuded of troops, all available forces being concentrated near Vologda. On 18th August Tchicherin addressed a request to the German Ambassador asking for German troops to cover Petrograd by occupying the River Svir. The German G.H.Q., however, not sharing the Bolsheviks' apprehensions, refused. As a matter of fact, the rigour of the

[1] The Moscow General Staff estimated the total Allied contingent at fifty-eight thousand men.

climate and the barrenness of the region on the one hand, with the trend of Russian policy in London on the other, prevented any serious developments on the northern front. The withdrawal of fifteen to eighteen thousand Red troops from the main theatre of the anti-Bolshevist struggle was to us the only tangible advantage of the Allied occupation of the northern territory.

*

In Moscow, the heart of Russia, an anti-Bolshevist rising was also being prepared. Boris Savinkov, a notorious revolutionary, at whose door lay many terrorist acts under the Tsarist regime, arrived thither from the Don Cossack territory. Advertising himself as an envoy of Generals Alexeyev and Kornilov, which was false, Savinkov secretly set about mustering an armed force. Both the right and left anti-Bolshevist organizations eyed his activities with suspicion and treated him as an adventurer. He obtained foreign support, however. Thanks to his irrepressible energy and temerity he succeeded in gaining admittance to the Allied Missions, which had hitherto turned a deaf ear to the petitions of the organizations in touch with the south and east. Savinkov received a subsidy, first from President Masaryk and then from the Allied Missions.

The organization consisted mainly of officers, alien in their views to Savinkov himself, but trusting the generals in whose name he was supposed to be acting. By his own statement about five thousand five hundred men scattered in Moscow and many provincial towns enlisted by the middle of June. It was with such paltry forces that Savinkov intended, simultaneously with an attempt to kill Lenin and Trotsky in Moscow, 'to surround the capital by a ring of rebel towns assisted by the Allies in the north and the Czecho-Slovaks on the Volga!' The utter foolhardiness of his calculations was obvious from the fact that the British only landed in Archangel on 15th August, while the advance Czecho-Slovak units were not nearer than Samara, both towns being more than one thousand kilometres distant from Moscow.

The rising was timed for the night of 18th to 19th July 1918, 'because the French Mission was anxious to hasten it.'

The rising in Yaroslavl and two other towns was drowned by the Bolsheviks in torrents of blood; numbers of defenceless citizens as well as officers were massacred, and the entire organization collapsed.

*

Far more serious was the movement spreading throughout eastern Russia, beyond the Volga, in the Urals and Siberia, the main impetus to which was given by the Czecho-Slovaks.

The Czecho-Slovak army corps, after the peace of Brest-Litovsk, was wending its way across Siberia to the Pacific Ocean. In the spring of 1918 its separate units were stretched over this vast territory, eighty-three hundred kilometres long, between Pensa and Vladivostok. At the demand of the German Ambassador, Count Mirbach, Trotsky ordered all the Czech contingents to be stopped, disarmed, and interned in concentration camps.

The Czechs mutinied.

With no definite plan or guidance, merely to save their own liberty and lives, the Czech troops assailed the Bolsheviks, seized railway lines and stations, and dispersed the local Soviets and Red Guard. As Bolshevist forces in the Volga region and Siberia were insignificant, the prowess of the Czechs met with overwhelming success. They were everywhere joined by Russian Volunteer bands, mainly composed of officers, which increased their forces and lent the Czech movement the character of a national crusade, though primarily undertaken for the sole purpose of opening up a way to the Far East.

The numerical strength of the corps, consisting of four brigades, varied from forty to sixty thousand men.

In the beginning of June several important events occurred almost simultaneously. A Czech brigade under Colonel Tchetchek occupied Pensa, capturing large quantities of arms and munitions. Pushing further towards the Volga it occupied Syzran and Samara. At Tcheliabinsk Colonel Voitsekhovsky's brigade routed the local Soviet and subsequently captured Ekaterinburg. In Siberia the first Czecho-Slovak rising took place between Tomsk and Omsk, where the brigade under Colonel Gaida, joined by Volunteers attached to the chief organizer of the Russian armed movement in Siberia, Lieut.-Col. Grishin-Almazov – overthrew the Bolshevist Government in several towns. Gaida then proceeded to push on eastward towards Irkutsk. By this time the fourth Czecho-Slovak brigade had already reached Vladivostok.

There existed no eastern front in the generally accepted sense of the word. Conditions changed almost daily in connection with the advance of the Czechs, and the success of the widespread local risings. Neither was there a common strategical plan. Some of the senior Czech leaders, fearing to scatter their forces, endeavoured to concentrate them at the railway centres. Others, responding to the appeals of the Russian organizations, swerved aside, despite orders from their superiors. The methods and behaviour of the Czecho-Slovak units also varied considerably. The Siberian population wished to look upon them as their deliverers, but many detachments treated the Russian towns which lay on their way as their booty. Trainloads of 'booty' were constant accompaniment to the Czech advance, with a demoralizing effect on the troops, crippling their fighting efficiency, and rousing the bitter and bewildered comments of the Russian population.

The general situation was becoming exceedingly complex and was unravelled only by midsummer: the Entente Powers, in pursuance of the plan to create an eastern anti-German front, desired to take advantage of the existing circumstances. By their order the Czecho-Slovak corps was to form a vanguard screen along the rivers Volga and Kama, under cover of which the transport of Allied troops would be carried out.

The Czech contingents which had pushed through to the east now trekked back to the west.

*

Whatever their motives, the revolt of the Czecho-Slovaks played an important part in the history of the anti-Bolshevist movement. During that *first period* they rendered a signal service to the cause of Russia's liberation.

The result of the Czecho-Slovak move was the spontaneous rising of whole provinces in the Urals and on the Volga. 'The Constituent Assembly Committee,' composed of members of that body[1] belonging mainly to the Social Revolutionary party, formed a government with its seat in Samara on the Volga. The Committee looked upon itself as the All-Russia State authority in embryo and as such enjoyed the special patronage of the Czech National Council which administered the Czech military forces. The Committee set about raising a so-called 'People's Army.' At first it was recruited mainly from Volunteers – officers, Cossacks, bourgeois youth

[1] The All-Russian Constituent Assembly in Petrograd was dispersed by the Bolsheviks on the first day of its existence.

(about eighty-five hundred in all), none of whom shared the political views of the ruling party, but joined the army as the sole means of fighting the Bolsheviks. Nor did the party find any support among the people. When a compulsory mobilization was ordered it failed. At the head of the army stood a group of civilians, while the military command was entrusted to a Czech, Colonel Tchetchek, on account of the mistrust felt for Russian generals, as 'Counter-Revolutionaries.'

The Cossacks of the Ural territory rose in a body, mobilized all the male population between nineteen and fifty years old, and turned out twenty regiments. As arms ran short many old men went into the field armed only with pikes, pitchforks, and flails. . . .

The Orenburg Cossacks rose also.

Following on two local *coups d'état* and the complex political struggle, a moderate government was set up in Siberia by a certain Vologodsky. Gradually, by dint of the arduous work and energy of the Minister for War, Lieut.-Col. Grishin-Almazov, the motley crowds of Volunteer territorials were shaped into a Siberian army, which by August numbered forty thousand men, fairly well disciplined but badly lacking in equipment. This army for fighting purposes was also subordinate to the Czech command.

In the Far East and Manchuria numbers of independent guerilla bands of adventurers were operating. Various rival governments were set up, including a Socialist one under Derber, styling itself an All-Siberian Government, and another under General Horvat, presuming to call itself All-Russian.

The vast territory from the Volga to the Pacific became the arena of continuous political strife between numberless Soviets, committees, governments and rulers, all hating and overthrowing one another. The situation was further aggravated by the intervention of the Czecho-Slovaks and Japanese. Meantime, blood flowed freely on the numberless internal fronts. Strategy was completely subordinate to politics, which brought confusion and a gambling element into military operations, chaos in the supply service and demoralization to the troops.

The strategic position in August was as follows:

Under the nominal command of the Russian General Shokarev, Commander of the Czecho-Slovak corps, one hundred and twenty thousand Russo-Czech troops were concentrated; but they were only in part subordinate to him, one-half belonging to the principal western front, the rest being quartered along the River Ural, in Trans-Baikalia and Vladivostok. Against these were the Red Armies, numbering eighty to one hundred thousand men, on the Volga-Kama front, and numerous Red Guard detachments impossible to estimate, scattered throughout Siberia and the Maritime Province.

Operations developed independently of one another and mainly along the railway lines.

In the middle of August the Bolsheviks started a big offensive in the direction of Perm, but were repulsed near Ekaterinburg.

In the Kazan sector the town was seized by a bold surprise raid, due to the initiative of the gallant young leaders – a Russian, Colonel Kappel, and a Czech, Captain Swetz. This operation had important consequences. The Russian State gold reserve of 651,500,000 gold roubles, and in addition 110,000,000 roubles in banknotes stored in Kazan was taken possession of and handed over to the Samara Government, thus placing the eastern front on a firm financial basis and considerably compromising the stability of the Soviet Government.

Further south, towards Saratov, the Ural Cossacks were putting up a heroic fight. Their territory was constantly

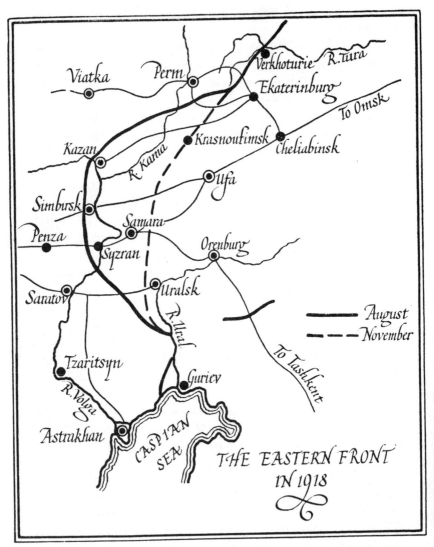

THE EASTERN FRONT IN 1918

changing hands, with all the dire effects of such changes on the population. By September, however, the Bolsheviks were repulsed on all sides, and the Ural Cossacks were

144

approaching the Volga along the roads to Saratov and Astrakhan.

On the other fronts small skirmishes went on with alternating success. In the depth of Siberia Captain Gaida, dealing successfully with the local Bolsheviks, was nearing Tchita, and soon cleared the way to Vladivostok.

September, however, saw a drastic change in the situation, brought about by two factors: considerable improvement in the organization of the Red Army and symptoms of unrest among the Czech contingents. The Bolshevist offensive, launched in mid-September and directed mainly against Ufa, was crowned with important success: Kazan was taken by them on the 10th, Simbirsk on the 12th, and by 8th October they occupied Samara and continued their victorious progress to the east.

The Czechs, spoilt by their easy victories over the Red Guards in spring and summer, now that they were faced with a serious foe, were no longer willing to fight. The shot by which that gallant Czech, Captain Swetz, put an end to his life, unable to bear the sight of what he deemed to be a betrayal of the Russian cause, sounded muffled and forlorn, and failed to rouse anyone's conscience.

The 'People's Army' disbanded after his death; crowds of demobilized soldiers trekked to their homes carrying away their arms. Only the Russian Volunteer formations continued to resist the enemy and were the last to retreat.

The Czechs were free to decide for themselves from alternatives, which to us were a tragic dilemma: either to shed their blood for Russia's salvation or to go away. They chose the latter. This gives us the right to regard the halo of 'heroism' which envelops the Czecho-Slovak movement with scepticism, and exonerates us from any debt of gratitude towards them.

Since the autumn of 1918, particularly in November,

when the last units abandoned the fighting front, the Czecho-Slovak corps became an alien and malignant growth on the organism of Siberia. It sapped material resources of which the Russian Army stood in such dire need, and obstructed and paralysed the working of the Siberian railway with countless stationary trainloads of idle troops and 'booty.'

*

As a result of reverses on the front and pressure on the part of the Czecho-Slovaks, a united government was at last established in Siberia. A 'state conference' met at Ufa in September, at which all political parties and local governments were represented. On 23rd September an Act was published announcing the formation of 'a Russian Supreme Power vested in the Provisional, All-Russian Government, formed by a Directory of five members.' The agreement was concluded under compulsion and lacked sincerity. The new Government, in which Social Revolutionaries predominated, pledged itself to be responsible to the Congress of Members of the Constituent Assembly, who were also almost entirely composed of Social Revolutionaries; the Government therefore, far from being a coalition, was purely party, and was extremely unpopular. From the earliest days of its existence friction arose between it and the local governments, which eventually led to the downfall of the Directory.

The troops of the eastern front were placed under the command of a member of the Directory, General Boldyrev. After the dissolution of the 'People's Army' and the appearance at the front of the Siberian army corps, the total armed forces by the beginning of November consisted of four armies, ninety thousand strong with two hundred and sixty-three guns, holding the line Verkhoturie-Krasnoufimsk-Guriev, on the roads to Perm, Kazan, Samara, Astrakhan, and Tashkent. Three divisions of mobilized Siberians stationed near Ekaterinburg, half trained and only partially equipped, served as reserves.

Against them six organized armies of the eastern Red front were advancing, numbering one hundred thousand men and three hundred guns, under command of Colonel Kamenev. Their chief blow was aimed at Samara. Hard pressed and morally weakened, the centre of the eastern White front slowly receded eastward. In front of the retreating troops all the roads were congested by a torrent of miserable fugitives fleeing from Bolshevist atrocities.

*

The period of the Soviet Government's military impotency was allowed to slip uselessly by.

And yet from August onwards the dream of those Russians who saw Russia's salvation in an Allied intervention seemed to materialize. That dream, figuratively speaking, sustained the despairing 'rear' and the vacillating 'front.'

In August and September transports landed the long-expected Allied troops in Vladivostok; among them were a Japanese division, five battalions of Americans, a small British contingent, a French battalion, and two companies of Italians. The numerical strength of these troops was obviously out of proportion to their objective as announced in the statements of the Allied Governments (except the American), and particularly the statements of their official representatives. Still more bewildering was the effect produced by the use and distribution of these troops. The Japanese occupied the railway from Vladivostok to Tchita; the Americans held the line between Irkutsk and Verkhneudinsk and the Ussuri railway; the battalion of British was transferred to Omsk, the residence of the High Commissioner, Sir Charles Elliot.

Sir Charles Elliot, who arrived on the Ekaterinburg

front before the other Allied representatives had solemnly declared: '. . . Already the Allied troops are on their way to Siberia and will soon fight on the front. Help is also coming from another quarter, from Kotlas (on the northern front). Everything is being done to speed it up.'

That help never came.

The port and millions' worth of Vladivostok stores were safeguarded, the way for the Czecho-Slovaks open, the contingents of Austro-German prisoners of war localized, and the political and military situation on the European theatre of war gave hope of its speedy and victorious ending.

What motives, then, could move the practical politicians of the west to take a more active share in the destinies of a country which was a menace in its tempestuous agitation, and in the misfortunes of a people they were unable to understand?

CHAPTER 12

The Liberation of the Don Territory – The Consolidation
of the Volunteer Army – The Organization of the Red
Army.

SUCH was the external situation at the beginning of the
mass movement in the south.

After the deliverance of Novocherkassk from the
Bolsheviks, a 'Krug (assembly) for the Deliverance of
the Don,' composed of delegates from the neighbouring
stanitsas and Cossack territorial units, met on 11th May.
This 'Krug' assumed constitutional functions, and pending
the summoning of a lawfully elected Cossack Krug, issued
provisional statutes, which laid down: (1) That all authority
within the territory was vested in the person of the Ataman
(chief); and (2) all laws passed during the Revolution were
abolished. General Krasnov was elected ataman, and
exercised sole and absolute power until the middle of
August, *i.e.* until the meeting of the 'Great Krug.' He
governed autocratically, with great energy, nor was he
particular as to methods. The main purpose of his
Government was to restore pre-revolutionary order, and
only occasionally did some liberal measure bring discord
into the general uniformity. However that might be, the
territory was settling down to normal life – but for one
circumstance. More than half its population consisted of
so-called 'aliens,' who were not Cossacks but mainly
peasants. As an aftermath to all their calamities, the
Cossacks were filled with a fierce spirit of revenge against

the 'Bolsheviks,' which they in all sincerity considered the 'aliens' to be. This feeling manifested itself not only among the ignorant masses but in the policy of the Government. The internal strife weakened the Cossacks, and by creating an unsatisfactory atmosphere fostered Bolshevism. The German orientation was the principal factor influencing the trend of events within the territory.

On 25th April 1918 German troops, under the command of General von Knertzer, entered Rostov; in the beginning of May they occupied Bataisk; then with three infantry divisions and two brigades of cavalry they took possession of the western and northern part of the Donets basin. The primary objective of the German occupation was purely economic – Donets coal. Later, however, the German command was confronted with the menacing problem of the creation on the Volga of an Allied eastern front. General von Knertzer's task, therefore, was increased by the necessity for creating strategic and political conditions to resist this new front.

The policy of Ataman Krasnov was particularly favourable to this. The very next day after his election he addressed a letter to the Kaiser. This and another letter dated 5th April, the contents of which were kept secret from us, practically petitioned the Kaiser to extend his patronage to the Don territory and the projected 'Dono-Caucasian Union' by recognizing the *independence* of these new formations, clearing their territories of the Bolsheviks and providing them with war supplies.

In return for this Krasnov pledged himself on behalf of the non-existent 'Union,' 'to prevent the access into his territory of any armed forces hostile to the German people,' and offered Germany certain economic privileges.

Krasnov's action found favour with the German authorities, and their representative, Major von Kofenhausen, declared that 'they would in every way support the Ataman and his authority.' Russian public opinion, however, took umbrage at the Ataman's policy. It was severely censured by the majority, who saw in it separatist tendencies, servility, oblivion of Russia's interest and a betrayal of the Russian Volunteer Army. A sentence in Krasnov's letter to the Kaiser, which transpired by chance, produced a particularly painful impression on the officers. He wrote: 'The friendship cemented by the blood shed on common battlefields by the warlike German and Cossack peoples (!) will become a powerful force for the struggle against all our foes. . . .'

There was one peculiarity, however, in all the Ataman said or wrote which rendered any confidence in his actions utterly impossible.

He assured the *Germans* of his and the 'Union's' loyalty to them and of their common struggle *against* the Entente Powers and the Czecho-Slovaks.

To the *Allies* he said 'that the Don had never forsaken them and that his pro-German activities were due to compulsion.'

He invited the *Volunteers* to unite with the Don Cossacks in a march to the north to join the Czecho-Slovaks.

The *Don Cossacks* he reassured by saying that they would not be called upon to quit the borders of their territory.

And lastly, to the *Bolsheviks* he wrote of peace.

Such a policy was either too astute or too unprincipled. In any case, in the light of current events, it was sufficiently unintelligible.

*

The Germans, meanwhile, were busy tapping the country's grain and raw materials, abusing requisitions, flooding the territory with their secret service agents, and persecuting the press unfavourable to them. Kofenhausen brought strong pressure to bear on the foreign relations of the Don Cossack Government, on the re-election of Ataman Krasnov and the composition of the Government. Otherwise, contrary to what was taking place in the Ukraine, the presence of the Germans had little influence on the life of the Cossacks, and in any case did not interfere with their struggle against Germany's Allies – the Bolsheviks. The German divisions, holding a line of more than five hundred kilometres, acted as a safe cover to the Don territory from north to west, strong not by their numbers, of course, but by the still surviving prestige of force and by their treaty with the Soviets.

The first concern of the Don Cossack Government was to create an army. The Ataman had succeeded in introducing some discipline and order into the formerly raw militia. A mobilization was announced for ten classes for the acting army and of four for the standing army. The Don Cossack Army, which in May numbered seventeen thousand men, increased to forty thousand, with fifty-six guns, by July.

The morale and fighting value of the Don Cossack Army varied. There was a little of everything. There was attachment to the paternal stanitsas, beyond the limits of which some did not wish to fight. At times there glimmered a clearer consciousness of the interests of the Don territory and the Cossack force. And lastly, a vague idea of the motherland, embracing Russia as a whole. There were: hatred of the Bolsheviks and fraternization; deeds of valour and greed; reckless gallantry and desertion; discipline and a passion for meetings. This heterogeneous compound resulted in those extraordinary fluctuations – from lightning successes to total collapse – which befell the Don Cossack front.

By the spring of 1918 the Bolsheviks had overrun the northern and eastern portions of the Don territory, proceeding mainly along the three railway lines running to Tsaritsyn. They numbered about seventy thousand men with two hundred guns. The north was thus cut off from the south.

Then began the systematic process of clearing the territory from the Bolsheviks.

The Don Army, in the very first month of its existence, launched an independent offensive, and after many days' fighting defeated the central group of the Reds on the road from Lisky to Tsaritsyn. Simultaneously the Cossacks of the northern districts revolted and swept the whole of the adjacent country up to the Povorino-Tsaritsyn railway.

*

With the arrival of the German troops in the Don territory, the position of the Volunteer Army became extremely difficult. The German headquarters at Kiev, and General Arnim's staff at Rostov made 'friendly advances' to us, but these were invariably waved aside. The Volunteer Army command, while avoiding active anti-German demonstrations, definitely refused to have anything to do with the invaders. A curious situation arose, and one which, to a certain extent, approached a state of 'armed neutrality.'

The actual intentions of the Germans were unknown to us. It was apprehended that the German troops would advance east towards Tsaritsyn and south to Ekaterinodar, and cut off the Volunteer Army from the Volga and Kuban. These fears had some foundation, both in the fact of the Germans having occupied the Taman peninsula, and in General Krasnov's secret request to General Eichorn, transmitted by the Hetman Skoropadsky, 'That he should occupy Voronezh, Kamyshin, and Tsaritsyn with German troops and secure Torgovaia and Tikhoretskaia for him.' The situation finally cleared when information was obtained from the head of one of the Central Soviet Institutions concerning a Note sent in the middle of August to the Soviet Government by the German Minister for Foreign Affairs, Herr Hintze. In it Berlin insisted on the Soviets taking decisive steps to suppress the Czecho-Slovak movement, force the Allies to abandon Murmansk and Archangel, and *suppress the 'rebellion'* of Generals Alexeyev and Denikine. To this was added the threat that should the Soviet Government fail to do so, it must put no obstacles in the way to free action of German forces across Russian territory.

All these developments were the outcome of a conflict between two currents of German policy. Foreshadowing the advent of a catastrophe since the spring of 1918, the German Command of the eastern front, particularly General Hoffman, supported by Helfferich, insisted on the overthrow of the Bolsheviks, which for the Germans was perfectly feasible, with a view to enlisting the sympathies of the new Russia on the side of Germany. The German Government and G.H.Q., on the contrary, regarded the disruption of a great country as a conducive factor to their policy and strategy, and were in favour of supporting the Bolsheviks. The latter opinion carried the day, and among other things, determined the German attitude towards the Volunteer Army.

Why, then, were these plans frustrated?

Any armed intervention against the Volunteer Army would undoubtedly have roused national feeling even among the pro-German section of the Russian community; it would have created a split in the Don Cossack Army, brought about Krasnov's fall, and much chaos in the rear of the advancing troops. The penetration into Northern Caucasia in pursuit of the rapidly moving Volunteer Army, if carried out by the small German force which was all that could have been spared from

General Knertzer's army corps, would have meant a protracted operation and rendered German communications particularly vulnerable to attacks by guerilla bands.

Without attacking us by armed force the Germans nevertheless tried to demoralize the Volunteer Army by other means. In Kiev they raided the local Volunteer centre, and since June 1918 they began to detain and arrest officers' columns going to join the army. To divert reinforcements from us the German staff at Kiev subsidized and controlled the formation on the Don territory of the Southern and Astrakhan armies. The former was under the command of the Duke of Leuchtenberg, a member of the House of Romanov; the second had as its leader a certain Tundutov, an adventurer styling himself Ataman of the Astrakhan Cossack Force, who managed to obtain an audience of the Kaiser and gain his approval. These 'armies,' with a pro-German and reactionary commanding staff, met with no response from the Russian officers, barely attained two thousand in number, and when the German subsidy was withdrawn in the beginning of 1919, ceased to exist.

The Germans similarly refrained from quarrelling with the Soviets. Only once in June were they forced to fight the Bolsheviks, who without Moscow's knowledge undertook a rash landing operation from Azov to Taganrog, which ended in a complete rout of the Bolsheviks. In the middle of June, as a result of supplementary agreements to the Brest-Litovsk Treaty, General Knertzer received an order to conclude an armistice with the Bolsheviks on all fronts.

Thus a curious situation arose! German troops 'friendly' to the Bolsheviks occupied the Don Cossack territory, assisted the Cossacks, and did not prevent but merely hindered the Volunteer armies in an armed struggle against their country's Ally – the Soviet Government. . . .

*
155

The position of the Volunteer Army was also extremely difficult for other reasons. Continual friction with the Don Ataman, due to his political orientation, the divergence of our strategic views and his personal qualities, further complicated our temporary sojourn in the Don territory. Conflicting political passions naturally found an echo in the army. Two burning questions stood out for all: that of 'orientation' – the Germans or the Entente? – and of political slogans – Monarchy or Republic? If pro-German influence found but slight response in the army the question of slogans was more complicated. 'Great Russia, One and Indivisible,' sounded clear and distinct to the mind and heart of one and all. But further – a vast majority of the commanding staff were monarchists. Influenced by active monarchist circles, many considered the acceptance of a monarchist slogan by the army to be imperative.

This was impossible. In giving way to what were then the wishes of the officers, we should also be in accord with the views of considerable groups of the non-Socialist intelligentsia, but would run the risk of totally alienating the people, especially the Cossacks, who at the time were not only unprepared to accept the monarchist idea but were definitely hostile to it.

General Alexeyev and myself spoke on these two subjects at large officers' meetings. He urged the inexpediency and inadmissibility of an alliance with the Germans, who aimed at Russia's economic enslavement, the proof of which could be found in the Ukraine – and who were on the eve of losing the war. I spoke of our duty to fight for Russia but not for a particular form of government, and for the sake of drawing the masses into that struggle – of the necessity honestly to adopt the principle of *not forestalling the form of Government.*

Those principles we succeeded in upholding to the very end.

*

The Volunteer Army, quartered in the Trans-Don region, took advantage of the Bolsheviks' two months of inactivity to recuperate and absorb into its ranks Drozdovsky's detachment, officers from the Ukraine and Cossacks escaped from the Kuban. It was just the time when the majority of the Volunteers, having served their term in the Army, were officially free to leave it. Yet almost every one remained.

Material equipment, however, was still disastrously lacking. Our financial resources all the time fluctuated between the army's fortnightly and monthly needs. General Alexeyev strained every nerve to obtain money from the wealthy bourgeoisie and the Allies. The Allies vacillated. They and particularly the French Ambassador in Moscow, M. Noulens, did not realize the significance of Northern Caucasia as a flank sector in relation to the eastern front they were creating, or as a prolific food-supply base for the Germans, should they assume control there. Finally, after lengthy delays, we received from Moscow, through 'the National Centre,' a secret anti-Bolshevist organization, ten million roubles, *i.e.* a sum equal to the upkeep of the army for six weeks. This was the first and the *only* financial aid ever received by the Volunteer Army from the Allies.

Consequently, on the day the army commenced a new campaign (23rd June), General Alexeyev disposed of a sum barely sufficient to cover its needs for six weeks. And when later we had pushed on much further and were fighting near Tikhoretskaia, I received a letter from him warning me that if he failed to obtain five million roubles for the coming month, we should be compelled in two or three weeks' time to raise the question of whether finally *to disband the army.* It was only after the territory occupied by the army became subordinate to the Command that our financial position improved somewhat. Nevertheless we reduced our necessities to a minimum and lived in dire want and poverty, of which neither our western friends nor our foes ever had any idea.

Owing to German opposition our 'technical equipment,' besides field artillery, was limited to two heavy guns and one whole and two damaged armoured cars. We started on our new campaign with two million rifle cartridges and several thousand rounds of artillery ammunition. This was a ridiculous, or rather an alarmingly small amount; but being accustomed to low standards, we considered the state of our ammunition park almost excellent.

By June 1918 the Volunteer Army consisted of three divisions of all three branches of the service, one cavalry division, and one cavalry brigade. Total: five infantry and eight cavalry regiments, and five and a half batteries – nine thousand men and twenty-one guns in all.

*

The total inefficiency of the *Red Guard* became finally apparent in the spring of 1918.

By a decree of the Fifth Congress of Soviets compulsory military service was restored, and citizens of the classes from eighteen to forty years of age were called to the colours, the bourgeoisie being drafted into special fatigue companies.

Thus the foundation of the new *Red Army of Workers and Peasants* was laid. It was being built on the old principles repudiated both by the Revolution and the Bolsheviks themselves at an early stage of their career, namely on normal organization, discipline, and unity of command. This was only natural as the Red Army was being completely organized, thanks to the experience and intellect of 'former Tsarist generals.' The part played in this matter by the commissars, Trotsky, Podvoisky and others, was at first quite fictitious. They merely acted as supervisers over the 'arrested' officers, while at the same time learning from their 'prisoners' the novel art of war. Some remained ignoramuses to the end, others succeeded at least sufficiently to avoid being duped.

The generals of the old regime gave of their wisdom, those of the new brought will power.

What reasons prompted Russian generals to enter Bolshevist service? With the exception of an insignificant percentage which joined the Communists, all the rest were hostile to them. At first they justified their conduct by the necessity for stemming the German invasion, later by the assumption of the short duration of the Bolshevist regime; finally – and this was also General Brussilov's plea – by the wish to save the starving and persecuted officers. Fate's reply to them was years of terror, 'internal fronts' and their direct participation in the fratricidal war against the Whites. A number of them crossed over to us, others were exterminated by the Bolsheviks; the rest were sucked down in the Bolshevist mire, wherein human depravity and real human tragedies found oblivion.

The rank and file officers who joined the Red Army shared a like fate.

The backbone of each regiment was usually formed by the 'Communist cell' sailors and various de-classed elements and old soldiers who had made soldiering their profession. These latter though ignorant of military science were generally appointed as company commanders, as men possessing certain practical experience and a knowledge of their subordinates' mentality. Frequently the men themselves elected ex-officers bound with them by common misfortune and equal oppression from the Communists. Finally the detachments of mercenaries, Letts, Chinese and

Hungarian and German prisoners of war greatly contributed to consolidate the Communist regime. Inability to discern the meaning of events, contempt of the country and people, cruelty and sadism coupled with the fear of future retaliation prompted these people into becoming the blind and submissive tool of the Soviet Government.

The first conscription was called in the beginning of August. It yielded eight hundred thousand men. This number very soon dwindled through desertion. Nevertheless by the autumn of 1918 the Soviet Government had at its disposal an armed force of *half a million* men.

Life in Russia in those days presented a striking anomaly. Throughout its wide territory about a dozen governments and armies had sprung up of all shades of political opinion. All of them carried out mobilizations within their territories. The people responded to all, most unwillingly, offering passive, seldom active resistance; but they obeyed nevertheless, and fought, *lightly deserting from the vanquished to the victors*. In all those eleven years of turmoil deep internal upheavals took place, outbursts of popular wrath, phantoms of a national impetus, but of a *national* struggle in any real sense of the word there was none.

When the *nation* does rise, the struggle will be short and sharp, and Bolshevism will be at an end.

*

In the summer of 1918, the Red Army was passing through a transition stage. The army consisted of a mixed type of contingents, partly Red Guards and partly men mobilized by order of the local Soviets and military authorities. Its fighting value was negligible, but it advanced *en masse*, driven by the machine guns of the 'punitive detachments,' egged on by fear as much as by wrath, sustained by the hope of a speedy end to the bloodshed. The population of the territories affected by the civil war also rose, destroyed their homesteads and trekked off at random knowing neither why nor whither. The Red Army was followed by a huge baggage transport with the men's belongings – their own property and plunder; with women who demoralized and made them quarrel, and children who were a burden.

Such were the forces against which the Volunteer Army was to be pitted a second time. . . .

CHAPTER 13

The Second Kuban Campaign of the Volunteer Army in Summer 1918 – The Capture of Tikhoretskaia

DIRECTLY facing the Volunteer Army was the North Caucasian Red Army, but imperfectly subordinate to Moscow and loosely bound together owing to the rivalry of four – the Kuban, Black Sea, Terek and Stavropol – independent Soviet 'republics.' Their common Commander-in-Chief was General Snessarev. But he lived in Tsaritsyn, which was soon cut off by us from the Caucasus. He was therefore replaced by his next in command, Lieut.-Col. Kalnin, a Lett.

The actual strength of the Reds was never actually known either to us or even to the Red General Staff. Their main groups were distributed as follows:

(1) Thirty to forty thousand men with eighty to ninety guns, under Sorokin (a Kuban Cossack formerly a medical assistant by profession, an able leader), were stationed near Rostov.

(2) Numerous detached contingents, numbering about thirty thousand with feeble artillery, occupied the region of Tikhoretskaia-Torgovaia. The best among them were an infantry brigade under Zhloba and a cavalry brigade under Dumenko.

(3) In the angle between the rivers Manytch and Sal were twelve thousand troops with twelve guns.

(4) All the big towns (Novorossisk, Ekaterinodar, Stavropol and others) as well as many villages were

garrisoned by detachments of varying strength. Another
fifteen thousand men were employed in the Terek region
in quelling a Cossack rising.

According to our estimates the sum total of the forces we
were about to encounter amounted to eighty to one hundred

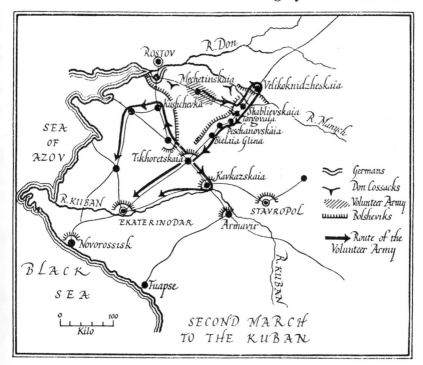

R. Don

ROSTOV

Mechetinskaia

Velikoknidzheskaia

Kushchevka

Shablievskaia
Torgovaia
Peschanovskaia
Bielaia Glina

R. Manych

SEA
OF
AZOV

Tikhoretskaia

Kavkazskaia

R. KUBAN

STAVROPOL

EKATERINODAR

Armavir

Novorossisk

BLACK

SEA

R. KUBAN

Tuapse

Germans
Don Cossacks
Volunteer Army
Bolsheviks

Route of the
Volunteer Army

0   100
Kilo

SECOND MARCH
TO THE KUBAN

thousand; while the Bolshevist Command in their reports
to Trotsky put them at two hundred thousand.

*

When I drew up the plan of the coming operations at
the end of May, neither the Volga nor the Czecho-Slovak
movements as yet existed. The only external factors
determining the political side of the problem were the
Germans, Krasnov and the perishing Ukraine.

The ultimate goal of the Volunteer Movement was clear to all: to reach *Moscow, overthrow the Bolsheviks and deliver Russia*. The ways and means to achieve this, however, raised controversies. General Krasnov spared no pains to divert us towards Tsaritsyn. My immediate *local* objective was to liberate Kuban. General Alexeyev vacillated, but in the end shared my view.

My starting-point was this: –

(1) An immediate march to the north, in the absence of any base save territory under German occupation and in view of the hostility of the Germans, who could easily push us beyond the Volga, might end in disaster to the army. On the other hand, a retreat *beyond the Volga, i.e.* to renounce the idea of raising the wealthiest southern provinces together with the east against the Soviets, was absolutely inexpedient.

(2) By delivering the southern districts of the Don and Kuban territories, we gained possession of the whole, more than four hundred kilomètres long, southern front of the Don Cossack territory, which gave us a wealthy base and a certain source of renewed man-power. Lastly, this would open up access to the Black Sea and guarantee rapid and reliable communication with the Allies in the event of their victory.

(3) We were bound by a moral pledge to the Kuban Cossacks, who formed about half of our army and had joined our colours to fight not only for 'Russia,' but also for 'their own Kuban.'

The strategic plan of the operation consisted in the rapid capture of the station Torgovaia, thus cutting off railway communication between Northern Caucasia and Central Russia; then, after protecting ourselves from the north-east, in turning towards Ekaterinodar to obtain possession of this military and political centre of the whole of Northern Caucasia. Our numbers were small: nine thousand against one hundred thousand. But we had military skill on our side. The army was enthusiastic, had faith in the righteousness of its cause, confidence in its strength and hope for the future. It had one thing more. – 'Our strategy was in accord with the qualities of a young army more capable of enthusiasm than of slow movements demanding patience and self-control, and one which could become tempered only by victories, victorious only in an offensive and triumphant over its enemies only by force of impetus.' These words – of the historian Sorel – refer to the French army of the Convention. But they exactly represent the fighting image of the Volunteer Army.

*

The army, having posted one regiment and two guns at Mechetinskaia to act as cover against Sorokin, set out on 22nd to 23rd June along a wide front in several columns, its main blow being directed on the station of Torgovaia. Skirmishing in every village along the route, and clearing the district of small Bolshevist bands, the columns emerged on to the railway line on the 25th. Then by a concentric attack with three divisions Torgovaia, together with artillery, machine guns and prisoners, was taken after half a day's fighting. Immediately after occupying the station the Volunteers equipped several trolleys on which were placed machine guns, and started in pursuit of the retreating Bolsheviks. Others began constructing a home-made 'armoured train' of platforms with ramparts of sand-bags, on which they placed a gun and machine guns. That same evening 'Armoured train No. 1' – a wooden one! – moved off to the station of Shablievskaia.

This first and signal success of the Volunteer Army had most important effects. From that day, 25th June, for twenty months, Northern Caucasia was cut off from Central Russia, while Central Russia in turn was cut off from the All-Russian granaries (the Kuban territory and the province of Stavropol) and from Grozny oil, a fact which greatly undermined the Soviet Government's economic foundations.

Night came on. The last echoes of the artillery firing were dying down, and still there was no news of General Markov's northern column. A report arrived at last:

'The Station of Shablievka is captured!
General Markov is fatally wounded.' . . .

Next morning the regiments bade a last farewell to their beloved chief. The command was given: 'Attention. Present Arms.' Never before had the regiments saluted their general in such strange fashion: rifles dropped from their hands, bayonets unsteadily wavered, officers and men sobbed aloud. . . .

I lost a friend and a trusted old comrade in arms. The army lost one of its most gallant, able and beloved leaders.

*

Posting one division as cover from the south-west with the rest of the army I forced the River Manytch and threw back the Bolsheviks concentrated at Velikokniazheskaia. Here in the Tsaritsyn direction my task was ended. After handing over the district to the Don Cossacks who continued to clear it of Bolsheviks, I turned back towards Torgovaia, and on 1st July started an offensive against Tikhoretskaia.

Once more on the move in three columns along a wide front. Sharp fighting for every village and heavy casualties. I marched with the centre column under Colonel Drozdovsky. Many stirring scenes were enacted before my eyes: the officers' infantry attack across a smooth open field under a hurricane of Bolshevist fire; the unequal duel between our wooden 'armoured' train and two real ar-

moured trains of the Reds. In this encounter the engine
was smashed by shells, the engine-driver killed and all the
officers wounded, while the train wrapt in flames slowly
retreated. Behind it, firing one shell after another, followed
the armoured trains of the Bolsheviks. Suddenly from
behind the embankment came salvos of rifle fire from a
company of Drozdovsky's men, which inflicted serious
losses among the crew of the leading armoured train, unnerved by the unexpectedness of the attack. Both trains
backed, and *pursued by a company of infantry* rapidly
disappeared.

Always advancing, the infantry being driven in carts,
we reached Pestchanokopskoe on the 2nd, and after two
days of fighting captured it. In the evening, after dark,
Borovsky's and Drozdovsky's columns rushed into the
village. The Bolsheviks made a disorderly retreat towards
Bielaia Glina; detached groups of them, wandering in the
darkness, fell into the hands of the Volunteers and were
destroyed.

The defeated and retreating Bolshevist units numbering
about ten thousand were gathering at Bielaia Glina under
the command of an energetic leader, Zhloba. These units
were reinforced by the villagers of the conscript classes,
who joined the ranks to a man. They knew nothing about
the Soviet Government; but utterly bewildered by propaganda and with no idea of the Bolsheviks' real intentions,
they determined to 'defend their village' from the
Volunteers!

Our plan was completely to surround Bielaia Glina.

In the night of 6th July in absolute silence the columns
left their bivouacs intending to attack the Bolsheviks at
daybreak. Drozdovsky's (III) division advanced along the
railway; Kutepov's (I) division in a right flank movement;
Borovsky's (II) to the left. The cavalry under Erdeli was
to cut across the line of retreat far in the rear to the station

of Yeia. The Bolsheviks had fortified the position in front of the village by two lines of trenches. They exhibited great nervousness, and that night continually fired rockets to light up the approaches.

Drozdovsky's column plunged too far forward. In the dark the regiment of that bravest of all men, Colonel Zhebrak, butted against an advance position of the Reds. Met by point-blank fire the head of the column wavered Zhebrak rushed forward shouting, 'To the Attack!' but immediately fell, mortally wounded. Twice the regiment attacked but without effect. Everybody became mixed up in the dark. Drozdovsky's battalions drew back and lay down.

The 3rd Division paid a heavy toll that night; besides a regimental commander, it lost more than one hundred men.

Meantime events were developing favourably on the other sections. At daybreak Borovsky from the north and Kutepov from the south rushed the village; the cavalry regiment pursued and hacked the Bolsheviks; our famous armoured car 'Trusty' paraded the village, fired upon in the heat of battle both by friend and foe!

About nine o'clock, conscious of being enveloped, the formations facing Drozdovsky wavered too. Disorderly groups ran to and fro in search of an outlet. I stood by the railway signal-box to the north of the village. Not far from it ran a road, the only one which by some misunderstanding had not been barred by Borovsky's column. Hither rushed the human torrent – all that was left of the Bolshevist detachment. Our artillery speeded them with heavy fire; the armoured car, a chance squadron, my escort and staff officers all joining in the attack.

That same day, after hard fighting, Erdeli captured the station of Yeia and the stanitsa Novopokrovskaia, the *first* stanitsa in the Kuban territory.

Besides its general strategic importance, the Bolshevist rout at Bielaia Glina produced a moral effect on the Caucasian Red Army and population of Stavropol. We captured a great number of arms and ammunition, as well as over five thousand prisoners. Of these, men of two conscript classes were drafted into the army, and the rest allowed to go home.

This was our first experiment of a method which both we and the Bolsheviks resorted to so freely later on, namely, reinforcing the army by drafting in *prisoners of war*.

As the Drozdovsky battalions entered the villages, they met a repelling sight: in front of the deserted trenches lay the wounded, dying, and the disfigured corpses of their comrades. On Colonel Zhebrak's body gaped seventeen bayonet wounds! Till late at night every one was busy collecting the wounded and bringing in the bodies of the literally tortured Volunteers. And the wrath of the living grew more intense.

It needed time, it needed much patient work and psychological change to overcome the bestial element infused by the Reds and which was reflected both in the Whites and among peaceful Russian people.

*

While the army was thus fighting its way towards Tikhoretskaia, an offensive, begun on 1st July by Sorokin's troops, was developing against our Trans-Don Cossack cover on its right flank, with the obvious intention of cutting off our communications in the rear and thus frustrating our whole operation.

General Pokrovsky with one regiment and Don Cossack territorials was with difficulty holding back the enemy, who had already reached the Rostov-Torgovaia railway line. I ordered two Volunteer regiments which had been recuperating at Novocherkassk and were now on their way to rejoin the army, to render assistance to Pokrovsky. By joint efforts they succeeded in the night of the 8th in inflicting severe casualties on Sorokin's detachment and threw it far to westward. Equally unsuccessful for the Bolsheviks was their twofold offensive against General Erdeli. From 8th July onwards the North Caucasian Bolshevist Army, renouncing all active operations, passed to the defensive all along the front.

I took advantage of this to give the Volunteer Army a rest, bring up the reserves and by means of light skirmishes facilitate our general deployment.

Before us in the region of Tikhoretskaia – an important railway junction – with a vanguard a day's march in front of them, a group of Reds was concentrated about twelve thousand strong with sixteen guns and three armoured trains. There, too, were the staff headquarters of the Bolshevist Commander-in-Chief, Kalnin. Between them and Sorokin a cavalry liaison detachment was stationed at Nezamaevskaia. South of us were another cavalry detachment and several peasant militia bands, numbering in all six thousand five hundred men and eight guns.

It was necessary as a preliminary to the main operation to deal with this latter group first. The blow would have to be swift and decisive. General Borovsky in command of the 2nd Division was essentially the right man for such a feat. My conversation with him on the 10th was brief:

'It is essential within three days to smash the Bolsheviks at Medviezhie, Uspenskaia and Ilyinskaia, in order to concentrate at Ilyinskaia on the 13th, because on the 14th we start a general offensive against Tikhoretskaia.'

'Very good, sir! I obey!'

'General, have you weighed the fact that you have 130 kilometres to cover, and six thousand of the Red Army to encounter?'

'Your order will be carried out!'
'Can you start to-morrow at daybreak?'
'I will start to-night!'

That evening I saw Borovsky's column off from Bielaia Glina, the infantry driven in carts. In the afternoon of the 13th a car drove up to the staff premises, now transferred to Novopokrovskaia: it was Borovsky, who alone with his aide-de-camp, traversing a road still infested with Bolshevist patrols, had come to report from Ilyinskaia! 'Borovsky's raid' as this exploit was called, was carried out with truly cinematographic rapidity.

On the morning of the 11th, fifty kilometres ahead of Bielaia Glina, the column encountered a four-thousand strong Bolshevist detachment with four guns. Borovsky attacked it, and sending part of his men to wade neck-deep across the river in the rear, routed and pursued the Bolsheviks, and captured Medviezhie. Pushing on further that same night, at daybreak on the 12th he attacked and defeated the second group (fifteen hundred men and two guns) at Uspenskaia. Here, 'Trusty' our marvellous armoured car, attacked an enemy battery. Having slain the horses, the crew captured the guns and immediately opened fire on the retreating Bolsheviks. On the 13th Borovsky, having routed the Bolsheviks a third time, occupied Ilyinskaia.

The remnants of these southern Bolshevist bands partly dispersed and partly retired to Tikhoretskaia, so that we were no longer molested from that quarter.

On 13th July the army was finally deployed upon a seventy-five kilometre front along the line Nezamaevskaia-Ilyinskaia. Here all our forces were collected; only one Kuban Cossack brigade remained to cover our rear and line of communication with Torgovaia.

The plan of the offensive to be launched that night consisted in *surrounding* Tikhoretskaia. The central column under Drozdovsky was to strike at the Red vanguard at Ternovskaia and attack Tikhoretskaia from the east along the railway. Kutepov's column was to envelop it from the north and Borovsky's from the south-east. The cavalry division under Erdeli was dispatched by a distant circuitous route to the rear of Tikhoretskaia, to the stanitsa Novorozhdestvenskaia, in order to cut off Kalnin from Ekaterinodar. The troops would have to cover forty to sixty-five kilometres at least between two battles. But this extra weariness would save many lives, while the suddenness of the blow would paralyse the enemy's will power.

*

The columns set out on the night of the 14th. By 9 a.m. the Bolshevist vanguard was completely routed. The Red divisions beat a hasty retreat and we soon lost touch with them. The field lay deserted and silent. Prisoners told us later that Kalnin's staff that day felt completely 'done for.' They had expected our offensive to start only on the next day. After a sleepless night Kalnin and his staff went to bed.

Meantime our columns, after having eaten and rested, resumed the offensive.

I was with Drozdovsky's division. By 5 p.m. it deployed within six kilometres of Tikhoretskaia. The formations advanced along a field of high growing corn. At about a thousand paces from the enemy trenches they were met by quick fire and lay down. An hour went by. Suddenly we noticed a strange commotion near the southern exit from the Tikhoretskaia station: men and vehicles were rushing to and fro, riders galloped about. – A good omen! Twice Drozdovsky attempted to raise his men, but each time, swept by heavy fire, they lay down again. A short while later the thick lines of the Bolsheviks, lying alongside the railway, suddenly rose up and ran, not back towards the station, but away to the north-east.

The station of Tikhoretskaia, as it turned out, was already in Borovsky's hands.

A quarter of an hour later I arrived at the station. It was deserted. The Volunteers were fighting in the station settlement; the railway employees had hidden themselves. All the lines were blocked up by trains, that of the Red Commander-in-Chief and his staff also stood there intact. Kalnin himself, we were later told by the railwaymen, alone and without a cap, had crept between the cars and disappeared. His Chief of Staff, a colonel of the General Staff of the old army, had remained behind and locked himself up in his compartment. On forcing the door, the Volunteers discovered the body of the colonel lying in a pool of blood on the floor, and beside him, still alive, his wife whom apparently he had shot before committing suicide.

Meanwhile, fierce fighting still went on near by. From somewhere heavy guns were shelling the station. Men were rushing about within the narrow circle, in search of escape, only to find death on every side. In the gathering darkness the battle appeared particularly sinister and threatening.

The enemy only fled from Drozdovsky's left flank. On the right the Reds were only repulsed after a fierce bayonet attack. Those left, fled north-eastwards, there to be rounded up by General Kutepov's detachment.

Kutepov's division after a fight for it occupied the stanitsa Tikhoretskaia at 4 p.m., barred the northern road of retreat for the Bolsheviks and launched an attack against the station. This met with desperate resistance. Fighting lasted well into the night, and in the darkness our units became intermingled with the Bolsheviks. Notwithstanding these complex conditions, Kutepov continued his offensive across a field of tall wheat. Here, too, the Reds were completely routed.

By morning a report came from Erdeli that his division

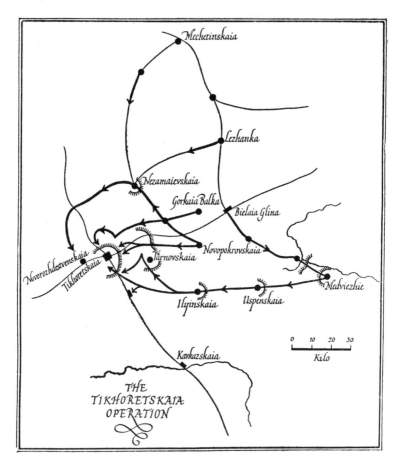

had reached Novorozhdestvenskaia the night before. The circle round the Tikhoretskaia junction was thus completely closed.

*

The significance to us of the victory at Tikhoretskaia was enormous.

Strategically we had (1) routed the thirty thousand troops of Kalnin's group; (2) obtained freedom of action and the chance to transport our troops by three main railways; (3) divided the groups of Bolsheviks, among other things placing Sorokin's army under menace, so that it was now compelled to hold the front both against the north (the Germans and Don Cossacks) and the south, with its line of communication with Ekaterinodar exposed.

In the way of material advantages the army, according to our standards, acquired huge and priceless trophies; a mass of rolling-stock, three armoured trains, an aeroplane, armoured cars, about fifty guns, a large quantity of rifles, ammunition and supplies.

Finally, in a moral sense, the Tikhoretskaia success had the effect of still further strengthening the army's confidence and of raising its prestige in the eyes of friend and foe alike. There was great rejoicing within the Don Cossack Force, while the German Command at Rostov manifested a growing interest and nervousness in our doings.

The Volunteer Army covered 360 kilometres in three weeks and fought a series of sanguinary battles. The Bolsheviks turned out steadier than we expected. We lost more than *a quarter* of our contingents, and these, it should be remembered, were the backbone of our army, the first idealists of the Volunteer Crusade. . . . But others came in their stead. . . . In August, in place of the nine thousand with which the army started its second campaign, it counted over twenty thousand fighting men in its ranks.

CHAPTER 14

The Fall of Ekaterinodar – The Beginning of Civil
Administration within the Occupied Territory.

AFTER a couple of days' rest in the vicinity of Tikhoretskaia, the Volunteer Army set about preparing the *operation
against Ekaterinodar* by enlarging and safeguarding the
arena for its movements.

The large enemy forces we were now about to confront
consisted of:

(1) Sorokin's Army – about thirty thousand men, still
stationed in the region of Kustchevka and near
Rostov.

(2) The Ekaterinodar group – from five to eight
thousand, and in the vanguard at Korenevka a further
two to three thousand, the remnants of the Tikhoretskaia group arrested in flight.

(3) The Caucasian group, consisting of strong garri-
sons in the towns of Armavir and Maikop and a detachment four thousand strong posted at Kavkazskaia
junction.

(4) The Stavropol group (about six to eight thousand).

The task I set the army was as follows:

The approaches to Ekaterinodar were to be covered by
a detachment of three thousand under Drozdovsky; a
further detachment of four thousand under Borovsky was
to capture Kavkazskaia in the south and Kustchevka in the
north, while the main blow was to be struck at Sorokin's

army by a force of ten thousand, jointly under Erdeli, Pokrovsky and Kutepov.

Only the incomparable efficiency of the Volunteers enabled me with an army of twenty thousand men to carry on simultaneous operations upon a front reaching from Kustchevka to Armavir, 245 kilometres apart.

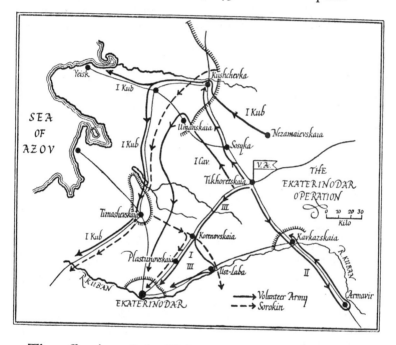

The offensive of the Volunteer Army opened on 16th July.

The troops on our northern sector advancing against Kustchevka met with desperate resistance. Continuous fighting lasted five days, both sides giving evidence of great tenacity and conspicuous bravery. Success alternated from one to the other. Sorokin already abandoning both the Bataisk (German) and the Kagalnitsky (Don) fronts was hastily withdrawing his troops, transport and

M   177

trains to Kustchevka and sending fresh batches of reinforcements to the south against us. But towards evening
on the 22nd, Sorokin, defeated finally at Kustchevka and
threatened in the direction of Umanskaia, retreated rapidly
and unnoticed along the Black Sea railway towards
Timashevskaia.

The Volunteers entered Kustchevka on the morning
of the 23rd. It was deserted. Simultaneously there
approached from the north Don Cossack contingents and
German patrols! Fearing a possible German advance into
Kuban territory I ordered the railway bridge at Kustchevka on the main line to Rostov to be immediately blown
up. This was a heavy tax paid to the political aspect of the
situation and one which severely handicapped our movements. The blowing up of the bridge roused General
Krasnov's intense anger and made a profound impression
on the Germans. Nevertheless, 'armed neutrality' was not
violated.

In consequence of Kustchevka's occupation the Trans-
Don Cossack region was soon completely cleared of
Bolsheviks, the southern Don front ceased to exist and we
obtained a free exit to the Sea of Azov (the port of Eiesk).

Borovsky in the south, after advancing sixty-five kilometres in three days, fighting all the way, seized the
Kavkazskaia junction in a brilliant attack. Having consolidated his position there, he pushed forward on his own
initiative to Armavir, which he occupied after two hours'
fighting in the streets. However, he under-estimated the
enemy's strength, and moreover at Armavir the Volunteers
behaved with too much careless unconcern. On the 30th
Borovsky, hard pressed by newly arrived Bolshevist reinforcements, was compelled to withdraw to Kavkazskaia.

The Armavir failure, which did not on the whole affect
the army's strategic position, nevertheless had a tragic
sequel for the unfortunate town itself.

The population, worn out and exasperated by the Bolshevist regime, welcomed Borovsky and his men with an ovation, and made much of them during the few days of their stay. With the return of the Reds came the reckoning: the Bolsheviks murdered more than fifteen hundred innocent people. The report of the Judiciary Commission of Inquiry thus described the events of that terrible day: '. . . incessant rifle fire, the intermittent rattle of machine-guns, the howls of the frenzied mob, the crunch of skull bones smashed by rifle-butts, the groans and hoarse gasps of the dying, cries for mercy from the tortured living, and blood, blood everywhere. . . .'

From behind the abstract premises of strategy, between the lines of the reports extolling victory or masking defeat, there stood out the blood-stained and tortured countenance of the ordinary Russian man in the street.

Drozdovsky's centre column was widening its sphere of action and gradually advancing towards Ekaterinodar. Acting swiftly and surely, Drozdovsky threw back the feeble enemy detachments grouped along the railway line, and by the 26th reached the station of Plastunskaia, one hundred kilometres distant from Tikhoretskaia and only forty kilometres from Ekaterinodar.

While the above events were in progress, another unexpected surprise took place: on 21st July I received news that Stavropol had fallen.

A guerilla chief, Colonel Shkuro, appeared in the Caucasus. A brave, rollicking, scatter-brained man of somewhat loose morals, he had collected a band of Kuban Cossacks and led them against the Bolsheviks. He captured Kislovodsk, a rich watering-place, but a few days later was again evicted by the Reds. Shkuro's raid, however, gave the signal for severe Bolshevist reprisals against the Kislovodsk bourgeoisie. Shkuro himself dashed off to the province of Stavropol in search of the Volunteer Army, rumours of which were current in the Caucasus. His movements were heralded by exaggerated legends of 'countless' forces, the persistent luck of their 'Ataman' and his cruel reprisals against the Soviet authorities. On arriving at Stavropol he sent the town an ultimatum demanding the exit of the Red garrison and threatening to bombard the town with 'heavy artillery' – although he did not possess a single gun. Strange as it may seem, the terrified Commissars evacuated their troops without fighting.

The joy of the long-suffering population knew no bounds.

Soon, however, the Bolsheviks recovered their senses and started an offensive against the town. The guerilla troops were little adapted to stubborn defence fighting, and moreover they ill-treated and annoyed the inhabitants by their debaucheries. The occupation of Stavropol which lay 150 kilometres from the centre of the army, placed upon us a moral obligation to defend it. This, on the other hand, compelled us to send reinforcements and by prematurely diverting troops and munitions from the main objective, interfered with the organized plan of operation.

*

Immediately after the fall of Kustchevka I left the pursuit of Sorokin's bands to the cavalry and transferred the 1st Division by rail in the direction of Ekaterinodar.

Sorokin's army was retreating, abandoning baggage, stores and trainloads of supplies in its endeavour to escape from a strategic envelopment. Its pursuit was neither impetuous nor energetic. Erdeli (from Uman) tarried, Pokrovsky busied himself with Eisk. Several days were thus lost, and by 26th July Sorokin succeeded in concentrating his troops at the railway junction of Timashevskaia, protected from the north by a strip of marshes and lakes.

The concentration of the main forces of the Volunteer

Army for the operation against Ekaterinodar was completed by 27th July. The 1st and 3rd Divisions were stationed at Plastunskaia, the cavalry division under Pokrovsky was approaching from the north, with Erdeli's cavalry division between them. Borovsky with part of his troops was to start a decoy offensive from the station of Kavkazskaia.

The question was, where to strike the main blow? If Sorokin's main forces still occupied Timashevskaia, then it was necessary to attack Timashevskaia with all our forces, placing a screen in the direction of Ekaterinodar. If, on the contrary, Sorokin's rearguard alone was at Timashevskaia and he with his main forces was advancing on Ekaterinodar, then after leaving General Pokrovsky's division to deal with that rearguard, all our remaining forces should attack Ekaterinodar sufficiently rapidly to prevent the Reds from escaping across the River Kuban.

The concensus of reports of the army and secret intelligence service agreed that Sorokin's army, weakened and demoralized, was making its way towards Ekaterinodar. Witnesses narrated how a continuous stream of thousands of waggons laden with infantry, and huge baggage transports was moving day and night along the roads to Ekaterinodar.

The second course was therefore adopted. On the 27th I visited the centre column and gave directions to the troops. I returned to Tikhoretskaia late at night in order next morning to transfer our headquarters to Korenevskaia. But in civil war surprises abound. News arrived that shortly after I passed through it, *Korenevskaia was attacked and captured by large enemy forces*. Its garrison was partly killed and partly captured. Our centre column was cut off from headquarters and the rest of the army, the Tikhoretskaia junction was threatened, and no troops were left for its defence except two battalions in process of formation, and my own escort.

The situation became extremely menacing.

I ordered the immediate recall of one of Borovsky's regiments and a battery, in order to attack Korenevskaia from the north-east with the help of armoured trains. Pokrovsky and Erdeli received the order to strike at the enemy from the north at all costs. A message was sent by aeroplane to the centre column to inform them of the coming assistance. The plane was to land in the vicinity of Plastunskaia with the risk of falling into the enemy's hands.

There followed twenty-four hours of weary, anxious waiting.

*

The reports of the Bolshevist exodus from Timashevskaia to Ekaterinodar were not without foundation: transports, fugitives, deserters, and small bands which had detached themselves from Sorokin were trekking thitherward. His main forces, however, remained at Timashevskaia. They were now put in order, their losses made good by drafting in fresh conscripts and their number was once more brought up to twenty to twenty-five thousand men. As it turned out, Sorokin decided to leave his crack 'Taman' division to deal with Pokrovsky and subsequently retreat to Novorossisk, and himself to break through with his remaining forces then at Korenevskaia, reach the crossing at Ust-Laba and retreat beyond the River Kuban. It was only later, on the 27th, having easily repulsed Erdeli's cavalry, holding it in check with his vanguard and having occupied Korenevskaia, that he decided to take advantage of favourable conditions and attempt to smash the Volunteer Army.

The plan testified to his daring, and its execution to his skill.

When on the morning of the 28th our centre divisions found themselves cut off from Tikhoretskaia and held in a vice, Kasanovitch and Drozdovsky, by mutual consent, placing a screen against the Bolsheviks of Ekaterinodar, moved to attack Korenevskaia. Fighting against considerably superior enemy forces lasted all day. In vain were the numerous attacks by our divisions, our field battery raids right into enemy lines or the personal example of the division commanders who themselves led the attacks. The divisions suffered heavy casualties, were routed and repulsed to westward. The infantry's retreat, impeded by a marshy river, was full of tragedy. Some of the Volunteers, utterly exhausted, dropped to the ground, and to escape being made prisoners by the Bolsheviks, committed suicide. The wounded and those left behind in the field met with a horrible death: the Bolsheviks pricked their eyes out, hacked off their limbs and then burned them alive.

The divisions halted in a field for the night and counted up their losses and the all but spent cartridges. The view of the situation taken by a council of war held that night at the staff quarters of the 3rd Division was of the gloomiest. Drozdovsky said that the only means of saving the army from complete annihilation was to withdraw east under cover of darkness and by a circuitous route to try and rejoin the Army Commander.

Kasanovitch protested: 'Such a withdrawal would leave the Bolsheviks a free hand. They would take Tikhoretskaia, disconnect various parts of our army and beat us in sections. On the other hand, it is impossible to think that General Denikine would not throw all available troops against the Bolsheviks.'

Kasanovitch settled the dispute by announcing that in view of their having lost touch with the Army Commander, he as senior assumed the command over the group according to the statutes, and ordered the attack on Korenevskaia to be resumed to-morrow at daybreak.

An attempt at an offensive was made on the morning of

the 30th. Sorokin, however, forestalled it by hurling his troops against the whole front of the 1st and 3rd Divisions. Fierce hand-to-hand fighting was going on in many places, the Volunteers were at their last gasp. At that very moment our airman landed, bringing the longed-for message of hope. The spirit of the fighters rose at a bound. At noon bursts of shrapnel high in the sky above Korenevskaia heralded the approach of reinforcements. Both groups of Volunteers from north-east and south-west hurled themselves against the Bolsheviks. Korenevskaia was captured, the enemy vacillated and began to withdraw in two groups. One completely routed, fled southward; the other retreated in comparative order and halted about three kilometres from Korenevskaia.

We were once more in touch with Tikhoretskaia, the front facing south-west. The Bolsheviks had sustained heavy casualties: we gave them no quarter. But the Volunteer Army too had been severely bled: the 1st and 3rd Divisions had lost twenty-five to thirty per cent. of their contingents and several of their most gallant officers.

This, however, was by no means the end.

By an order from Moscow Sorokin was appointed Red Commander-in-Chief in Northern Caucasia, and this distinction probably influenced his tenacity. His northern group resumed the offensive against Korenevskaia on the 31st, and from that day onwards fierce fighting went on for a week. We strained our every nerve, but to no purpose. Only on 7th August did we win at last. This time Sorokin's army sustained a crushing defeat and retreated all along the front, being pursued and massacred by our cavalry, armoured cars and trains.

On that day I regained complete freedom of action and was able to proceed with the carrying out of my original plan.

*

Sorokin's army was retreating towards Ekaterinodar, to the south and in part towards Timashevskaia, where the Taman division was still stubbornly resisting Pokrovsky's cavalry attacks.

Notwithstanding the extreme exhaustion of the troops, worn out by the continuous fighting, I kept the army in continuous pursuit of the enemy: that is to say, I sent Kasanovitch's and Erdeli's divisions in the direction of Ekaterinodar and Drozdovsky's – along the River Kuban. On 14th August, Pokrovsky at last took Timashevskaia after fierce fighting. In the night of the 3rd, after a series of battles on the approaches to the town, our troops dashed into Ekaterinodar itself.

Next morning our columns and the army staff made their entry into the delivered town, which greeted the Volunteers with wild enthusiasm. We entered that town with feelings of emotion, for during the previous six months' struggle, it had ceased in the eyes of the Volunteer Army to represent merely a political or strategical centre, but had acquired a kind of mystical significance.

Shells still burst in the streets of Ekaterinodar and machine guns rattled across the river, but these were the last echoes of the storm which had raged outside the town. The 1st Division seized the bridge and threw the Bolsheviks back from the river.

*

Beneath the sun's burning rays a *Te Deum* of thanksgiving was sung in the cathedral square. The prayers of the multitude seemed to reconcile them with the past, to deepen their faith in the future. These sentiments were reflected in all faces, they united the crowds, the smart ranks of the Volunteers, the officers and government authorities grouped round the lectern in a common fervour.

In their addresses of welcome to me and General

Alexeyev just arrived in Ekaterinodar, the members of the Kuban Government exalted the merits of the army and its leaders and assured us of their loyalty to the national idea.

'The Kuban territory,' said the Ataman, 'realizes full well that her happiness lies only in a close union with her Mother-Russia. Therefore, having ended the struggle for the deliverance of the Kuban, the Cossacks will fight in the ranks of the Volunteer Army for the liberation and regeneration of Russia.'

*

The celebrations were over, the speeches finished and stern everyday business began. Politics made a rude and imperious intrusion upon the domain of the White Movement.

The first important question to be settled was that of the delimitation of the sphere of authority between the military command and the Kuban Government. The men who stood at the head of affairs in the Kuban territory were above all concerned with its 'sovereignty.' On the other hand, neither General Alexeyev nor myself had any desire to interfere with territorial administration. Circumstances, however, proved stronger, and laid their rigid claims on us all. Whatever might be said, upon that 'sovereign' territory a 'sovereign' army lived and fought. The enemy, still numerous and strong, occupied one-half of the region. The whole situation demanded that the Government's activities and the life of the country should be completely subordinated to the interests of the armed struggle.

Acute friction arose, therefore, on the ground of the army's finance and supplies. But the chauvinism of the Kuban Government went still further. They claimed that the Kuban Army should form a separate unit from the Volunteer Army, a measure which, if carried out, would completely disorganize the latter. 'To round up their frontiers,' they laid claim to a portion of the provinces of

Stavropol and of the Black Sea. They oppressed the non-Cossack, 'alien' population, inflicting upon them severe penalties, including confiscation of property and the death sentence for real or more often imaginary Bolshevism. With the enemy at their door, these men suffered so much from swollen heads as to declare in their official press that: 'The Kuban in the future will never acquiesce even to an autonomy. The Cossacks desire to be absolute masters in their own house. They need ports and communications of their own, and independence in their relations with neighbouring peoples and states'(!) This was already absolutely opposed to the idea of a One and Indivisible Russia, which was what the Volunteer Army was fighting for.

At first, however, these separatist tendencies found little response among the Kuban troops and the mass of the Cossack population.

We could easily have overthrown the Government by means of the Kuban officers themselves.

Neither General Alexeyev nor I wished, however, to begin the task of the Kuban's regeneration by an act of violence. Moreover, another display of internecine strife would bode no good.

We might abandon the Kuban territory. In that case the Volunteer Army would become depleted and disorganized, the guiltless Kuban stanitsas flooded with Bolsheviks and all our efforts and sacrifices be in vain.

We therefore determined to carry on the campaign in the hope that the Kuban Rada (Parliament), due to assemble shortly, would inaugurate a new policy.

I have purposely dwelt on our inter-relations with the Kuban Government because, as will be seen later, their continual and unalterable deterioration became one of the chief factors of the ultimate collapse of the White front in South Russia.

At the outset of the campaign General Alexeyev looked upon our advance into the Kuban territory as temporary. Thinking that a civil government on an All-Russian scale would be established on the Volga with his concurrence, he therefore refrained from setting up bodies of civil administration in the army. As the territories under our occupation became wider, particularly after the liberation of the Stavropol and later of the Black Sea provinces, their provincial administrative centres were reinstated and military governors directly subordinated to the Army Commander placed at their head.

Our scope of action was being continually widened by the trend of events. Soon it became imperative to create a body capable of undertaking the all-round organization of the liberated territory. This task was assumed by General Alexeyev. He set up a ' Special Conference,' at first a consultative body, but which later became invested with the functions of a normal government.

The difficulties confronting the new government were appalling. A ruined administrative apparatus, a convulsed economic system, an empty exchequer, acute social strife and boundless class exactions, a general decline of morals – such was the outcome of four years of war, revolution, and mob-and-soldier law, etc.

I, personally, exercised absolute authority over the army. In civil administration, however, General Alexeyev's and my functions were not clearly defined, and our relations rested mainly on my consideration for him and recognition of his seniority. Neither did we differ concerning the principles of the task before us: without infringing on fundamental Russian law, to establish conditions enabling the Russian people to live more or less peacefully till the overthrow of the Bolsheviks and the reinstatement of legal All-Russian government.

Although we enjoyed practically absolute power over

the territories occupied by the Volunteer Army, we never laid claim to represent an All-Russian Government.

Heated arguments were carried on in political circles over the question of creating such a central authority. The more conservative public opinion proposed the Grand Duke Nicolai Nicolaevitch as its candidate for the post of Dictator. But such a dictatorship, foreshadowing as it were the restoration of the monarchy, did not correspond at the time to the wishes of the people and the Cossacks. The liberal groups desired to see General Alexeyev as sole ruler at the head of a triumvirate, but waited for him to reach the Volga, where, they surmised, lay the centre of future developments. Finally, as we already know, a 'Provisional All-Russian Government' was set up under pressure from the 'left' politicians in Siberia, which owing to its extreme unpopularity was recognized by none of the newly established southern state formations.

Soon all the schemes connected with General Alexeyev collapsed. A malignant disease, the hardships of the first campaign and the strenuous, exhausting work of these last years had undermined his strength.

He passed away on 8th October.

A vast concourse of people accompanied him to the grave, rendering homage to a man who had done such signal service to his country. General Alexeyev's death was received with profound sorrow by the Volunteer Army.

In consequence of our heavy loss, I assumed the title of 'Commander-in-Chief,' uniting the dual functions of military command and civil administration.

CHAPTER 15

The Volunteer Army reaches to the Black and Azov Seas – The Battle of Stavropol – The Meeting with the Germans and Georgians.

CONTRARY to all the rules of logic, the Volunteer Army, severely depleted, had by September *increased fourfold.* By the influx of volunteers the mobilization of four classes within the occupied territory and ten classes of Kuban Cossacks, we succeeded in raising its numerical strength to forty thousand men, exclusive of local militia of older Cossacks raised in every stanitsa close to the front. We possessed eighty-six guns and two hundred and fifty-six machine guns. All these forces were organized in three and a half mixed and four cavalry divisions.

By the middle of August the front of the Volunteer Army ran from the lower Kuban to Stavropol, a distance of four hundred and forty kilometres.

Over this area the Reds were grouped as follows: (1) The lower reaches of the Kuban, covering the approaches to Novorossisk, were occupied by the Taman group of ten to fifteen thousand men; (2) in the region between the River Kuban and the line Maikop-Armavir, Sorokin's retreating troops, added to those stationed there before, formed a group twenty-three thousand strong; (3) another eight to ten thousand men were advancing on Stavropol; (4) troops stationed along the railway south of Armavir, about ten thousand in all, acted as reserves to the former groups.

The total strength of the Red forces in Northern Caucasia at that time amounted to seventy to eighty thousand men and eighty to a hundred guns.

Under such conditions, to fight the Bolsheviks unaided was beyond the strength of the Kuban Cossacks. Circumstances, therefore, drove us to seek natural frontiers – the Black and Caspian Seas and the Caucasian mountain range.

The strategic task of the army consisted in safeguarding our flanks by occupying the Black Sea coast and consolidating our precarious position in Stavropol. After which we could hurl ourselves against Sorokin's main forces.

Not only Northern Caucasia was to be saved by this sanguinary struggle. The Don territory and Georgia owed their very existence to it. That alone saved these regions in 1918 from being overrun by the more daring bands of the North-Caucasian Bolsheviks.

The Georgian as well as some of the Don Cossack leaders refused to realize then the full portent of that struggle.

*

The Taman Red Army group under Matveyev was hard pressed. Pokrovsky after six days' fighting had seized the crossings on the lower reaches of the Kuban River, while another Volunteer brigade was marching from Ekaterinodar to cut off his retreat. The Reds were hastily falling back upon Novorossisk, fighting stubbornly all the while, suffering heavy casualties, and sacrificing their rearguard. On 26th August our brigade overthrew Matveyev's rearguard and dashed into the town. Matveyev himself succeeded somehow in dodging our blow, and, crossing Novorossisk, escaped further south along the coast.

With the fall of Novorossisk the Volunteer Army obtained a firm footing on the *Black Sea coast*.

The Taman group, however, maintained its discipline and firmness. It was joined on its peregrinations by all the desperadoes collected on the seaboard, and by those who feared the Cossack vengeance. This avalanche of men and horses rolled along the coastal high-road, destroying like a swarm of locusts all the meagre supplies of the local population. On reaching Tuapse they halted. Obviously such numbers could neither exist nor act in this empty corner of the Black Sea province. It was to be expected that the Taman group would move along the Tuapse-Armavir railway to effect a junction with Sorokin. Leaving one brigade in pursuit of the Taman Reds, I therefore dispatched Pokrovsky along the southern bank of the Kuban River to cut the railway line near Maikop.

Covering nearly two hundred and twenty kilometres, Pokrovsky defeated the Maikop Bolsheviks on 8th September and occupied the town, cutting off the railway. The Taman group eventually arrived three days later, after which, for ten days, the Kuban Cossacks (three thousand men) with their *backs* to Sorokin, kept up an uneven combat against fifteen thousand Taman Reds. The latter eventually broke through, crossed the River Laba and rejoined Sorokin. Pokrovsky then veering his front faced east.

During the whole of September fierce fighting went on in the region between the River Kuban and the Caucasian range, with heavy casualties on either side. Towns and stanitsas constantly changed hands. The unfortunate town of Armavir did so three times. Our troops fought valiantly, captured thousands of prisoners and large quantities of munitions and transports, but were unable to break the enemy's resistance. Nevertheless, the circle of Volunteers surrounding Sorokin was narrowing more and more. By 23rd September the main bulk of the North Caucasian Red Army was strategically almost completely surrounded: Pokrovsky to the west, Wrangel and Drozdovsky to the north (at Armavir) the foothills of the Caucasian range to the south, and to the east – the River Kuban and Borovsky. The latter, having swept the Stavropol region clear of Bolsheviks, attacked Nevinnomysskaia, Sorokin's staff headquarters, whence he himself barely escaped. Further south-east Shkuro's partisans were blowing up the railway. At the same time came the first news from Mozdok in the depths of the Caucasus that the Terek Cossacks also had revolted.

At the end of September, however, the Bolsheviks, by dint of strenuous fighting, succeeded in breaking our ring: by a brief offensive they repulsed us from Armavir and Nevinnomysskaia, thereby opening for themselves a line of communication along the Vladikavkaz main line. Simultaneously, two newly arrived Red divisions menaced Stavropol.

I concentrated *all* the forces of the Volunteer Army within the Armavir-Stavropol area.

The morale of the Bolshevist Army, however, was shaken. In the beginning of October they decided *to abandon the Kuban, and leaving strong detachments at Armavir and on the River Laba to act as cover, to withdraw to Nevinnomysskaia.*

No sooner did the Bolshevist retreat become apparent than one of our divisions stationed before Armavir made an attack on the town, but without success. The cavalry, on the other hand, pushing back the Bolsheviks, reached the River Urupa. Within this curiously sharp angle formed by the rivers Kuban and Urupa about forty-five thousand Reds were grouped.

Their further destination was unknown to us.

The Bolshevist Army might retreat on Vladikavkaz,

Astrakhan, or via Stavropol to Tsaritsyn, whence the
Tenth Soviet Army was advancing against the Don
Cossacks. As it turned out, the Bolshevist command, after
prolonged arguments and vacillations, resolved to head
for Stavropol.

*

Sorokin no longer took any active part in the operation.
His ill success had engendered a doubt as to his abilities
both among his troops and in the Soviet Government; he
was even suspected of treason. Sorokin dealt cruelly
with the commissars and commanders who had com-
promised his reputation, and many were shot. Among
them was Matveyev, the highly popular commander of
the Taman group, who was shot for alleged disobedience.
In the beginning of October 'The Central Committee of
the North Caucasian Republic' abolished the individual
authority of the commander in the army and substituted
a 'Revolutionary Council,' drawn from civilians and the
army, of which Sorokin was merely an ordinary member.
He was at Piatigorsk with his staff and escort. To protect
himself from the vengeance of the Bolshevist chiefs whom
he had ill-treated, he attempted a *coup d'état*. On 26th
October he arrested the chairman of the Central Committee
of the 'republic,' one Rubin and four of his assistants,
and shot them that same day.

The army, however, did not declare for Sorokin. The
congress of delegates from the front assembled at Nevinnomysskaia declared him 'an outlaw and a traitor to the
Revolution.' . . . Sorokin fled in the direction of Stavropol, but was caught by one of the Taman regiments
and assassinated.

Sorokin's *coup* had a disastrous repercussion on the fate
of the intelligentsia living at the Mineral Waters Spa.
Already, at the time of Shkuro's raid, hundreds of 'hostages'
were flung into prison by the Bolsheviks, liable to be shot

in the event of a 'counter-revolutionary rising.' Now in retaliation for the revolt of a *Red* commander, the Tcheka ordered the death of one hundred and six innocent hostages, among whom was the former Commander-in-Chief of the Russian northern front in the Great War, General Ruzsky, and the Bulgarian General Radko-Dmitriev, the hero of the last Balkan war, who had later commanded one of the Russian armies. Both had several times been offered high posts in the Red Army, which both had firmly refused to accept.

The protocol of the Commission of Inquiry thus described their last moments: 'Dressed only in their underclothes and with hands bound, the prisoners were led to the cemetery where a large hole had been dug. The executioners ordered the victims to kneel down and stretch their necks. Then they struck them – sometimes as often as five times or more! Some groaned, but most died silently. The Red soldiers pushed them all into the hole. . . . Next morning it was covered up. The low moans of those buried alive came from the newly filled grave. These were heard by the overseer and gravediggers. They approached and saw one of the hostages, a priest, still alive, peering out and imploring them to drag him out from the heap of corpses. . . The diggers, fearing the Red soldiers, threw on more earth. . . . The moans ceased. . . .'

A record exists of General Ruzsky's last conversation with his executioner:

'Do you acknowledge now the great Russian Revolution?'

'I see nothing except great banditism.'

*

On 23rd October the Reds at Nevinnomysskaia launched an offensive to the north. This marked the beginning of the *decisive battle for the possession of Stavropol, which lasted twenty-eight days.*

195

Drozdovsky's division, which protected the town from the south, was repulsed at its very outskirts, and after severe fighting was forced to abandon it and retreat north. Crowds of peaceful citizens, forsaking their homes and belongings, followed in the wake of this division. The Red troops entered the town, and reprisals set in. . . .

However, the Bolsheviks were unable to develop their initial success. With the arrival of Borovsky, who united three divisions (the 2nd, 3rd, and 2nd Kuban) under his command, our northern front was consolidated some thirteen to twenty kilometres' distance from Stavropol.

I was at the time near Armavir. Deciding that the best way out of the situation lay in a success on our western front, I ordered the divisions under Generals Kasanovitch, Wrangel, and Pokrovsky to spare no efforts in driving the left-bank enemy forces across the River Kuban, thus giving us a free hand in the Stavropol region.

By a surprise attack on the 26th October Kasanovitch captured Armavir, drove the Reds beyond the River Urupa, and pursued them to the distance of a day's march. Within the next few days the cavalry under Pokrovsky and Wrangel completely routed the Bolshevist forces facing them, captured numerous trophies, and emerged on to the River Kuban. By 5th November Pokrovsky had finally consolidated his position at Nevinnomysskaia.

All these divisions, including Shkuro's guerilla troops, were then diverted to Stavropol, only a small screen of Kuban Cossacks being left to protect Nevinnomysskaia from the south.

Flushed by these successes, Borovsky undertook a general offensive along the whole front on 4th November. His troops, in spite of heavy casualties, reached the outskirts of Stavropol, and next day one of the regiments dashed

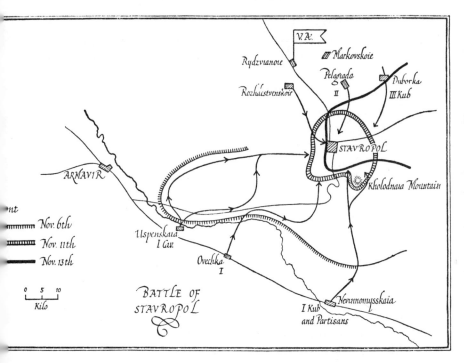

V.A.

Rydzvianoie

Markovskoie

Pelagrada
II

Duborka
III Kub

Rozhdestvenskoie

STAVROPOL

ARMAVIR

Kholodnaia Mountain

nt

Nov. 6th

Nov. 11th

Nov. 13th

0 5 10
Kilo

Uspenskaia
I Cav.

Ovechka
I

BATTLE OF
STAVROPOL

I Kub
and Partisans

Novunomysskaia

into the suburb. Here, however, the offensive was
stemmed. For four days after this the Bolsheviks kept
up stubborn counter-attacks. For four days blood flowed
freely and our ranks were thinned.

Meantime, troops were advancing from the south, and
by 11th November Stavropol was surrounded by the
Volunteer Army at a distance of one to twelve kilometres.
This fact greatly unnerved both the inhabitants of the
town and the Red troops. The town was crowded with
many thousands of sick and wounded, whose number
increased daily. All means of reaching the outer world
were cut off. Once more ominous rumours of treason
crept through the Bolshevist camp. Deserters began
to join us. . . .

The Bolshevist command determined to break through the blockade. On 11th November large forces were hurled against Borovsky's divisions, and after inflicting severe casualties drove their wing two kilometres beyond the town. Other numerous Red attacks on different sections were unsuccessful. Exhausted by even heavier casualties than ours, the Bolsheviks did not resume their attacks next day. Meantime, from the south, the circle was narrowing. Our divisions in places were within five kilometres of the town. They occupied Kholodnaia hill, where they seized and shut off the town's water supply.

The position of the besieged became critical. On the 13th they made a final effort to break through the envelopment, and started an offensive to the north and south-east. This time the completely depleted regiments of Borovsky's 2nd and 3rd Divisions, unable to hold out, were routed and pursued by the enemy, and hastily retreated to the north-west, halting only some twenty kilometres away from Stavropol. In endeavouring to parry the Bolshevist assaults by personally leading his broken units to counter-attack, the gallant commander of the 3rd Division, Colonel Drozdovsky, was severely wounded and died a few weeks later. The cavalry in the southern section was also somewhat hard pressed. But Wrangel's division, stationed to the west, taking advantage of the enemy's inactivity on its own section, attacked Borovsky's pursuers in the rear and reoccupied the suburb abandoned by Drozdovsky.

Nevertheless the Bolshevist break-through was successful. They evaded the enveloping circle. Having formed a new front north-west and south-west of Stavropol, they began hastily to organize their baggage. Whole arrays of waggons began trekking eastward.

Wrangel's vanguard, on the 14th, occupied the Stavropol railway station, and next day his division, reinforced on my orders by two regiments, definitely took possession of the town.

Stavropol had fallen. Two thousand five hundred corpses and four thousand wounded had been abandoned by the Bolsheviks. On the doors of the hospitals were inscriptions: 'Entrusted to the honour of the Volunteer Army.' They had every reason to trust! *We* – never. . . .

Notwithstanding the men's extreme exhaustion and weariness, I nevertheless resumed the general offensive on the 16th. Simultaneously the Bolsheviks did likewise, giving proof of extraordinary energy and tenacity. For four days longer the fighting raged upon the fields round Stavropol, and the fortunes of war fluctuated. It was only on 20th November that our onslaught upon the crack Red troops, the Taman group stationed to the north-east, settled the issue of the combat. Attacked from the front by remnants of our infantry, and from north and south by two cavalry divisions, the Reds were smashed and fled in panic, the whole *Bolshevist* front crumbling behind them. The fugitives were pursued by our cavalry.

The battle of Stavropol was of intense significance for the Volunteer Army. Another two and a half months were to be spent in incessant fighting; there were to be many hard moments to face, but never again would the Red North Caucasian Army recover from its crushing defeat.

The original cadres of the Volunteer Army, it seemed, were perishing a second time. In some regiments not more than one hundred men remained. But men might perish, yet tradition lived, together with the principle of the struggle and the indomitable will to carry on.

Another notable event took place within those memorable days which produced a profound impression throughout South Russia. The Allied Fleet entered the Black

Sea, and on 22nd November its first ships appeared in the bay of Novorossisk.

*

The consolidation of our position on the Black Sea and Azov seaboard in mid-August brought us in touch with the German Army and Fleet. In the western part of the Kuban territory a German brigade occupied the Taman peninsula with the object of controlling the Straits of Kertch and the economic exploitation of the region. A detachment of the German Army of Occupation in Georgia had landed at Adler and was digging trenches facing north. A German flotilla appeared now and again in Novorossisk and Eisk harbours. At the same time representatives of the German and Austrian command addressed several requests to the local authorities for permits to proceed to Ekaterinodar, which were always politely declined.

Nevertheless 'armed neutrality' remained unbroken, and the German command, while consistently remaining our enemy, treated the Volunteer Army with unfailing respect.

When the German flotilla appeared at Eisk, the officer in command thus explained its arrival to the Volunteer commandant:

'At the time of their campaign on Taganrog the Bolsheviks seized a transport steamer with Austrian officers which they brought to Eisk. These officers were barbarously murdered and thrown into the sea. In addition, many boats with Bolsheviks fleeing from the Volunteer Army have lately been landing along the coast. The flotilla's task consists in quelling atrocities at sea, *in preventing the ruffians from landing, and exterminating those who do*; as no state would willingly tolerate them within its bounds.'

Such an unexpected attitude towards Germany's allies

and satellites surprised the commandant so much that
the German officer hastened to explain:

'Oh, yes; officially Germany has signed a treaty with
Soviet Russia, but unofficially I may express to you my
wishes for a speedy victory over the Bolsheviks for the
sake of pacifying the country and establishing a strong
and orderly government.'

The German officer, I am convinced, was sincere, and
this way of thinking was predominant in the German
Army. But it bore no influence whatever on Germany's
cruel and short-sighted policy over the Russian question.

Personally, I came into contact with official Germany
only once. At the beginning of October Major von
Kofenhausen, then in Rostov, on behalf of the German
Government handed me a demand that I should place
the Indo-European telegraph line running through our
occupied territory at the disposal of the German military
authorities. I refused. The demand was shortly repeated
in the form of an ultimatum, the reply to be given within
five days. Again I refused. Whether the presenting of
this ultimatum was prompted by a desire to create a
casus belli remains unknown, for within the next few
days the situation underwent a radical change. An
appalling catastrophe broke over Germany, and her
'High Emissary' von Kofenhausen disappeared from
Rostov, no one knew whither. For a long time after he
became the bogey of the Allied Missions, which set up a
fruitless search for him throughout the south territory.

*

When our troops in pursuit of Matveyev's Red bands
along the Black Sea coastal route reached Tuapse in
September, their further progress within the Black Sea
province was unexpectedly arrested by the Georgians.
They had commenced fortifying many points of the coast

against attack from the *north*, while an advance detachment of their semi-Bolshevist 'National Guard,' deploying south of Tuapse, threatened Novorossisk.

General Alexeyev, considering all this to be due to a misunderstanding, and the Georgians as natural allies in the struggle against the common foe – the Bolsheviks – sent a message to Tiflis, inviting representatives of the Georgian Government to a conference. On 25th and 26th September a meeting took place at Ekaterinodar between the Volunteer Army Command, the Kuban Government, and Georgian delegates (the former member of the Russian Imperial Duma, Gueguechkori, and General Mazniev). The following outstanding questions were placed on the agenda: (1) Our alliance; (2) mitigation of the regime practised with regard to unfortunate Russian officials mercilessly dismissed from their posts by the Georgians; (3) consideration of our rights to a portion of the enormous Russian Empire war supplies on the former Caucasian front; (4) guarantees that in our mutual trade exchange Russian corn should go to the Georgians but not to Germany; and finally (5) the evacuation of the Black Sea province by the Georgians.[1]

We encountered stubborn opposition from Gueguechkori, and no settlement was reached on any of these questions. With regard to the first point, Gueguechkori declared that there could be no question of an alliance, but merely of 'jointly carrying out a common task,' and even that only upon the Black Sea coast. He likewise refused point-blank and for no reason whatever to reinstate the southern part of the Black Sea province.

In view of the failure of the negotiations I closed the frontier, prepared, however, for recourse to hostilities with regard to the Georgians.

---

[1] Within the disputed region only *one* village out of fifty had a Georgian population.

Our troops 'stood by,' ready for action at Tuapse, and a state of 'neither war nor peace' was established between us and the Georgians.

Such was the beginning of our co-existence with Georgia, charged with many consequences, which gave rise to legends regarding the intolerant policy of the Volunteer Army, accused of rebuffing its 'natural ally.'

When in 1921 the Soviet Government put an end to Georgia's existence as an independent state, its former rulers, in an appeal to 'the proletariat of the world,' endeavoured to justify themselves against the charge of opposing the Soviet Government: 'Georgia was always opposed to intervention in *Russian affairs*. It refused decisively to collaborate with General Denikine at a time when the Volunteer Army was at the zenith of its power and sought an alliance with Georgia, threatening to go to war in the event of refusal.'

As enemies of the *Russian* Volunteer Army they failed to realize that by undermining its existence they thereby worked the ruin of their own people.

CHAPTER 16

The Liberation of Northern Caucasia by the Volunteer Army.

THE further the Volunteer Army penetrated into the depths of Caucasia, the more complicated became its position.

Various processes had marked the end of the year 1917 and the beginning of 1918 in that region. There was the antagonistic split within the Russian population of the territory (Terek Cossacks versus 'aliens,' who formed forty per cent. of the population), moral degeneration among the Cossacks themselves, and the ceding of the North Caucasian small nations (fifty per cent. of the population). Five new 'states' and 'governments' appeared on the scene,[1] some of which quarrelled both with the Russians and among themselves, were divided into antagonistic groups, and settled their disputes and right to live by violence and bloodshed. As these small peoples were still on a low plane of civilization, the struggle here assumed a cruel and ugly shape.

Owing to such a division of forces, the Soviet Government found no difficulty in establishing itself in Northern Caucasia by the spring of 1918. The province of Dagestan, situated in the east, adjoining the Caspian Sea, being under Turkish influence and provided by Turkey with arms and instructors, was the only one to offer any resistance.

[1] Dagestan, Tchechnia, Ingushetia, Ossetia, Kabarda.

The Soviet Government considered the Terek Cossacks to be the most hostile element, and treated them with particular cruelty, frequently using the local alien tribesmen to ruin and plunder Cossack territory. This policy eventually led the Terek Cossacks to revolt. This was timed for the autumn, but Shkuro's raid on Kislovodsk at the end of June gave the signal for a premature rising. Its centre was the town of Mozdok. The Cossack forces numbered about ten thousand men and forty guns; they were also joined by small bands of Ossetin and Kabarda mountaineers. For five months from July onwards the rebels, wedged in the narrow space between Prokhladnaia and Kizliar, cut off from the outside world and surrounded on all sides by enemies, fought on fiercely and stubbornly. Their firm stand diverted Bolshevist forces from the Volunteer Army. It was only in September that we managed to send the Terek Cossacks a message by air and cheer them by the promise of coming aid.

But it was too late.

Upon the narrow strip of the free Terek Cossack land a big Socialist 'Government' established itself, primarily concerned with the solution of questions relative to the 'Terek and Russian constitutions.' The troops gradually became demoralized. Notwithstanding the protest of the commanding staff the Government introduced 'conscious discipline,' together with soldiers' meetings and elected officers. General mobilization was superseded by fortnightly 'service shifts,' owing to which the units became a heterogeneous compound of men for ever moving to and fro, and frequently going home before the arrival of the next shift. The 'Government' changed three commanders, but this did not improve matters. One of the three, the gallant and honest General Mistulov, unable to bear the sight of the army's disruption, committed suicide.

When the Bolsheviks, under pressure from the Volunteer Army and fearing to lose their line of retreat, undertook a serious operation in November to clear a way for themselves across Mozdok, the Terek front collapsed. Part of the force retired to Petrovsk, there to join Bicherakhov's

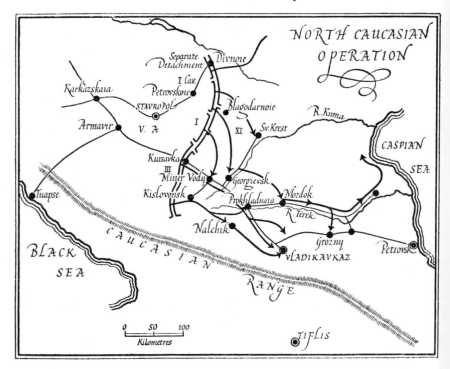

contingent,[1] another by circuitous mountain paths pushed westward and joined us, while the rest dispersed to their homes.

*

As had become customary, the Volunteer Army, after the heavy fighting and severe casualties sustained at Stavropol, increased in volume and again numbered forty

[1] See Chapter 10.

thousand men. The greater part of these, namely, twenty-five thousand, were divided into three army corps, and formed the Caucasian group stationed between the River Manytch and the Caucasian foothills. Confronting them was a body of Red troops reorganized and brought up to strength, forming the Eleventh Army, and numbering a great quantity of men, not less than one hundred and fifty thousand, of whom only one-half were actually capable of fighting. Moreover, a new army (the Twelfth) released after the fall of the Terek territory, occupied the Mozdok-Kisliar line. The total Bolshevist forces on the Caucasian front were estimated at seventy-two thousand fighting men. Their main base was at Astrakhan, while the nearest, and a very wealthy one, was in the town of Sviatoy Krest.

The task I set the Volunteer Army was the final liberation of Northern Caucasia to the Caucasian range, and the occupation of the Caspian western seaboard and lower Volga. This, while cutting off Soviet Russia from the Baku and Grozny oilfields, would enable us to come in touch with the Ural Cossacks at Guriev and with the British at Enzeli.

For six weeks exhausting local fighting went on along this front, both sides, alternately worn out and repleted, endeavouring to improve their strategical positions. At last I ordered a general offensive of the Volunteer Army to begin on 3rd January. The main blow was to be directed east of Stavropol and the Bolshevist front subsequently enveloped from the north.

Leaving a small detachment to hold the northern Bolshevist group, the two crack army corps united later under the command of General Wrangel, attacked the enemy's centre in the direction of Sviatoy Krest and Georgievsk. The attack was crowned with complete success. The Bolshevist centre was smashed and the troops took to flight. The Red front ceased to be. In its place there remained three groups, completely detached the one from the other: one on the River Manytch, another Vat Sviatoy Krest, and the third at Mineral Waters Spa.

The Manytch group was making desperate efforts to alleviate its position by an offensive; however, within the next few days it was defeated and repulsed far back into the Astrakhan steppes. General Wrangel's troops, continuing in pursuit, captured Sviatoy Krest after fierce fighting on the 17th, and Georgievsk on the 19th. This facilitated the task of the Third Corps, advancing along the Vladikavkaz railway, and which next day occupied the Mineral Waters Spa. Its vanguard division, under General Shkuro, by a rapid flank movement from the south, seized the Prokhladnaia railway junction, thus cutting off the Bolshevist retreat to Vladikavkaz.

No other way of retreat was possible to the remnants of the Red Army except over a long and difficult route by Mozdok-Kisliar, and along the Caspian coast to Astrakhan.

The enemy was completely routed both physically and morally, but demanded incessant pursuit, notwithstanding the terrible exhaustion of the Volunteers.

By this time, as will be seen from the subsequent pages, the Don Cossack Army recognized my authority, and the Volunteers having occupied the Crimea and the Donets coal-mining area, I no longer was able personally to lead the Caucasian detachments. They were formed into the Caucasian Volunteer Army which I placed under the command of General Wrangel, who had greatly distinguished himself in the recent fighting.

To this army was entrusted the task of finishing off the enemy.

*

Two army corps were told off by the army commander for the pursuit of the Reds along their principal routes of retreat: that of General Liakhov in the direction of Vladikavkaz and Grozny, and of General Pokrovsky towards Mozdok and the Caspian Sea.

The human torrent rolled incessantly eastward, flooding all the roadways for scores of kilometres, obstructing them with broken waggons, abandoned luggage, corpses of men and beasts. Those who escaped death from bullet or sword fell victims to spotted typhus, which raged unrestrained. Many campaigners, inured one might think to the horrors of war, never could recall these nightmare visions without a shudder: wildly rushing crowds, trainloads of the sick and wounded abandoned on the sidings, thousands of people worn out with fever and delirium, crawling along the rails and railway banks, and ruthlessly crushed to death by the passing trains.

At times the crowds of Bolsheviks would halt and, driven by an instinct of self-preservation, hurl themselves against their pursuers in a last desperate, cruel combat. Thus, on 28th January, Pokrovsky having encountered stubborn resistance near Mozdok, charged the Bolsheviks on a front thirty kilometres wide, drove them with their backs to the river, and routed them completely. The fugitives tried to cross to the other bank, but the only wooden bridge collapsed, and many who tried to swim across were drowned in the Terek.

After another two days' successful fighting, the corps, while dealing swift and effective blows to the enemy, advanced uninterruptedly, and by 10th February its vanguard reached the Caspian. Remnants of the Red forces dispersed, partly throughout the Tchechnia region, and partly were overtaken and massacred north of Kisliar. Only a few succeeded in escaping to Astrakhan.

This unequalled march of three hundred and ninety kilometres, with constant fighting, was accomplished by Pokrovsky's corps in fourteen days.

Meantime, General Liakhov's corps encountered in its progress the stubborn resistance not only of the Bolsheviks but also of a small but warlike and well-armed people – the Ingush. The Ingush became the *Landsknecht* and support of the Soviet Government. While intolerant of any manifestations of Communism at home, they willingly assisted the Bolsheviks to plunder and do violence to all their neighbours, owing to which they made common cause with the former. In every aoul, in every cottage was an ambush against our troops. Nevertheless, by 3rd February General Shkuro's vanguard approached Vladikavkaz and dashed into the suburb. The combat for the possession of the town and the Ingushetia territory adjacent to it from the east lasted six days. It was only on the 9th that the Ingush National Council volunteered submission, and the next day, after nine hours of fighting in the streets, our troops occupied Vladikavkaz.

The next few days were spent in rounding up the Bolsheviks scattered in the narrow valley of the River Sunzha between Vladikavkaz and Grozny.

*

Northern Caucasia was delivered from the Bolsheviks. The one hundred thousand Red Army had ceased to exist. It left on our hands fifty thousand prisoners, one hundred and fifty guns, and an enormous quantity of various war supplies. The foothills of the Caucasus were strewn with the bodies of its fighting men, slain for the sake of ideas and aims which they neither shared nor understood.

For seven and a half months that army, beaten more than once but reviving again and again, had drawn upon itself nearly all the Volunteer forces of the south. That struggle had cost us much bloodshed, many lives, and strenuous efforts, but it was rich withal in glowing examples of gallantry and skill, both among leaders and men.

In the middle of February the Caucasian Volunteer Army, its rear safeguarded and to a certain extent pacified, was able at last to turn its face to the north – in fulfilment of its original task.

This was all the more urgent as the Don front was on the verge of collapse.

PART III

CHAPTER 17

The Defeat of the Central Powers – The Evacuation of
their Armies – The Political and Military Situation in
Soviet Russia – The Formation of the Western Front.

THE collapse of the Central Powers, long heralded by a
number of ominous signs, nevertheless came as a surprise
by reason of its suddenness and disastrous extent. Victors
and vanquished alike were overwhelmed, not merely by
its actual consequences, but more so by the gigantic scale
of the event. It also was bound to produce a radical
change in the Russian situation.

Both Whites and Reds felt assured that the change
would affect merely the outward setting; that the Austro-
Germans would be *superseded* by the Allies, and the
military and economic blockade of Soviet Russia would
assume the form of active intervention. We regarded it
as a direct continuation of the war and of relations morally
binding to the Allies and also as corresponding to the
interests of the Entente Powers themselves, to which the
spread of Bolshevism presented a direct menace. The
Bolsheviks thought likewise. Trotsky said: 'There is
grave danger. All history for us is now condensed in the
one question of the Entente intervention.'

Hope on the one side and apprehension on the other
were nourished by actual developments. By the terms of
the Armistice Germany was bound to evacuate the
territories which before the war formed part of Russia,
'in so far as this was justified by the internal conditions of

the same,' and simultaneously allow for the free passage of Allied fleets through the Kattegat into the Baltic, through Danzig and the Vistula to the east, 'to maintain order.'

Meantime a revolution broke out in Germany, filling the Bolshevist camp with wildest hopes. Enthusiastic greetings were broadcast from Moscow to Berlin, with expressions of such selfish rejoicing as to be directly insulting to a country laid low and plunged into national mourning. Only the Berlin Council of Workers and Soldiers' Delegates responded to the greeting. The Ebert-Haase Government openly avoided too close relations with Moscow. And the Moscow wireless soon sent out complaints to 'Germany's revolutionary masses.' 'Sorrow and irritation are growing at the news that the German revolutionary workers and soldiers do not even attempt to express their unity with us.'

The German people were, at the time, occupied in settling their destinies without the aid of Moscow. The rising of the Spartacists was suppressed with bloodshed and all the Moscow Communists' hopes of a World Revolution in the near future were for a long time to come buried beneath the new German Constitution.

*

Having failed to obtain the desired results in the relations with the Central German Government, the Soviets set in operation all their means of propaganda and agitation among the troops of the Austro-German eastern front. They were saturated with the mentality and practice of Russian Bolshevism, among other things with the necessity 'to make short work of their officers and generals.' Active tasks were also set: 'In Russia – in the Ukraine, the Don, and Kuban territories – there is sufficient grain both for us and for you. That is why the

English are hastening to assist Generals Skoropadsky, Krasnov, and Denikine to wrest the bread from the workers. Together we should be able to crush them in a fortnight.'

All such appeals, while contributing to quicken the general process of disruption among the Austro-Germans, were powerless to move to action men whose every thought was occupied with anxiety to return to their native country aflame with revolution.

The disintegration of the multi-national Austrian army was immediate and final. Austrian officers fled by the hundred into the German occupation zone, while the soldiers dispersed, swelling the ranks of freebooters and spreading anarchy throughout the land. The German Army also became demoralized. From all sides came news of unrest, soldiers' meetings, desertions by whole contingents, insult to and even of the murdering of officers. At the same time, within the seething soldier masses the struggle was going on between anarchist elements and the inborn discipline of the German mind and spirit. The latter got the upper hand and prevented the rest from overstepping the limit beyond which commences the suicide of the army and of the nation. Not only the Government, but nearly all Soldiers' Committees issued sober appeals: (1) for the maintenance of organization without which no orderly return home was possible; (2) until the time of departure that no advance of Soviet troops be allowed; and (3) in the event of internal risings that neutrality should be preserved.

*

When this stake – the roping-in of the revolutionary German Army – was lost, the Soviet Government made every attempt at a *rapprochement* with the Entente Powers, were it even at the price of heavy sacrifices. The length to which it was ready to go is proved by the contents of Tchicherin's Note of February 1919, in which, in exchange for peace, the Soviet Government offered 'to recognize Russia's financial liabilities to all creditors belonging to the Entente Powers,' expressed itself willing 'to grant concessions for mines, forests, etc., to citizens of the Allied Powers,' and even 'to conduct negotiations on the question of territorial concessions.' How far these proposals were sincere may be judged from the fact that *simultaneously* drastic appeals were being broadcast to Europe from Moscow in the name of the Soviet Government and the newly created Third International for the overthrow of the bourgeois governments.

All these futile endeavours of the Bolsheviks merely testified to the plight in which Russia was then placed, both with regard to her internal as well as international status. It also proves *the enormous potentialities possessed by the Allies for the solution of the Russian problem.*

Simultaneously the Soviets were busily engaged in organizing the Red Army. Seventeen classes were called up for service, as well as those members of the former General Staff and 'Tsarist' officers who were still in Soviet territory. At the beginning of 1919 the armed forces of Soviet Russia nominally amounted to eight hundred thousand fighting men, formed into twelve armies consisting of separate infantry and cavalry divisions.

A meeting of the Council of People's Commissars at the end of November 1918 revealed the desperate position of the country, cut off from sources of food supply and raw materials; the stocks of copper, pig-iron, cotton and coal were completely exhausted. The Soviets' only means of salvation lay in widening their territory, and in a campaign for the recovery of Donets coal and Tashkent cotton. These considerations, coupled with Trotsky's schemes to 'drive a wedge between the departing German militarism and the approaching Franco-British,' formed the basis of the winter campaign of 1919.

The Red Army was given the following task:

(1) On the northern front and the approaches to Petrograd to limit itself to active defence.

(2) On the western front, following on the withdrawal of the Germans, to occupy the most important railway junctions such as Riga, Dvinsk, Kovno, Brest-Litovsk, and so forth.

(3) On the Ukrainian front, by means of small bands, to foster revolt, taking advantage of the population's discontent with German occupation.

(4) On the eastern front (more than a hundred thousand men), active defence in the Urals and an advance on Tashkent.

(5) On the southern front (more than a hundred thousand men), as a primary objective to occupy the Donets basin and repulse the Don Cossack force beyond the River Don.

The main blow was aimed at the southern front, at the long-suffering Don Cossack force, and incidentally at the Volunteer Army.

'The pulse of the Soviet Republic beats on the southern front,' said Trotsky. 'We have sounded the call to the Soviets. Hundreds of fresh workers, motor-cars, rifles, and guns are being rushed thither. We must occupy the Don territory, Northern Caucasia, and the Caspian, and retain the Ukraine. In the Don territory we must cut the knot of counter-revolution that is being tied there.'

*

The German exodus commenced in December.

There had been more than ample time for the arrival of the 'substitutes.'[1] For the evacuation, even from the

---

[1] *I.e.*, the Allies.

technical side, was fraught with stupendous difficulties: throughout Russia's vast territory, aflame with revolution, her railway traffic crippled and almost destroyed, a German army of half a million men was quartered – thirty-six Austro-German divisions, separated from their state frontiers by a distance of from six hundred and sixty (Pskov) to four thousand (Tiflis) kilometres.

But the 'substitutes' did not come.

The Germans abandoned Finland. That country's practical politicians soon changed their orientation for the sake of British goods, American wheat, and even French ammunition. The strategic position of this new state in relation to Soviet Russia was extremely unfavourable. Finland owned the coast-line and the *scheere* route of the Gulf of Finland; its army, forty-five thousand strong, had its outposts only thirty kilometres from Petrograd and close to the Murmansk railway, thus threatening the rear of the Red Army operating against General Ironside, as well as the undefended Russian capital. The Entente Powers, which at that period exercised absolute control of the Finnish Government, merely claimed loyalty to themselves and the cancellation of all obligations towards Germany.

So Finland took no part in the campaign against the Soviets, preserving an armed neutrality to the very end.

The evacuation of Esthonia and the north-western province was accomplished under different circumstances. In the wake of the outgoing Germans the Bolshevist forces, numbering three divisions, advanced, seizing one western town after another and meeting with no resistance. They thus occupied Vilna, Minsk, Baranovitchy. Only at Pskov they had a short encounter with a small Russian Volunteer force (about four to five thousand men), formed there with the assistance of the Germans, but unable to expand owing to the opposition of – the same! The

Bolsheviks had already invaded Esthonian territory, but were held up by Russian and Esthonian detachments a hundred kilometres from Reval.

The anti-Bolshevist struggle in Esthonia assumed an exclusively national character, under the slogan of that province's independence of Russia. This was also upheld by the British Government, which established a secret protectorate over Esthonia. A British squadron appeared off Reval. British economic assistance and military supplies were placed at the disposal of the Esthonian Government, whose policy became entirely subordinated to British influence.

Once on the territory of 'independent' Esthonia, the Russian detachment was forced to submit to its military authority (General Laidoner) for 'concerted action against the Bolsheviks and anarchy.' The Esthonians, who were fighting for their independence, demanded unconditional recognition of the same. The Russian officer in command could not assume the responsibility of such an act. Consequently, this led to mutual mistrust, although the Russian corps throughout its stay in Esthonia remained strictly loyal.

Howbeit, the Russian and Esthonian troops by their joint efforts succeeded in throwing back the Bosheviks beyond Lake Tchudskoe, and by the spring of 1919 Laidoner's army was firmly established as cover on the ethnographical borders of Esthonia. The Russian army corps under the command of General Rodzianko, smashed the Seventh Bolshevist Army at the end of May, and supported by an Esthonian division which captured Pskov, occupied portions of the Petrograd and Pskov provinces. This corps swelled to thirteen thousand men, and on acquiring its *own* territory, was renamed the North-western Army, acting quite independently of the Esthonian command.

When General Yudenitch, appointed by Admiral Kolchak as commander-in-chief of the north-western front, joined the army in July he was met by a force truly gallant and brave, but lacking the barest necessities. They were clothed in rags, their supplies consisted almost exclusively of what had been taken from the Bolsheviks, and their pay was practically nil.

The British, so lavish to the Esthonians, would as yet spare nothing for the Russian Army. Added to this, the continuous friction between it and the Esthonian Government, and the latter's peace negotiations with Soviet Russia placed the North-western Army under a constant menace from the rear.

*

If Allied and mainly British influence was paramount on the northern Baltic seaboard, in the southern part of the territory it had to compete for a long time with that of Germany. Conforming to the demands of the Allies, the German troops were hastily evacuating these territories. The local Russian and Lettish forces were small, and consequently the Bolsheviks were able to advance rapidly, and already, on 15th January 1919, occupied Riga.

The Bolsheviks' rapid advance to the Nyeman and the alternative of their juncture with the German Spartacists, roused the keen apprehension of the Allies. Their views underwent a drastic change. M. Clemenceau formulated the idea, taken up by Mr. Lloyd George, of creating a *barrier of small buffer states and national armies for the defence of Europe against Russian Bolshevism.* Primarily, it became necessary to have recourse to the Germans, and the Entente gave corresponding instructions to German headquarters. The German evacuation was suspended, and the Bolshevist offensive stemmed by the Germans on the line of Windava, Kovno-Grodno, and the River Pripiat.

By an agreement between the Latvian Government and the German Command, a strong Volunteer force was organized by General von der Goltz which, together with local formations, towards the summer numbered forty thousand men. The German Volunteers were attracted by the promise of grants of land held out to them by the Latvian Government; an extremely onerous promise, and practically impossible to carry out. This added bitterness to the age-long feud between the Baltic Germans and the Letts. The Germans deposed the Ulmanis Socialist Government and established a Conservative one, with Nedra as premier, in its stead. The Entente refused to recognize the latter. Complete confusion ensued. Nevertheless, by the middle of March von der Goltz undertook an offensive against the Bolsheviks, and having thrown back the Reds, occupied Riga in June. The further progress of the 'cordon' into the interior, however, was impeded by the jealous and suspicious policy of the Entente Powers.

Farther south seven thousand Westphalian Volunteers, together with Lithuanian units in process of formation, were covering the frontier of Lithuania. Here, too, on this small strip of land, sharp conflicts raged: the Lithuanians were quarrelling with the Poles, who were trying to take possession of disputed territories; Germans, out of pique towards Poland, were assisting Lithuania with supplies, while the Allies were hindering Germany by prohibiting the export of war supplies across the German frontier.

Still farther south lay the Polish cordon.

Thanks to liberal assistance from the French, Poland by the spring of 1919 already possessed on her external front a more or less organized force of eight to nine infantry and four cavalry divisions. But a menace from the west still loomed over the country. Field-Marshal Hindenburg still tarried with the demobilization of the German Army corps stationed upon Germany's eastern frontier. In Eastern Galicia, where pro-Russian and pro-Ukrainian tendencies united in a common hatred of Polish domination there was fierce warfare. Military activities among anti-Bolshevist Poles, therefore, were none too energetic. Only in spring 1919, jointly with the Lithuanians, did they start an offensive, taking Vilna and approaching Minsk in May; cleverly taking advantage of the war between the Ukraine and Moscow, they seized part of Volhynia, with the town of Lutsk.

The territories thus seized, the Polish population of which did not exceed five per cent., were annexed to Poland. From that time pressure was brought to bear more and more unbearably for the Polonization of the Russian border territories, while blind hatred became the mainspring of Poland's policy in the East.

*

From the standpoint of strategy the north-western anti-Bolshevist front was of immense importance. The reasons for this were manifold: the proximity of Petrograd;[1] the possibility of organizing a well-equipped base on the Baltic Sea close to British and French shores; the potential assistance of the Allied Fleet; large stores of both Russian and German war supplies in the territories adjoining the front line; a whole army of over a million Russian prisoners of war in the concentration camps of Central Europe from which many Volunteers could be drawn. And finally, the presence on this area of over eighty thousand men, now disunited, but capable of forming an efficient fighting force.

A smashing blow from the west would be disastrous to the Soviets.

[1] Twenty-eight kilometres from the Finnish frontier; one hundred and fifty kilometres from Narva.

Unfortunately, with the exception of the feeble Russian detachment embroiled in a complex political situation, no one, not a single Power nor any local national government, aimed at the *overthrow of the Bolsheviks.*

The Entente Powers were solely concerned with the *barrier.* Germany – besides the barrier – by maintaining a strong army of occupation, envisaged the opportunity of circumventing the clause limiting her army to one hundred thousand men to create a mailed fist against Poland on the outskirts of East Prussia. Even if the German war party, from purely selfish motives, was actually in favour of a more serious intervention, this would certainly not be under the flag of the Entente, while the latter above all things feared a 'Russo-German *rapprochement.*' Speaking in the House of Commons, Mr. Winston Churchill said he was obsessed by the idea of the terrible danger which would arise if Russia, becoming an enemy of the Entente, and Germany thirsting for vengeance, were to realize that by uniting they might once more become powerful.

With regard to the new border states, their sole aim was to safeguard their independence and round up their frontiers at Russia's expense. In this they were assisted by the policy of M. Clemenceau and Mr. Lloyd George, at a time when another British statesman, Mr Churchill, strenuously opposed such a short-sighted policy.[1] He clearly saw that the 'barrier' was not solid, and the young states behind whose back Europe was screening herself were holding their own merely 'because no one was seriously attacking them.' For 'two-thirds of the entire

[1] Both Admiral Kolchak's Government and mine recognized in principle Poland's independence within its ethnographical borders, and Finland's independence on terms of strategical guarantees. With regard to the other formations, these were recognized as autonomous. The final solution of these questions was to be referred to the All-Russian Constituent Assembly.

Bolshevist Army were engrossed in fighting Kolchak and Denikine.'

Having correctly gauged the political impotency of the north-western front, Trotsky left ridiculously negligible forces to face it, and concentrated all that were available in the south.

CHAPTER 18

The Entente Intervention on the Black Sea Coast –
British Material Support – The Ukraine and Don
Tragedies.

ON 23rd November the Anglo-French squadron cast
anchor in the bay of Novorossisk, and ten days later a
British Military Mission arrived under General Poole. The
whole town of Novorossisk, as also later of Ekaterinodar,
turned out to greet them. Joyous crowds flooded the
streets in an outburst of welcome. The toasts and speeches
at numerous banquets were full of optimism.

'Welcome, dear friends!'

'Salut à nos Alliés!'

These exclamations resounded wherever the Allied
pennants flew over the Black Sea. They were expressive
of the feelings of keen joy, warm friendliness, and boundless hopes which the sight of this mission roused in the
population. Never had the Entente Powers been offered
such a golden opportunity for cementing firm and enduring
ties with a country now poverty-stricken, it is true, but
possessing boundless wealth; with a people who, though
now struck by madness, under normal circumstances
acquitted themselves honourably under international
obligations and remembered the good done to them.

'We have a common aim to achieve,' said General
Poole. 'We never forget for a moment that Russia is our
old and trusted Ally. Nor have we forgotten that, in spite
of being placed in extremely difficult circumstances, you

have refused to side with the Germans and remained loyal to your Allies to the end. . . . I am sent by my country to see what we can do for you. We shall be only too ready to assist you.'

'You may implicitly rely on the aid of Great Britain and free France. We are with you! We are for you!' said the French diplomatic representative, M. Erlich.

Far be it from me to doubt the sincerity of these first Allied representatives. But, estranged by years of war from the workaday policy of their governments, their speeches were expressive of their own feelings and convictions rather than the outcome of actual fact. In any case they did not carry sufficient weight and influence with their respective governments to alter the Russian policy of the Entente. At the time, however, Russian public opinion was assured that such were the actual feelings of the Allied peoples and the intentions of their governments.

To define the exact nature and extent of the Allied assistance to the southern armies was no easy task.

Their own mutual relations were not defined. The British and French Commanders-in-Chief, Generals Milne and Franchet - d'Espérey, to whom the missions at Ekaterinodar were subordinate, resided at Constantinople. At the same time Bucharest was the headquarters of the staff of General Berthelot, who himself bore the title of 'Commander-in-Chief of the Allied Forces in Rumania, Transylvania, and South Russia.' On behalf of the latter, General Stcherbachev forwarded me, as representative of the Volunteer Army, a detailed scheme which opened up most favourable prospects: (1) it had been decided to dispatch for the occupation of Russia twelve French and Greek divisions, which would rapidly occupy Kiev, Kharkov, and the Don and Kuban territories in order to enable the anti-Bolshevist armies to organize themselves for the march on Moscow; (2) the main Allied base would be at Odessa, whither enormous quantities of war supplies were being transferred. With regard to financial assistance a special plan was being worked out.

On the strength of this letter and the French delegate's proposals, my staff drew up and transmitted to the French a report on the military and political situation in South Russia with the plan of a joint campaign with the Allies. Its main idea was that the Allied Army should deploy along the line of the German cordon, viz., Pskov-Bielgorod-Tsaritsyn, to cover our mustering and formation. 'No active intervention will be necessary. What we need is not force but the promise of friendly support.'

Under cover of the Allied troops, the Russian armies were to start their advance on Petrograd, Moscow, and Kazan.

*

Time went on. All the fine speeches had been made, and still help was not forthcoming. A whole series of episodes had aroused suspicion. . . . In Sevastopol the Allies refused to hand over to us the ships of the Russian Fleet on the pretext that 'they might do great harm to the Allies should they be seized by the Bolsheviks.' Ships fit for navigation were ordered to be taken to Izmet and interned. Under a similar pretext Allied crews, by order of Admiral Leger, were sinking and blowing up munition stores at Sevastopol, destroying the engines of the submarines, dismantling the guns, and carrying away the gun-locks. All this resembled a winding-up rather than the beginning of the anti-Bolshevist campaign.

The telegraph soon brought us news of the existence of 'a demarcation line between the British and French zones of action.' It ran from the Bosphorus via the Gulf of Kertch to the Don estuary, then up the river and on to

Tsaritsyn. From a strategic standpoint this line had no significance whatsoever, as it took no account of the meridian-wise lines of operations in the direction of Moscow. Neither did it correspond to the object of a rational provisioning of the southern armies, for, by dividing the Don territory in two, it favoured the interests of occupation and exploitation.

The unrest in the Ukraine fostered both by the Bolsheviks and the Ukrainian extremists (under Petliura) was spreading and threatening to sweep away both the Hetman and the German 'cordon.' In order to safeguard this vast area as a base rich in food and war supplies, and defend the already fluctuating Don territory from being submerged in a Bolshevist avalanche, I repeatedly urged the French command to dispatch, if only two, divisions into the Kharkov and Ekaterinodar regions.

In December the Allied forces began to arrive: a French division under command of General d'Anselme in Odessa; British contingents under General Thomson in Baku; and under General Forestier-Walker, a further division in Batum. At a time when the Ukraine and the Don territory were on the verge of collapse, the Allies sent troops to areas of then secondary importance, or rather possessing a world importance of an *economic* nature.

The only problem satisfactorily settled was that of material assistance. A representative of the British Military Mission called one day on my Chief of Staff, and said:

'Whether the French will give you war material is open to doubt. Be so good as to order complete lists of your wants to be sent to us.'

Two months elapsed, and with the arrival of General Briggs – the new head of the British Military Mission – the first eleven transports carrying war supplies entered Novorossisk.

This timely aid was of tremendous importance to us, as it extricated us from a very difficult position. For by the end of 1918 periods occurred when there remained only some twenty thousand rifle cartridges for the whole army, and the supply of shells did not exceed twelve thousand; there was not a single first-aid individual packet, no medicines or medical appliances, no linen, and in the hospitals wounds had to be dressed by stripping off the dirty linen of the wounded.

The news of the Allied assistance spread to our front and revived the will to carry on.

*

The collapse of Germany resulted in a prolonged period of anarchy in the Ukraine. The Germans had prevented the Hetman from organizing an army, and now that the Bolsheviks and the Ukrainian extremists once more raised their heads, the only forces available to defend the territory were weak Volunteer detachments of Russian officers and raw youths, equally hostile to Ukrainian independence and to the Hetman. These detachments declared themselves to be subordinate to the Volunteer Army, though remaining under the orders of the Hetman for military operations. Meantime the Ukrainian Socialists, led by two members of the former 'Rada' – Vinnichenko and Petliura, formed a Directory and carried off a successful *coup d'état*. Troops were hastily recruited from among straggling remnants of Austrian formations, peasant bands and Galician regiments retired from the Polish front. Some of these detachments occupied Kharkov and Poltava without resistance from the Germans; others, under command of Petliura, advanced on Kiev.

The German Government was obviously favourable to the Directory. As, however, the movements of Petliura's bands were impeding the German evacuation, a detachment of the latter, sent to open up a passage, easily repulsed them from Kiev. Next day Petliura's staff and the German soldiers' 'Soviet' came to an agreement on the strength of which the German marching columns obtained free passage to the west, and Petliura's bands to Kiev. On 14th December, having overthrown the feeble Volunteer forces, Petliura entered Kiev.

The Hetman disguised as a wounded German major fled to Berlin; the commander, General Prince Dolgorukov, fled to Odessa, while of the hapless officers left in the lurch some escaped, but the majority were massacred by Petliura's men.

Petliura's bands, unmolested by anyone, spread themselves throughout the Austro-German occupation zone and advanced towards Odessa. In Odessa itself a Volunteer unit of about fifteen hundred men had been formed by that time, but it was still unorganized and placed under a double command: the unit held itself to be subordinate to the Volunteer Army only, but for military purposes were *nolens volens* obliged to obey the local Hetman officers. In the city complete panic and chaos reigned supreme. When Petliura's bands approached Odessa, Biskupsky, the Hetman's general-in-command, opened a parley with them for the surrender of the town. The Volunteers were placed on board a transport which remained at anchor in the harbour. On 11th December Petliura's troops entered Odessa.

And the duration of their power lasted only seven days!

In the middle of November a conference of Russian public leaders,[1] representing all shades of political opinion, together with the ministers of Great Britain, France, and the United States, met at Jassy, in Rumania. The Russians handed the Allied governments a Memorandum, the

[1] Among them were Krivoshein, Miliukov, Fedorov, Bunakov, and others.

contents of which the latter fully endorsed. The Memorandum required: (1) the unity of Russia and unity of the Russian command; (2) the substitution of the German cordon by Allied forces; (3) immediate assistance to the Volunteer Army.

Already, before the end of the conference, the French Consul, Henno, was dispatched by the Allied ministers to Kiev on a special mission and bearing the text of a proclamation containing a solemn assurance of Allied assistance.

Out of touch with their centres of government, these diplomats undertook this serious step at their own risk, convinced that it would receive their governments' approval. A general mystification, tragic in its consequences, was on the point of being enacted.

When Petliura's band entered Odessa a Polish brigade, formed at Ekaterinodar and now on its way home, happened to be there, while three French ships – the symbols of approaching aid – rode at anchor in the harbour. That part of the boulevard adjoining the sea was guarded by French and Polish sentries and formed a 'neutral zone,' to which the Petliurites had no access.

Meantime, M. Henno, newly arrived in Odessa, and members of the 'Special Conference' Shulgin and General Grishin-Almazov, stranded within the 'zone,' were eagerly seeking for some issue. On 14th December the first transports with a French landing division arrived at last. To forestall the French and deprive them of a pretext *for military occupation* of Odessa, Shulgin and Grishin-Almazov offered to clear the town by Russian forces alone. The Volunteer detachment landed from the steamer and led by Grishin-Almazov, after ten hours of fighting, was master of Odessa, having lost only a hundred and fifty men. The Petliura troops retreated, but continued to lurk in the vicinity forming a semicircle round Odessa.

Grishin-Almazov, at the proposal of the French, and with my consent, became Military Governor of Odessa and exercised authority on behalf of the Volunteer Army.

This unexpected augmentation of our territory, while conforming to the idea of the unification of South Russia, laid upon us a heavy responsibility for the care and safety of a large and distant city surrounded by enemies. But the Russian tricolour once raised we were in honour bound to defend it.

*

As it was in the past, so now; the advent to power of the 'Ukrainian Rada' and Directory was merely a transitionary stage towards Bolshevism. The Ukrainian Government was a purely Socialist one. More moderate members were grouped round the 'Chief Ataman' Petliura, while the extremists inclined to Bolshevism sided with Vinnichenko, another member of the Directory. As the latter were in the majority, nearly all their legislative measures were a repetition of the Bolshevist programme, and only drew the line at open Terror, which, however, was everywhere practised without restraint both by the troops, unbridled as nowhere else, and by the mob whose slogan was: 'Down with the Jews and gentry.' The anti-Jewish pogroms during the period of the Directory were particularly fierce and sanguinary. The whole country became a prey to anarchy.

Ukrainian nationalism had little to do with these events.

The Directory's 'second-rate Bolshevism' alienated the bourgeoisie and failed to satisfy the proletariat, which inclined more and more to Bolshevism of the Soviet stamp. The governing body and the army were both deteriorating. The greater portion of the latter – fourteen thousand Galicians and ten thousand demoralized Ukrainians – were quartered in the Tchernigov and Kharkov areas, facing the Bolsheviks.

The Directory declared a 'friendly neutrality' towards the Germans, but the people hated them fiercely, and the German marching columns were continually being attacked and despoiled. Railway traffic ceased. Particularly hard was the plight of the First German Army corps farthest away in the province of Kharkov. To push its way to Germany it had to enter into a compromise with the Soviet Government for evacuation via Soviet Russia – at the price of surrendering their arms and artillery to the Bolsheviks and raising the cordon.

The road to Kiev lay open.

As soon as German and French non-interference became certain, two Soviet divisions consisting of Ukrainian Bolsheviks of no strength whatever, under the command of Antonov-Ovseenko, commenced an offensive, one against Kharkov and the other against Tchernigov. These towns were occupied in the beginning of January 1919. A month later the Directory surrendered Kiev – without fighting – to the Bolsheviks and its members fled to Vinnitsa. The advance guard of the First Soviet Division penetrated into the city cautiously and somewhat surprised at their own temerity because no other serious Bolshevist forces were to be found either far or near.

*

The impending German evacuation and fall of the Hetman, with the prospect of a Bolshevist invasion from the north, prompted me already in December to adopt certain precautionary measures. At the request of a government newly established in the Crimea five thousand Volunteers from General Borovsky's contingent were moved thither to act as the skeleton of an army to be formed by means of mobilization. Owing to the weakness of the government and revolutionary propaganda, the mobilization was unsuccessful. To apply forcible measures was impossible, because all my requests to the French command – that they should post some of their expeditionary force as a screen to cover us during the formation of the

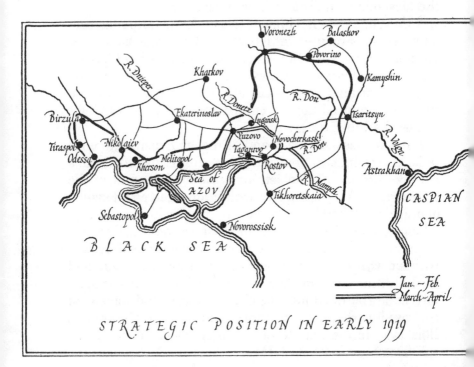

STRATEGIC POSITION IN EARLY 1919

corps, remained unanswered. Instead of occupying themselves with formations, our cadres were obliged to go to the front. They deployed before Melitopol, between the Dnieper and the Sea of Azov, and held their own against numerous (ten to twelve thousand) but ill-organized guerilla bands for over six weeks.

Immediately after the conclusion of the Stavropol operation in December I transferred to the north, to the district of Yusovka, a small but veteran Volunteer division (about three to five thousand men), commanded by General Mai-Maevsky, equipped with armoured trains and cars and with aircraft. The division was allotted the task of covering the Donets coal area, the left flank of the Don Army and the route to Rostov.

Mai-Maevsky found himself in a most intricate situation. The region swarmed with independent guerilla bands, Petliura's 'Atamans,' Soviet troops, and stranded German marching columns. By dint of strenuous energy and tenacity the general and his division bore the brunt of incessant fighting and repulsed the assaults of their numerous enemies.

Further east the Don army was fighting heavily.

In the middle of November, its front line forming a convex corresponded north and east to the limits of the territory, reaching Tsaritsyn within some forty kilometres, and in the south joining that of the Volunteer Army. Along this line the Don Cossack force disposed of fifty-two thousand men against more than one hundred thousand troops of the southern Soviet front (the Eighth, Ninth, and Tenth Armies). The Don Cossack Army was given the task of seizing the most important mainline railways with the stations of Lissky, Povorino, Kamyshin, and Tsaritsyn. The task of the Soviet Southern Armies was to smash the Don Cossacks and throw them back beyond the River Don.

In the second half of November the Cossacks defeated the Eighth Soviet Army in the direction of Voronezh and reached the points indicated. In the beginning of December, after receiving reinforcements, the Eighth and Ninth Armies resumed their offensive and penetrated far into the Don territory, but were again repulsed: the victorious Cossack regiments pursuing the retreating enemy as far as the Volga. But the Bolshevist hordes pressed on and on. All December of 1918 and January 1919 the Don Cossacks, having mobilized all men capable of bearing arms, exhausted by hardships, heavy losses, and continued fighting in the intense cold, nevertheless fought valiantly for their lives against a foe double their strength. The Cossacks invariably had the best of them, capturing thousands of prisoners and rich war booty. Strategically, the victory was already theirs, and the Reds carried on their frustrated winter campaign solely by force of inertia.

In civil war, more than in any other, the moral element is paramount. All that had been won during many months by moral impetus and the force of arms, was lost in a moment of depression. Weariness, bitter cold, skilful and frenzied Bolshevist propaganda, loss of faith in the Allies, of whose speedy arrival and aid Ataman Krasnov had so often and incautiously spoken to the wavering front: all this, taken together, drove the Cossacks, already duped once before, to believe again the possibility of peace with the Bolsheviks. The Red command, on the other hand, straining to the utmost, sent four fresh divisions to the south, and an entirely new army against Lugansk.

And suddenly, unexpectedly, and precipitately the Don Army rolled back. . . .

'Our well-armed detachments, equipped with machine guns and artillery, are retiring without fighting into the depths of the country,' said Ataman Krasnov, speaking at the Krug. 'They surrender to the mercy of the Red scoundrels and with them go and murder their own fathers and brothers. They arrest their officers and hand them over to the Reds to be shot.'

We all realized that the mere presence on the Don Cossack front of an Allied force, however small, might produce a complete change of spirit among the Cossacks exasperated by the taunts in Bolshevist proclamations:

'Show us but one British or French soldier and we'll lay
down arms at once.' I repeatedly appealed to the Allied
commanders-in-chief for help for the Don Cossacks. But
General Franchet d'Espérey made no reply whatever,
while General Milne expressed 'extreme regret that the
orders received by him from the British Government did
not give him the right to dispatch troops.' However, the
head of the French Military Mission, Captain Fouquet,
informed General Krasnov officially that a French division
would immediately be sent into the Lugansk area, if the
Ataman and Government signed a pledge that: (1) The
Don Cossack territory would repay all damages and losses
incurred through the Russian Revolution by French and
Allied subjects, not only domiciled within the territory,
but likewise in *the adjacent areas* . . .; (2) the Don
territory would recognize the authority of General Franchet
d'Espérey 'in all matters military, political, and of a
general order.'

I am inclined to think that this demand, waived aside
both by General Krasnov and myself, originated not with
the French Government at all but with the over-zealous
Fouquet.

In February the Don Cossack Army, continually
retreating, and melted down to fifteen thousand, retired
beyond the River Donets, where it halted owing to the
thaw, then to the spring floods, but mainly to the timely
aid of the Volunteer Army.

CHAPTER 19

The Amalgamation of 'The Armed Forces of South Russia' – The Evacuation of Odessa and the Crimea by the French.

Our hopes of carrying out a plan of campaign with the support of Allied armies were disappointed. Henceforth we had only to depend upon ourselves.

The North Caucasian operation being ended, the question arose as to the Caucasian Volunteer Army's next objective.

When at the outset the van of the Don Cossack Army approached Voronezh, I planned to transfer that army in the direction of Tsaritsyn with the object of occupying the lower Volga and getting in touch with the armies of Admiral Kolchak. By the time, however, this became possible, the Don Cossack Army was helplessly rolling back towards the River Don and Sea of Azov, the Bolsheviks were steadily advancing on Rostov and Novocherkassk, and the Krug, the Ataman, and the Government in view of the mortal danger to the territory were beseeching our help.

The route to Rostov, as before, was being gallantly defended by General Mai-Maevsky's Volunteers. This area attracted Moscow's particular attention. Trotsky in his proclamations and appeals never ceased to harp on 'the mortal need of coal.' 'A great treasure,' he said, 'is buried in the Donets basin, on which the welfare of the whole country depends. . . . In so far as the Soviet

Republic represents the citadel of the World Revolution, so the key to that citadel is to be found in the Donets basin.'

Taking all these circumstances into account I determined, without abandoning the Tsaritsyn area, to preserve the Donets basin and save the Don Cossack Army from utter destruction. So from the middle of February marching columns of Volunteers began to trek north. The appearance of our first contingents in the direction of Lugansk raised the morale of the Don Cossacks. The enemy, who had already broken through in many places across the River Donets, was repulsed by the Cossacks with heavy loss. Bolshevist divisions moved on towards Lugansk, where a fresh and powerful Red force was again concentrating. Further south the corps of Mai-Maevsky was again repulsing renewed Bolshevist attacks with much bloodshed and fierce fighting, forcing the enemy to retreat. Only on our right flank some Don Cossack regiments, no longer capable of fighting, having completely lost their nerve, were slowly but ceaselessly retiring towards the River Manytch.

*

By dint of strenuous efforts the southern armies grew in numbers and gained in strength as an organization. Their territory too expanded. On 8th January the single command of all the Volunteer forces was unified in my person, owing to the reiterated demand of Russian public circles and the pressure brought to bear upon Ataman Krasnov by the Allied Missions, particularly by General Poole. It is true that the legal relations between myself and the command of the Don Cossack Army were not definitely stated, but even that army's semi-autonomous status was a better alternative than the former divided authority which led to prejudicial and dangerous conflicts.

Soon after the Krug (Parliament) was assembled, and a new ataman, General Bogaevsky, elected, General Sidorin, a man who upheld the idea of Russia's unity, was appointed Commander of the Don Cossack Army.

I assumed the title of 'Commander-in-Chief of the Armed Forces of the South of Russia.' These forces were scattered over a vast area from Odessa to Vladikavkaz and Petrovsk (on the Caspian Sea), and distributed as follows: (1) One brigade, first of two thousand, later of five thousand men, in Odessa; (2) the Crimea group, five thousand; (3) the Caucasian Volunteer and Don Cossack armies deployed from the Sea of Azov along the rivers Donets and Manytch, about fifty thousand; (4) the North Caucasian troops and those on their way to the north, about ten thousand; (5) on the Georgian front, three thousand.

Amid the greatest difficulties we undertook the reconstruction of the Russian Fleet. As already mentioned, the Allies had hoisted their flags on all the navigable ships of the Black Sea Fleet and took them away to be interned. Soon after, fighting began on the Black Sea and Azov coasts, and the assistance of a fleet became imperative. Again, as in the early days of the Volunteer movement – the days of wooden armoured trains and stolen artillery – our young officers got hold of old slow-moving mercantile steamers and barges with broken-down machinery, equipped them with guns, and put to sea, keeping along the coast and fighting the Bolsheviks, with the constant risk of either sinking or falling into the enemy's hands.

After many efforts, and more than once deceiving the Allies, we succeeded in bringing several ships to Novorossisk, and by the summer of 1919 our fleet consisted of one cruiser, five torpedo boats, four submarines, and a score of small craft. It was only in the autumn that the whole of the captured fleet was returned to us by the Allies.

Against the Armed Forces of the South, the Soviet Armies of the Southern (commanded by Colonel Gittis) and the Ukrainian fronts (under Antonov-Ovseenko) were advancing with a total of a hundred and seventy thousand men. Their main offensive was directed against the Don Cossack force.

*

On our extreme west, Odessa, closely blockaded by Petliura's bands, was like a seething cauldron. Cut off from every source of supplies, the city ran short of food, and even the waterworks were seized by the Petliurites. No increase of the Russian contingent was possible within the narrow confines of the city area. The people openly expressed their dissatisfaction both with the Volunteer Command and with the French, whose prestige rapidly waned. General Grishin-Almazov persistently endeavoured to persuade the French command to occupy at least some of the neighbouring villages as a preliminary; but they considered the strength of their one brigade to be insufficient, and refused. Instead, the French started lengthy and perfectly useless parleys with the Ukrainian Directory, not realizing that co-operation with the independent and semi-Bolshevist Government and the Ukrainian guerilla bands would be impossible for us and futile for themselves. Grishin-Almazov offered to expand the zone by using his own troops, but was refused.

A month passed. Famine broke out in Odessa, strangled in the narrow ring of the blockade. The Directory was gradually crumbling to pieces, its troops were becoming demoralized, the Volunteer forces were not increasing, and the Soviet armies drawing nearer.

Since the arrival in Odessa of General d'Anselme, the Commander of the French division, and with the landing of the Greek contingents, the Allies advanced at last and occupied the line of Tiraspol-Birsula-Nicolaev-Kherson. Troops continued to arrive, and by the end of March there assembled, according to our standards, a very considerable force, viz., one and a half French divisions, two Greek divisions, one Polish brigade (two to three thousand) and a Volunteer brigade (five thousand) under General Timanovsky.

Widening the zone, however, brought no change to the situation. The French command refused permission to place the zone under the Volunteer Army administration or to lay at our disposal the enormous supplies of the former Russian-Rumanian front. Complete chaos therefore reigned within the zone, with keen rivalry between Petliura's agents and the Bolshevist Soviets. Thus, for instance, in the town of Nicolaev there existed simultaneously *five* centres of authority: the Town Council of the time of the late Provisional Government, a Bolshevist Soviet of Workers' Deputies, a commissar of the Ukrainian Directory, the German garrison Soldiers' Council, and a French commandant.

The sharp protests I addressed to General Berthelot and then to Franchet d'Espérey, in command of the Army of Occupation, remained unheeded.

The French Government had formulated no definite policy. Crowds of people of varied political opinions daily flocked to the French staff headquarters in Odessa, and its members built their plans on the basis now of a league with the Directory, now with the fragments of the Hetman Government, or again with organizations hostile to the Volunteers, who urged the French to carry out a military occupation pure and simple. Neither was there a strategic plan. Perhaps, because the *poilus* were too weary and no longer wished to fight. At least so General Franchet d'Espérey telegraphed to M. Clemenceau before the intervention in autumn 1918, expressing his doubt as to the success of a campaign 'into vast and cold Russia.' 'My men,' he wrote, 'who willingly advanced into Hungary as a foretaste of their triumphant entry into Germany, will hardly consent to take part in operations leading to the occupation of Russia.'

The main drafts of the landing forces, therefore, were quartered in Odessa, nearer to the ships, and only small advance units were posted at the front. Such a distribution was fairly safe during a quiet spell. By the end of February, however, the Bolsheviks drew near. Disorganized bands of about seventeen hundred men, with three guns, under Grigoriev, one of Petliura's chiefs, went over to the Bolsheviks and advanced on Kherson, garrisoned by a Franco-Greek contingent of about similar strength. After several days' fighting, the Allied detachment, having suffered severe casualties, was placed on steamers and brought to Odessa. After Kherson, the Allies hastened to abandon Nicolaev, though without any pressure from the enemy. A few days later they sustained another defeat at the station of Berezovka. Attacked by the Bolsheviks, they withdrew in disorder, leaving six guns and five tanks and abandoning their wounded, the baggage, and ammunition.

General d'Anselme withdrew his troops from the front to the nearest approaches to Odessa.

These events produced a most painful impression in the city and upon our troops, provoked friction between the French and Greeks, and shattered our last vestige of faith in the possibility of the Allied Command fighting the Bolsheviks or their desire to do so.

All the more so, that for the time being the only Bolshevist forces facing the Allies on the Odessa front were but a brigade of the Bolshevist 'Guerilla Division' and Grigoriev's bands.

Such a situation, it would seem, should have obliged

the French Command to act with extreme caution in matters of internal policy. Yet General Franchet d'Espérey informed me at the end of March of a *coup d'état* which had taken place at Odessa: that he had deposed the Russian authorities, transferred authority to the French Command and appointed as his Governor-General a Russian general named Schwarz.

This *coup d'état*, which raised profound indignation in Ekaterinodar and Odessa itself, was preceded by a telegram from General Berthelot to the French staff in Odessa:

'It is decided in Paris: (1) to concentrate forces for the defence of Odessa; (2) the city's food supply will be provided for up to one million inhabitants; (3) General Franchet assumes the command over the Allied forces in South Russia.'

Three weeks later, on 2nd April, General d'Anselme announced that 'he had received an order from the Entente to evacuate Odessa within forty-eight hours.'

To evacuate a large city at such short notice was unthinkable. The ships were commandeered for the troops. Persons in any way connected with the latest government or the rich bourgeoisie, who gave bribes, were practically the only ones to be saved. Crowds of unfortunate people, with their belongings, thronged the embankment, and unable to board the steamers, speeded the departing cargoes with curses.

General Timanovsky's Russian brigade was left behind.

Destitute of means, without food, the brigade pushed to the Dniester and into Bessarabia. Before they crossed the river, the French ordered them to leave behind their guns, horses, all their equipment assembled at such heavy cost and with such loving care. In Rumania, an attempt was made at disarming them, but this was met by a threat to open machine-gun fire. After long wanderings (of over a month), having suffered hardships, hunger, and humiliations alike from the French and Rumanians, the brigade arrived in Novorossisk.

A similar fate awaited the Crimea.

In the middle of December a small British contingent landed at Sevastopol. It left after a fortnight, to be replaced in the beginning of January by a French regiment and two batteries, under the command of Colonel Rué, and a Greek regiment. The object of their arrival was not clear; they did not intend going to the front. Rué bore himself in Sevastopol as a person in authority. The town (it was our base), infested with Bolshevist propaganda, was like a boiler ready to explode. Rué not only refrained from any precautions against the Sevastopol Bolsheviks, but would not tolerate the Russian Command's 'interference in the political strife' and released the agitators we arrested.

In the beginning of March, the forces of the Red Ukrainian front overthrew our feeble Crimean contingent and occupied Melitopol and Berdiansk. The Crimean front was cut in two: part of the troops withdrew to rejoin the Caucasian Volunteer Army, the other retreated beyond the Crimean isthmus. There a desultory, spiritless fighting went on – with 'eyes to the rear.' Local conscripts, drafted into the units, compelled to fight against their fellow-villagers mobilized by the Bolsheviks, began to desert. No reinforcements were available as all the reserves had been sent to the main front.

I asked General d'Anselme to transfer from Odessa to the Crimea Timanovsky's brigade, which was of no use to him there, but was refused; I also repeatedly requested the French Command to send us Allied troops, and at last obtained *two companies of Greeks*, which, dispatched to the isthmus, fought valiantly, but obviously without effect.

Having crossed the Dnieper at Kakhovka and advancing simultaneously from the north, the Bolsheviks, fifteen thousand strong, forced the isthmuses. Their main body pursued the Volunteer contingent of three thousand men, which retreated in a south-easterly direction, and by the end of April reached Akmanai, the narrowest and more easily defended part of the Kertch peninsula. Once there, the detachment was reorganized and reinforced and, supported from the Black and Azov Seas by the Allied, chiefly British, Fleet, held out for two months, stubbornly defending the last strip of Crimean land, which eventually became the base of our new and victorious offensive.

Another small contingent of Soviet troops was advancing towards Sevastopol without meeting any resistance. By that time over seven thousand French and Greek troops were quartered there under the command of Colonel Trousson. An Allied squadron, with powerful artillery, was at anchor in the bay. The French dreadnought, *Mirabeau*, was docked there for repair, and the French Command were solely concerned with her safety. Trousson engaged in a parley with a Bolshevist committee which had sprung up in Sevastopol. To propitiate this committee, the French authorities laid an embargo on some supplies belonging to the Volunteers, arrested all the members of the Crimean Government, and claimed the delivery to the Sevastopol exchequer – now in Bolshevist hands – of all state funds, even of those sums which had been dealt out to the unfortunate destitute refugees. To facilitate their negotiations with the Bolsheviks, the French Command took special pains to isolate themselves from the Whites. When small Bolshevist forces appeared before the town on 15th April, the French admiral, Amet, ordered all the Volunteers to leave the town and for our ships to follow next day. The evacuation of Russian nationals and Russian property was stopped. Few of either could be saved.

An episode occurred in those days which was characteristic of the whole evacuation process. Some ships, which had given shelter to the refugees, were still at anchor in the outer bay. On the French warship, *Duguay-Trouin*, was the Russian chief-of-staff of the fortress of Sevastopol, General Rerberg, with staff officers, who carried on their duties to the last. On 20th April, an order was received from the French flagship for all Russian officers to leave the French battleship. 'We were faced with the alternative either of falling into the Bolsheviks' hands or of jumping into the sea,' wrote Rerberg in his report. They were saved by the British admiral, who received the Russian officers and their families on board of one of his transports.

The French concluded an armistice with the Bolsheviks which lasted till 30th April, when the *Mirabeau* weighed anchor, and the leisurely evacuation of the French and Greek troops was over.

*

The cup of Russian sorrow and humiliation was full indeed. A wave of indignation swept the south. Relations with the French became extremely strained, more than once threatening diplomatic complications.

Six weeks after the tragic events in Odessa and the Crimea, at a time when the Armed Forces of South Russia were carrying off successes on all fronts and we were on the eve of re-occupying the Crimea, I received the Protocol of an Anglo-French conference held in Paris on 17th April (*i.e.* the day after the evacuation of Odessa was announced). In handing me the Protocol, the French Mission confirmed the existence of British and French 'zones of action.' The Protocol in question provided for intervention and complete occupation of the French zone and the formation therein of Russian contingents under the French high command 'from such units as would be unwilling to serve in General Denikine's army,' etc.

The reply to the French Mission ran as follows:

'I am greatly obliged for the text of the Protocol of 17th April, but am somewhat perplexed as to the possibility of carrying it into operation, when taking into account that: (1) upon the territories of the Armed Forces of South Russia I exercise Supreme Command over the armies, and in the territory occupied by the Volunteer Army, the Supreme Administrative Power likewise; (2) and that the participation of French troops in the operations of the Russian Armies is not anticipated.'

CHAPTER 20

The Fighting on the Don and Donets Territory in Spring 1919

WHILE these events were taking place, a fierce battle had been raging since the beginning of March on the northern front of the Armed Forces of the South.

Five Red armies, one hundred and fifty thousand men in all (*i.e.* treble our own strength) were advancing upon us with the object of 'exterminating the group of Whites who were covering the Donets basin.' The main blow of three armies was aimed at Rostov from the north-west, while the strong Tenth Army (thirty thousand) threatened our flank by an attack on Velikokniazheskaia from Tsaritsyn.

While the Bolsheviks were concentrating near Lugansk for the grand attack, three Cossack cavalry corps under Generals Pokrovsky, Shkuro, and Konovalov, by skilful manœuvring within that region, never ceased heckling the enemy by short swift attacks. In other areas we had meantime passed to active defence. In these constant cavalry attacks the three corps sustained heavy casualties, but the losses inflicted on the enemy were greater still. Moreover they created panic in their midst and paralysed their offensive. General Konovalov's Don Cossack troops had twice dashed into the town of Lugansk itself.

General Mai-Maevsky's army corps, on the western front, was conducting a 'railway war' under most exceptional conditions, and was obliged to adopt quite special tactics in view of the five-fold superiority of the enemy. By taking advantage of the thick net of railways in the Donets basin, he occupied the most important points of the front with small units, while at the railway junctions

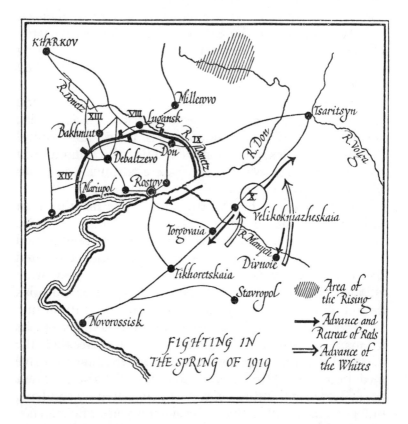

FIGHTING IN THE SPRING OF 1919

in the rear he kept 'moving reserves' in armoured and ordinary trains, which he would dash off to the point of pressing danger. The impression on the Bolsheviks was that of large forces on every point of the front. But they were always the same men fighting day after day without respite here, there, and everywhere, catching a bit of sleep in the train, physically worn out but alight with courage. For weeks and months on end firing never ceased along the front, railway stations changed hands, blood flowed freely, the Volunteer numbers dwindled away, and still they fought on.

At the end of March the general offensive recommenced with renewed force. The front of the Caucasian Army fell back slightly. But Shkuro's Kuban cavalry, cutting across the rear of the Bolsheviks from Debaltsovo, reached the Sea of Azov within a fortnight, striking panic among the Bolsheviks, massacring or making prisoners of several thousands. In an encounter with the Kuban Cossacks, a 'division' of Makhno, a notorious bandit and skilful guerilla chief – of whom more later – took to flight in a panic, leaving behind not only their arms, but, the easier to run, even their boots.

Simultaneously, the Ninth Red Army on the Don Cossack front was making a series of attempts to force the River Donets. These for a time were successful, and the Bolsheviks, pushing back the Cossacks, penetrated into the depth of the area. Soon, however, they were rounded up and hustled back across the river. Upon this section of the front of secondary importance a lull set in.

The Don Cossack force was visibly recovering from its erstwhile breakdown, especially those Cossacks of the northern districts, who last winter were the first to 'drive their bayonets in the ground' and ruin the front. Their revolt, far behind in the Bolshevist rear, flared up suddenly and spread like wildfire. Deceived by the Bolsheviks, completely ruined and driven to desperation, they fought valiantly against the punitive detachments of the Reds arrived from the front. By April, the rebels numbered thirty thousand. They lacked arms and ammunition, but had the courage of despair. When we succeeded in getting in touch with them by air across the Red front, their joy knew no bounds. They welcomed our airmen with peals of bells and smothered them in flowers. News from us strengthened the hope of the rebels; while their messages to us gave faint-hearted Cossacks on our front food for thought.

Finally, at the end of April, *i.e. a month and a half since the beginning of the Soviet offensive*, the White Army occupied the same line as at the start, having retained the Donets coal-mining area and the Don Cossack territory. All the efforts of our threefold superior enemy had been in vain.

*

Meanwhile a great danger was threatening us on the Tsaritsyn front.

The Tenth Soviet Army, under Egorov, pushed back the Don Cossacks beyond the River Manytch, and early in April began crossing in their wake. This placed the Vladikavkaz railway, Rostov, and the whole rear of the Volunteer and Don Armies under menace. Reinforcements had to be rushed to the Manytch area from Northern Caucasia, and even from the Donets basin. By 3rd May the concentration of three army corps along the line Bataisk-Torgovaia-Divnoe was completed, and I personally took over their command. The enemy had already by this time occupied Torgovaia and was only twenty kilometres distant from Rostov.

The instructions to the Manytch group were to throw back the enemy beyond the rivers Manytch and Sal, while the cavalry corps under General Ulagai, following the Stavropol-Tsaritsyn route, was to emerge in the rear of the enemy and cut their railway communication.

Within the next four days the Red Army was thrown back across the river by the spirited attacks of the Volunteers and Kuban Cossacks, leaving small units to guard

the lower reaches of the river. Therefore I massed five
and a half cavalry divisions to force the river and strike a
decisive blow from the south-east at Velikokniazheskaia.
General Ulagai's army corps was successfully advancing
along the Tsaritsyn main road, scattering the Bolsheviks
to right and left.

In the north, however, the pressure of the Red Armies
on General Mai-Maevsky's corps was becoming more and
more alarming, and the commander reported the necessity
for a general withdrawal. This idea met with the complete
approval of the Commander of the Caucasian Army,
General Wrangel. He had, from the very beginning,
criticized the plan of operation and insisted on its being
altered. In Wrangel's opinion, our 'main and only'
direction was to Tsaritsyn, to establish connection with
the armies of Admiral Kolchak. With this object in view,
he proposed that we should abandon the Donets basin,
'which, in any case, we would be unable to hold,' leave
only the Don Cossack Army on the right bank of the River
Don and transfer the whole of the Caucasian Volunteer
Army in the direction of Tsaritsyn, along which route an
advance could be developed under cover of the River
Don.

Such a decision would have led to fatal consequences.
The Don Cossack Army only held out owing to the
presence of the Volunteers. Had these departed, the
Cossacks could not have held out for *a single day*, but
would have rolled back beyond the River Don, where in
place of an army we should be overrun by crowds of
refugees and small guerilla bands. With our base at
Novorossisk, to advance on Tsaritsyn would be absurd
with eight hundred and forty kilometres of battle-area
to cover, running parallel or in close proximity to the
River Don, protected by a thin screen of Don Cossacks
and exposed to the attacks of the Soviet Armies (Eighth,

Ninth, Thirteenth, and Fourteenth) released from the front and able at any given moment to strike at our rear.

I still maintained my view that we could, if not attack, at least hold in check the activities of the four Red Armies north of the Donets, and simultaneously smash the Tenth Army on the Manytch. While our *victorious* offensive, by diverting more Bolshevist forces against us, would thereby greatly relieve the pressure on the other White fronts.

Was this possible? Events in the near future responded in the affirmative by the rout not only of the Tenth, but also of the Eighth, Ninth, Thirteenth, and Fourteenth Soviet Armies.

*

In view of the meancing situation on his front, General Wrangel early in May asked me to meet him in Rostov, and again raised the question of the withdrawal of the Caucasian Army. I replied:

'It is of primary importance to maintain the front. The order to retreat will not be given. It may only take place as the result of the sheer impossibility of holding out any longer. And I have implicit confidence in the Corps Commander General Mai-Maevsky's discrimination to determine when that moment has arrived.'

But, already, on 14th May the staff of the Caucasian Army was discussing with the staff of the corps the line of the forthcoming retreat. That same day Wrangel arrived at my G.H.Q. at Torgovaia to report that 'all limits have been surpassed, and a retreat is inevitable.' I maintained my former decision, and offered him the command of a cavalry contingent I had assembled for an attack on Velikokniazheskaia, which he readily accepted. Serious preparations for the crossing went on between 14th and 18th May.

Meantime, on our right wing, General Ulagai advanced

for more than one hundred kilometres north of the Manytch, having defeated the group of the Tenth Army, operating in the steppe, made prisoners of six regiments, their staffs, baggage, and more than thirty guns. To parry an impending blow from General Ulagai's corps at his communications, Comrade Egorov advanced six of his crack cavalry regiments under Dumenko against the former. On 17th May, at noon, the two masses of horsemen hurled themselves against one another to the north-east of Velikokniazheskaia. After a lively encounter, Ulagai defeated Dumenko's cavalry, which took to flight, pursued by the Kuban Cossacks. One of Ulagai's detachments emerged on the railway and destroyed the permanent way.

This success settled the issue of the Velikokniazheskaia operation.

Next day General Wrangel's cavalry group crossed the River Manytch. After three days of stubborn fighting, during which the Bolsheviks offered strong resistance, General Wrangel defeated the enemy's centre group and took Velikokniazheskaia.

The Tenth Soviet Army, utterly demoralized, having lost during this action fifteen thousand men as prisoners alone, and fifty-five guns, was hurriedly retreating towards Tsaritsyn pursued by the entire forces of the Manytch front.

These forces received the name of the *Caucasian Army*, and I appointed General Wrangel, so keen to push on to Tsaritsyn, as their commander. The troops operating in the Donets area were named the Volunteer Army, to the command of which I had appointed General Mai-Maevsky.

Since then no bad news had been received from Mai-Maevsky. On 17th May the Bolsheviks resumed a general offensive on the whole Donets front, but were repulsed with great loss. The Volunteer Army within a few days reoccupied the whole of the Yusovka district and Melitopol, and captured thousands of prisoners, armoured trains, artillery, etc.

A moral breakdown ensued in the Bolshevist camp. Their impetus was broken against the resistance of the Volunteers and Cossacks and their numbers were depleted by casualties and desertion. The appearance for the first time on that front of British tanks added to the Bolsheviks' nervousness. Rebellions led by Grigoriev, Makhno, and Ukrainian freebooters were spreading in their rear. The defeat and demoralization of the Red Armies were attributed by the staff of their southern front, and later by Trotsky, to the fact that 'Our armies were confronted by Denikine's numerous (!) and perfectly fresh (!) forces. On several sectors they were numerically two and three times our superior.'

The middle of May marked a sharp turning-point in the destinies of the Armed Forces of the South. The Bolshevist front had been shaken, and I launched all our armies – from the Caspian to the Black Sea – into a decisive offensive.

CHAPTER 21

The Struggle on the Eastern Front in the First Half of 1919 – General Denikine's Recognition of Admiral Kolchak's Supreme Authority.

ON 18th November 1918 a painless *coup d'état* was accomplished in Siberia: the Directory was deposed and Admiral Kolchak assumed sole power with the title of Supreme Ruler of Russia and Supreme Commander-in-Chief of the Russian Army. As soon as I received news of this I sent Admiral Kolchak and the Siberian patriots my heartiest greetings. Soon we started a correspondence, fraught, it is true, with the greatest difficulties, because letters took months to reach us, and telegraphic communication went via London and Paris. There was no subordination, but perfect solidarity was established between Admiral Kolchak and myself, and a complete amalgamation of our territories was agreed upon after they actually joined up. By mutual consent we temporarily divided the territories within the sphere of influence or government of Omsk and Ekaterinodar, the territory west of the Volga, and also the Transcaspian region falling to my share.

One of my letters to Admiral Kolchak on the question of an all-Russian Government contained the following words: 'Please God, we shall meet in Saratov and decide that question for the good of the Motherland.' As this letter was written under the immediate impression of the evacuation of Odessa and the Crimea, I added, in reference to the Allies: 'At present we are receiving ample assistance with supplies from the British and ample opposition on the part of the French.'

The fate of this letter was unexpected. It was dispatched with General Grishin-Almazov,[1] who was trying to reach Siberia across the Caspian. He carried a great deal of very important correspondence. Refusing to wait for the regular steamer, he hired a private cutter, and with his officers and the crew sailed from Petrovsk under the convoy of a British boat, heading for Fort Alexandrovsk. When in sight of Alexandrovsk the British ship steered northward, and the cutter was suddenly attacked by Bolshevist torpedo boats. The situation was desperate. General Grishin-Almazov retired to his cabin and there shot himself, dying later under the jeers and guffaws of the Bolshevist sailors. Four officers followed his example; one threw himself into the sea; the rest were carried off by the Bolsheviks to Astrakhan and were never heard of after.

This was one of the countless tragedies enacted during those terrible days of bloodshed and struggle.

The mail-bag fell into the Bolsheviks' hands; my letter appeared in a Moscow newspaper and was the cause of two important episodes.

According to Trotsky's testimony my sentence about meeting Kolchak in *Saratov* served as a foundation for the Bolshevist plan of military operations on the southern front in spring 1919, and led to the concentration of the main Bolshevist forces in the direction of Saratov. The unfavourable allusion to French policy roused the extreme wrath of M. Clemenceau and to a certain extent influenced the attitude of the French Government towards the Armed Forces of the South.

---

[1] Formerly in turn War Minister of the Siberian Government and Military Governor of Odessa.

THE WHITE ARMY

*

At the time when Admiral Kolchak assumed the supreme command the state of the Siberian front was disastrous. Beneath the blows of five Soviet armies, commanded by a former Colonel Kamenev, the Siberian front was falling back towards the Urals. Uralsk and Orenburg fell. The hapless Ural Cossack force were cut off from the rest of the front, and the Bolsheviks, overthrowing the screen covering the route to Tashkent, poured into Turkestan. Only in the north was the Siberian Army successful. Launching a counter-offensive at the beginning of January it inflicted heavy casualties on the Third Soviet Army and reoccupied Perm. In February severe frost set in, causing a lull in the military operations. The combatants occupied a line which could be roughly traced via Perm (Siberian Army), Ufa (Western Army), Orenburg (Orenburg Cossack Army), Uralsk (Ural Cossack Army). The numerical strength of both sides was nearly equal: one hundred and ten thousand men on the Bolshevist side and one hundred and twenty to one hundred and thirty thousand under Admiral Kolchak.

By far the strongest and best equipped was the Siberian Army, under the command of the Czech, Colonel Gaida – a sinister figure against the background of the White Movement.[1] This army was intended for the main

---

[1] Gaida's career is sufficiently picturesque. A Czech ensign, then commander of the Czech brigade, he almost entirely cleared the Siberian railway of Bolsheviks all the way to Vladivostok, thereby acquiring great popularity. Was instrumental in the fall of the Socialist 'Constituent Assembly,' while himself conducting Socialist propaganda against the Government within the army. Entered Russian service, was promoted general and given the joint command of two armies. Showed absolute lack of discipline and terrorized the G.H.Q. at Omsk. Was dismissed from service and deprived of his rank. Took part in a Social Revolutionary revolt against Admiral Kolchak in Vladivostok; failed, and surrendered himself, and was deported. Lately, in Czecho-Slovakia occupied the post of Chief of the General Staff, was charged with and tried for espionage on behalf of the Soviets.

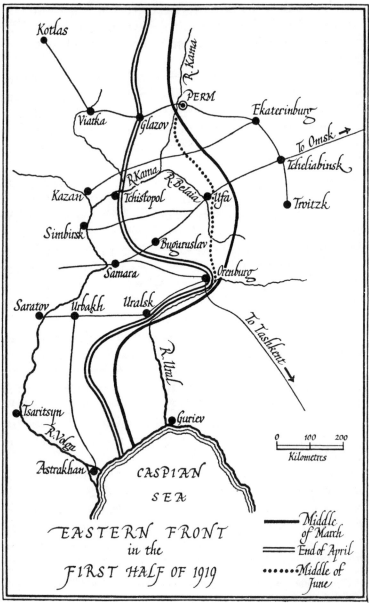

Kotlas

Viatka

Glazov

PERM

R. Kama

Ekaterinburg

To Omsk →

Tcheliabinsk

R. Kama

Tchistopol

R. Belaia

Ufa

Troitzk

Kazan

Simbirsk

Buguruslav

Samara

Orenburg

Saratov

Urbakh

Uralsk

To Tashkent →

R. Ural

Tsaritsyn

R. Volga

Guriev

0   100   200
Kilometres

Astrakhan

CASPIAN SEA

EASTERN FRONT
in the
FIRST HALF OF 1919

Middle of March
End of April
Middle of June

offensive in the direction of Viatka-Kotlas, which brought it in touch with the troops on the Archangel front. The way lay across a deserted region remote from all centres of supplies.

This plan, which those in favour of the southern orientation held to be the cause of most of the subsequent reverses and even of the collapse of the eastern front, was attempted mainly to satisfy Gaida's own ambitions. He had succeeded in winning Admiral Kolchak's confidence in his military talents and wished to make a name for himself. The British Mission, on whom the front depended for its supplies, was also in favour of it. This latter fact is supported by documentary evidence. The report of the British Military Mission in Omsk (20th to 30th June 1919) contains the following passage: 'Gaida's resignation is extremely unfortunate. It is to be feared that this change may divert the attention of the Russian headquarters from north to south, particularly since Denikine has himself become subordinate to Kolchak.'[1]

Operations commenced before they were due and on an unforeseen scale. Early in March the Western Army, in carrying out a local action for the occupation of the River Bielaia and particularly of the town of Ufa, inflicted such a crushing defeat on the Fifth Soviet Army that it took to flight. Following on the heels of the fugitives, the Western Army, unable to control its impetus, rushed onwards to the Volga.

This was the second crucial moment in the history of the war on the eastern front, when the command was accused of allowing the troops to run amok. Far better, said the critics, to have stopped the impetus and given the army time to rest and organize itself, and to continue the offensive in spring when the snow had gone and reinforce-

---

[1] This is not a verbatim quotation of the original, but a retranslation of the Russian version.

ments were at hand. Yet who knew but that the Fifth Soviet Army too would not be strengthened by that time? Who could with certainty anticipate developments, when with a nearly equal numerical strength and technique success depended on the morale of the troops, which always rose and fell with unexpected suddenness.

The Western Army occupied Ufa on 13th March. A month later, having covered seven hundred kilometres and captured numberless trophies, it was only one hundred and ten kilometres distant from Simbirsk and sixty-five kilometres from Samara, and threatened to cut off the Fourth Soviet Army operating in the direction of Tashkent. Further south the Orenburg Cossack Army under General Dutov was within a day's march of Orenburg, while a section of the Siberian Army, after repulsing the Second Soviet Army, marched along the River Kama down to the estuary of the River Viatka, and was within ninety kilometres of Kazan.

By the end of April the wave of successes on the eastern front reached its climax and then all of a sudden swiftly dropped.

One of the southern army corps suffered a serious reverse near Orenburg. A crack Red contingent concentrated to the east of Samara made a flank attack, and by seizing Buguruslan on 14th May, cut off a section of the Western Army. And then *the two armies* – the Western and the Orenburg (Southern) – rolled back. *They rolled back as rapidly as they had pushed forward, owing to a thousand and one reasons which depended on the very nature of these troublous times, the peculiarities of Civil War and the psychology of a people's army, and among which the purely strategical factor, however important, was by no means the decisive one.*

By 23rd May both armies had already recrossed the River Bielaia and abandoned Ufa. The Soviet Command then started rapidly transferring troops, partly to the northern front but mainly to mine.

Gaida's army of fifty thousand men was meantime still stationed in the region of Perm. All the endeavours of Kolchak's headquarters to move it south – first to develop the success of the Western Army and then for its relief – were met with absolute insubordination by Gaida, who shielded himself behind the immunity of a 'hero.' Only after the fall of Ufa did he start an offensive on his own account in the direction of Viatka, and took Glazov. This, however, was all. Under the influence of prevailing conditions, the Siberian Army too commenced a retreat, becoming more rapidly and thoroughly demoralized even than the rest.

By the middle of June the Bolshevist forces were approaching Perm, had passed Ufa, and were well on their way to Tcheliabinsk.

*

On 27th May M. Clemenceau on behalf of 'the Allied and Associate Powers,' addressed a statement to Admiral Kolchak to the effect that:

The Powers, aiming at peace with Russia and convinced of the futility of negotiating with the Soviet Government, are willing to render material assistance to Admiral Kolchak, and 'those associated with him' for the purpose of creating an All-Russian Government, but conditional upon: (1) the summoning of a Constituent Assembly 'as soon as Admiral Kolchak reached Moscow.' Should order by that time be not restored, then the summoning of a Constituent Assembly as elected in 1917; (2) reinstatement of Zemstvo and municipal self-governments; (3) repudiation of the 'former land policy' and establishment of 'freedoms;' (4) recognition of the independence of Finland and Poland; (5) regulation of mutual relations with the

newly formed border states, with the concurrence of the
League of Nations, pending which, recognition of their
autonomy; (6) recognition of the right of the Peace
Conference to decide the fate of Bessarabia.

Admiral Kolchak's reply was dispatched on 4th June.
It ran thus: The Constituent Assembly will be invested
with supreme power, but not the Constituent Assembly
of 1917, 'elected under a regime of Bolshevist violence,
and the majority of whose members belong to the Bolsheviks.' The independence of Poland is recognized, but
the final delimitation of her Russian frontiers, as well as
the final settlement of the Finnish and Bessarabian
questions rests with the Constituent Assembly. With
regard to the national groups of Esthonia, Latvia, Lithuania, the Caucasus and the Trans-Caspian region – their
autonomy was recognized in principle, its scope to be
determined for each nation separately; the collaboration of
the League of Nations was admitted as a means for
reaching a satisfactory agreement.

With regard to the remaining points at issue, the
Admiral, while emphasizing their purely internal
character, nevertheless assured the Powers of the
liberal trend of his policy, and that 'there could be no
return to the regime existing in Russia until February
1917.'

In informing me by telegraph of the contents of his
Note, Admiral Kolchak expressed the wish that we
should ensure 'the unanimity of our pronouncements
on state policy.'

Soon after, a delegation of Russian public men arrived
in Ekaterinodar. These were sent by the Conference
in Paris, which consisted of diplomatists and public
statesmen under the presidency of Prince Lvov, the
late Prime Minister of the Provisional Government,
with the mission to persuade me as to the necessity

for recognizing the supremacy of Admiral Kolchak's Government. To my surprise, in all their speeches, I noted great consternation – whether due to the now unfavourable situation on the eastern front and the growing successes of the armies of the south, or because the mission they had undertaken appeared to them as to be particularly delicate and complex, I could not decide.

Both my Government and the political organizations of the south treated this proposal either with extreme reserve or absolute disfavour. My own personal decision had been made long since. I intended at our projected meeting (which then seemed near), to proclaim to the armies unconditionally and without any bargaining, our subordination to the 'Supreme Authority of the Supreme Ruler,' as the natural outcome of our having joined territories. This decision was further facilitated by the fact that although I was not personally acquainted with Kolchak, I knew him to be a man of honour, intelligence, and great nobility of character.

The question, therefore, was reduced to whether such an act was justified by existing circumstances.

The prospect of our joining territories, however, seemed to be fading. The possible Allied recognition of Admiral Kolchak as head of an All-Russian Government seemed a factor of the supreme importance for raising the new Russia's international prestige. It was therefore incumbent on us all to give the Admiral political and moral support. The fact that all the Russian White forces would become united could not fail to raise the spirit of the army and of the people.

The conclusion to be drawn was therefore obvious.

On 12th June, at a farewell function in honour of General Briggs, the head of the British Military Mission, who was leaving for England, to the surprise of those present I made public my proclamation to the armies, which closed as follows:

'. . . The salvation of our Mother country lies in One Supreme Power and inseparably with it – in one Supreme Command.

'Profoundly convinced of this, and having dedicated my whole life to the service of my deeply beloved Mother country, and placing her good above all else, I submit to the authority of Admiral Kolchak as Supreme Ruler of the Russian State and Supreme Commander-in-Chief of the Russian Armies.'

The patriotic enthusiasm with which this pronouncement was greeted by Russian public opinion, testified to the passionate desire that Russia's broken and dismembered entity should once more become one. Only the Cossack governments looked upon this submission with disfavour and accepted it only in matters relating to military administration.

*

In spite of the great moral significance of this reunion of south and east, its practical political effects failed to justify our hopes. The decision of the Versailles Conference was received at Omsk in the middle of June. 'The Allied and Friendly Powers,' so it ran, 'are satisfied that the general tone of the reply of Admiral Kolchak and his fundamental statements are in conformity with their own suggestions. They are willing to render to the Admiral and his associates the assistance mentioned in their previous memorandum.'

The *recognition* by the Entente Powers of Admiral Kolchak as the head of the All-Russian Government did not take place. The *Russian Question* remained unsolved in all its magnitude, not excluding the alternative of a fresh attempt on the part of the Powers at arriving at an understanding with the Soviets, as, to wit, the unfortunate idea of inviting both Reds and Whites to a conference on Prinkipo.

The policy of the Entente underwent no change, nor was there an appreciable increase in their material assistance.

CHAPTER 22

The Advance of the Southern White Armies on Kiev-Orel-Tsaritsyn in Summer 1919.

THE armies of the south commenced their general offensive in May 1919 on a wide front.

A detachment of the *North Caucasians* was detailed to march on Astrakhan. The capture of Tsaritsyn became the objective of the *Caucasian Army*. To the *Don Cossack Army* was allotted the task of defeating the enemy force in the Donets territory, and by advancing to the line of Povorino-Lisky, to clear the northern part of this area of Bolsheviks, establish connection with the rebels there, and cut off Tsaritsyn from Povorino. The *Volunteer Army* was to push back the Fourteenth Soviet Army to the lower reaches of the River Dnieper, and defeat the Thirteenth and part of the Eighth Soviet Armies on the route to Kharkov. The Third Army corps stationed on the Akmanai heights was to advance to deliver the Crimea, while a special contingent of the Volunteer Army, by blocking up the isthmuses was to cut off the Bolsheviks' exit from the Crimea.

Towards the end of May our position on the northern front became easier: the Armed Forces of South Russia, fifty thousand five hundred strong, were now pitted against only ninety-five to one hundred and five thousand Red fighting forces under the command of Gittis.

*

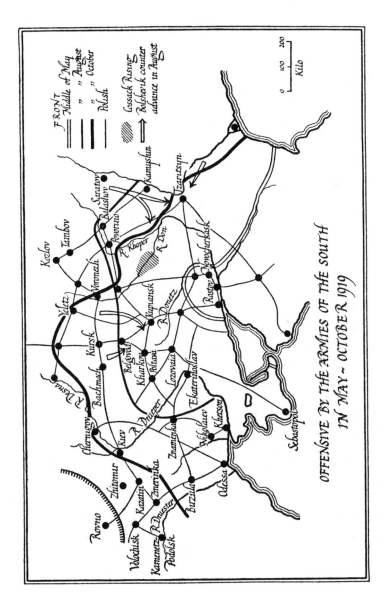

OFFENSIVE BY THE ARMIES OF THE SOUTH
IN MAY ~ OCTOBER 1919

By 4th June the *Volunteer Army*, developing a continuous offensive, repulsed the routed and demoralized contingents of the Eighth and Thirteenth Soviet Armies beyond the River Northern Donets. The resistance of the Thirteenth Army being completely broken, the Soviet Command was feverishly organizing new centres of defence in Kharkov and Ekaterinoslav. Reinforcements were being rushed thither consisting of crack Communist sailor detachments and Red cadets. Trotsky, with his usual gusto, urged the workers to arm as one man, and swore that they 'would never surrender Kharkov.'

A 'shock group' – the Fourteenth Soviet Army – was simultaneously concentrating at Sinelnikovo, under the command of Voroshilov,[1] a man without military training but cruel and determined. The Soviet Command intended by a flank movement of this army to check our advance on Kharkov and reoccupy the Donets basin.

This plan ended in complete failure.

Before the Fourteenth Army had time to concentrate, General Shkuro's division routed Makhno at Guliay-Pole, and pushing north towards Ekaterinoslav, in a series of encounters, smashed Voroshilov's forces and pursued them to the Dnieper. Simultaneously our troops were successfully marching on Melitopol, and the Third Corps having started an offensive on 18th June, was ousting the Bolsheviks from the Crimea.

Having thus protected himself from an attack from the west, General Mai-Maevsky was able to push the First Army Corps, under General Kutepov, and a Terek division under General Toporkov uninterruptedly towards Kharkov. These troops, everywhere overthrowing the enemy and giving him no chance of recovery, advanced over three hundred kilometres within a month. On 27th

---

[1] Now Commissar for War and Marine in the Soviet Government. – (Translator.)

June, following a five days' battle on the approaches to Kharkov, they dashed into the town, and after fierce fighting in the streets, at last occupied it.

The Crimea was finally cleared on 29th June, and by the end of the month we were in possession of the entire region of the Lower Dnieper up to Ekaterinoslav, which latter town was captured on 29th June by General Shkuro on his own *personal initiative.*

The enemy's collapse on this front was complete, and our trophies innumerable. The Army Order of 'the President of the Revolutionary War Council of the Republic' (of Soviets) contained a description of 'the humiliating deterioration of the Thirteenth Army,' which might equally well be applied to all the rest. 'The army is in a state of complete collapse. Its fighting efficiency is practically *nil*. Instances of senseless panic abound. The "save our skins" mentality is rampant.'

The remnants of the enemy armies withdrew: the Thirteenth towards Poltava, the Fourteenth and the Crimean group to the Dnieper.

*

The *Don Cossack Army* started its offensive at the end of May. Its right wing, under General Mamontov, forced the River Don above the Donets, covered two hundred and twenty kilometres in four days of tracking the enemy, clearing the right bank of the Don and raising the stanitsas in revolt against the Bolsheviks. They reached the Tchira on 7th June, and after destroying the Povorino-Tsaritsyn railway line, pushed on further, one section going up the River Medvieditsa and another to the rear of Tsaritsyn.

A second contingent of the Don Army advanced on Povorino; a third, after crossing the River Donets, pursued the retreating Eighth Army of the Reds in the direction of Voronezh; while a separate cavalry unit pushed directly north-east into the upper Don Cossack area, newly risen against the Bolsheviks.

As a result of this skilful and high-spirited offensive of the Don Army, the Ninth and part of the Eighth Soviet Armies sustained a severe defeat, the rebel Cossacks were reunited with their brothers, and the Don territory swept clear of the Bolsheviks.

In June the Don Cossacks crossed the boundary of their territory and emerged on the Balashov-Povorino-Lisky railway line, where during the whole of July fierce fighting went on, particularly severe in the Voronezh and Balashov areas.

Great enthusiasm reigned throughout the Don Cossack territory. On 29th June the Cossack Force celebrated the deliverance of their territory from the Red invasion. The Don Cossack Army, which in the middle of May had numbered fifteen thousand fighting men, was by the end of June increased to forty thousand.

Immediately on the fall of Velikokniazheskaia, the *Caucasian Army*, under General Wrangel, commenced their pursuit of the enemy retreating towards Tsaritsyn. The route lay across thinly populated steppes traversed by marshy rivers, each of which presented a convenient natural barrier of defence. The Tenth Soviet Army, screened by Dumenko's cavalry regiments, which had retained their efficiency, was retreating, destroying the only railway in the district and blowing up two bridges, thereby interrupting communication and the transport of supplies for several weeks. The campaign, therefore, had to be carried out under conditions of great hardship and privation.

On 24th May the Caucasian Army, after forcing it, overtook and overthrew the enemy on the River Sal. To save the situation the Soviet Army commander, Colonel Egorov, himself led a cavalry counter-attack in which he was wounded. Thus, advancing step by step, fighting heavily all the while and suffering severe casualties, the Caucasian Army in the battle of 2nd June captured the last serious barrier before Tsaritsyn. It was now faced with two alternatives: either to wait for the railway bridges to be repaired, traffic restored and armoured trains, tanks and aeroplanes rushed up; or by bringing into play the elements of speed and surprise, to develop the pursuit and dash into Tsaritsyn, as it were on the shoulders of the enemy.

General Wrangel chose the latter and by the middle of June the force of the Caucasian Army began the assault of the fortified positions round Tsaritsyn.

The Soviet Command had meanwhile rushed up nine regiments as reinforcements to Tsaritsyn. For two days the sanguinary attacks of the gallant Caucasian Army broke down before the enemy's stubborn resistance. We again sustained heavy losses, and the army withdrew to a distance of several kilometres, where it remained during the next ten days.

By that time railway traffic was restored, an infantry division transferred from the Volunteer Army together with technical equipment. On 29th June General Wrangel repeated the attack and Tsaritsyn fell.

The Tenth Soviet Army was again defeated, and retreated up the Volga pursued by the Kuban Cossacks.

In its advance General Wrangel's Army captured many prisoners, guns, and a quantity of war material from the Bolshevist base on the Volga, which they had intended to defend at all costs and failed to evacuate in time. The Caucasian Army paid a heavy price in blood for its triumph. In killed and wounded the officers' staff alone numbered five division, two brigade, and eleven regiment commanders – a proof of the high courage of the forces.

The only part of the North Caucasian force which

suffered a reverse was the contingent of five thousand men dispatched to Astrakhan.

The instability of the Caucasian formations, the remoteness of the area, the difficulty of revictualling the troops, the risings in the rear – in Tchechnia and Dagestan – all contributed to handicap the operations. Moreover, till the middle of July the British purposely withheld from us the Caspian flotilla, so that with the feeble craft then at our disposal, we were powerless to protect the coast-line from the attacks of the strong Red Volga-Caspian Fleet.

Towards the end of June the Caucasian columns approached to within fifty-five kilometres of Astrakhan, but were repulsed. The offensive on this front failed to develop even after the fall of Tsaritsyn. The morale of many units was low, and the whole operation gradually died down.

In the middle of July the British handed over to us all the ships of the Caspian flotilla – about ten to twelve armed steamers, and ten fast cutters. This flotilla, which it was found very difficult to man, successfully carried out its main task of blockading the Bolshevist Fleet in the estuary of the Volga, preventing the revictualling of Astrakhan and protecting our navigation in the Caspian.

*

In July the Armies of South Russia, in pursuit of the defeated enemy, emerged on to the front of Tsaritsyn-Balashov-Bielgorod-Ekaterinoslav, with their flanks firmly established on the Volga and Dnieper.

On 3rd July, at Tsaritsyn, I issued instructions to the armies to proceed with the general offensive, 'with the final objective of reaching the heart of Russia – Moscow.' According to these instructions the main blow was to be directed along the shortest lines converging to the centre: the Volunteer Army was to strike via Orel and Tula, the

Don army via Voronezh, and the Caucasian was first of all due to emerge on the line of Saratov-Balashov. To cover our west flank, part of the Volunteer Army was to advance towards the Dnieper and Desna and occupy Kiev; while an army corps, now in the Crimea, would emerge on the Lower Dnieper and occupy Kherson and Nicolaev. The Black Sea Fleet's orders were to support this operation and also to blockade Odessa.

The instruction of 3rd July henceforth became known as 'the Moscow Instruction,' and in the coming days of failure was severely criticized for undue optimism! Yes, in those days I was an optimist! But then optimism was general in South Russia in those days; it ruled over the population and the army. It was based on practical grounds. Never had the position of the Soviet Government been so precarious, never had it been a prey to such acute anxiety. 'Moscow,' of course, was but a symbol. All longed to march to Moscow, and the hope of this was held out to all.

The month of July was marked with fresh successes. In the west the Volunteer Army took Poltava, and the Third Corps Ochakov, thus consolidating the position on the Dnieper. The Caucasian Army in the east, jointly with the right wing of the Don Force, routed the Tenth Soviet Army which had restarted an offensive, and seized Kamyshin. Our advance guard was within ninety kilometres of Saratov.

*

Military operations developed in an atmosphere of serious internal friction. Our small numerical strength and the acute lack of technical appliances and supplies in general created a situation of continual shortage on all fronts and in all armies. Each commander considered his own front as the most important. Every strategical transfer of troops called forth a collision of conflicting interest, offence, opposition, and procrastination.

If, however, relations with other commanders were merely in the nature of an exchange of views on forthcoming operations and never transgressed discipline, the position with regard to the Caucasian Army was different. Not a day passed without a telegram from General Wrangel addressed to my headquarters – nervous, exacting, sharp messages, at times even insulting. Sometimes we received from him whole pamphlets in the form of letters, copies of which, as it appeared later, he circulated among the senior commanding officers. All this correspondence aimed at proving the superiority of his own strategical and tactical plans, alleged and premeditated negligence towards his army, and our responsibility for hindrance and the failures of his own operations. These systematic internal bickerings created a most unpleasant atmosphere and mutual antagonism. This state of mind infected the staff, penetrated the public and the army. The British Mission itself, as I learnt afterwards, was also drawn into this contention. Intrigue became a popular topic, and the political opposition acquired a recognized leader.

The campaign for power had commenced.

I cannot discuss with my foreign readers the detailed course of this intrigue against the High Command, described by me in volume five of my Russian work, *Sketches of the Russian Turmoil*. I mention it merely because it was fraught with the direst consequences for the future of the south.

*

The science of external war possesses its own laws – which are immutable and eternal. But their relative significance is sometimes displaced in *civil war*, so much so that unusual strategy and tactics are created. This fact was seldom appreciated by our Allies, accustomed to apply to it the standards of the Great War. And this is so among certain Russian military experts even to this day.

Strategy urges the consolidation of occupied areas, whereas, in the process of civil war, with its enormous distances and extensive fronts, and the preponderance of the psychological factor not only in the army but in the population itself, trench warfare becomes impossible. Strategy does not admit of a scattering of forces and demands that the front should be in proportion to the numerical strength of the army, whereas we allowed hundreds of kilometres to separate us[1] – sometimes purposely, at times under pressure. We occupied vast areas, because it was only by closely following on the enemy's heels and giving him no time for respite, that we had any chance to break the resistance of forces superior to our own. Exhausted by repeated mobilizations, Northern Caucasia could no longer serve as a reservoir of man-power for the armies and only new territories could save them from languishing away. Finally, in civil war the armies themselves, their leaders, discipline and so forth – all these possess distinctive qualities, marking them apart from armies of a normal type.

By expanding our front over hundreds of kilometres we became not weaker but stronger. The Volunteer Army, in the middle of May (in the Donets basin) numbered nine thousand six hundred fighting men. Notwithstanding continuous fighting and severe casualties, its fighting forces had increased to twenty-six thousand in July (Kharkov) and to forty thousand in August (Poltava). The Don Cossack Army, which in the middle of May possessed fifteen thousand men, had increased its numbers

---

[1] For instance, I did not intend to cross to the right bank of the Dnieper at Ekaterinoslav; but General Shkuro, having occupied that town on his own initiative, we were bound to defend it by moving to the front of it.

to twenty-eight thousand in July, and to forty-five thousand by August. The total strength of the Armed Forces of the South from May to October 1919 gradually rose from sixty-four thousand to one hundred and sixty thousand men.

Such was the result of our offensive on a wide front. It was only these conditions that enabled us to carry on. Otherwise we should long ago have been overwhelmed by the enemy's numerical superiority due to his boundless sources of man-power.

Our liberation of vast territories ought to have served as an inducement for all elements hostile to the Bolsheviks to rise against them. The question was: *had the masses of the people sufficiently outlived Bolshevism, and had they the will to overcome it? Would the people follow our lead, or as before remain passive between the two camps deadly antagonistic towards each other?*

The answer was in the negative.

The Soviet Command was making strenuous efforts to restore its southern front, shattered by the reverse of the previous spring.

Fresh mobilization of classes from eighteen to forty-five years of age provided new drafts of conscripts. The Ukrainian armies were being reorganized. Discipline was maintained by the cruel terror of the revolutionary tribunals and Communist punitive detachments. A number of inefficient commanders were dismissed. Colonel Kamenev, former commander of the Red eastern front, was now appointed Commander-in-Chief. All these measures improved the state of the southern armies, which by July numbered one hundred and eighty thousand men and seven hundred guns. In mid-August Colonel Kamenev launched a determined counter-offensive in two main directions: (1) from Kursk and Voronezh towards Kharkov, by an army group of forty thousand under

General Selivachev; and (2) from Balashov and Kamyshin Tsaritsyn and the Lower Don, by an army group under Shorin (fifty thousand). The latter direction was looked upon as *decisive*.

On 14th August Shorin's force, supported by the Volga flotilla, hurled itself against our Caucasian, and the right wing of the Don Cossack Armies. Hard pressed by a greatly superior adversary and fighting heavily all the time, the Caucasian Army for three whole weeks was compelled to retreat, and by 5th September withdrew as far as Tsaritsyn. That same day a decisive battle began. The Bolsheviks, attacking from north and south (from Astrakhan) broke through the fortified position near Tsaritsyn and reached the town. By rushing up his last reserves and sending the Kuban cavalry to attack, General Wrangel dealt the enemy a severe blow and threw them back in both directions. The Bolshevist attacks, though repeated on the following days, became weaker and gradually died down.

The right wing of the Don Cossack Army was thrown back on to the line of the rivers Khoper and the Upper Don, but by counter-attacking inflicted heavy casualties upon the enemy and restored the lost position. At the end of September the Red Army again defeated the Cossacks, who once more retreated beyond the Don. Taking advantage of this, the Bolsheviks resumed the attack of Tsaritsyn. There fierce fighting went on for nine days, but on the tenth Wrangel's troops repulsed the Bolsheviks, who retired in disorder eighty kilometres to the north. The Don Cossacks, too, threw back the enemy beyond the Khoper and themselves emerged again on to the Povorino-Tsaritsyn railway.

In October, after two months of incessant fighting, the right wing of the Armed Forces of the South still retained the line of the Khoper and the town of Tsaritsyn. The impetus of Shorin's 'shock group' had been broken, and weakened by enormous casualties, it forthwith took up a passive stand.

*

The Red 'shock' group under ex-General Selivachev was to have struck a combined blow on Kharkov on 16th August by an offensive of sections of the Thirteenth and Fourteenth Armies on Gotnia, and of main forces (Thirteenth and Eighth Armies) on Kupiansk.

Three days before the commencement of the operation, however, our First Army Corps under General Kutepov, in accordance with the general plan, started an offensive in a north-westerly direction, cut the Thirteenth and Fourteenth Soviet Armies in two and defeated them, repulsing the former towards Kursk and the latter towards Voronezh. Leaving screens to cover both routes, the corps concentrated part of its forces at Bielgorod.

Meanwhile the Voronezh group of Reds, having hustled the left flank of the Don Army, struck at the juncture between the Volunteer and Don Armies, and meeting with no resistance occupied Kupiansk. By the end of August the enemy had penetrated one hundred and ten kilometres into our rear and their advance guard approached within forty-five kilometres of Kharkov.

This constituted a serious menace to our rear.

But General Mai-Maevsky, having regrouped his forces, dealt a counter-blow with Volunteer units from the direction of Bielgorod, and General Shkuro's cavalry corps attacked likewise from the north-west. This assault met with resounding success. During the first half of September General Selivachev's Voronezh group retreated uninterruptedly to the north, leaving behind thousands of prisoners, and artillery. The Volunteer Army advanced on Voronezh, Kursk, and the River Desna, while a Don

Cossack cavalry corps under General Mamontov, which broke through the enemy front east of Lisky, raided the Reds' extreme rear.

This raid of eight thousand horsemen, who traced a circle via Tambov-Kozlov-Griazy-Voronezh, was an example both of brilliant and ineffective prowess. All along their route General Mamontov destroyed the enemy's stores and huge supplies, wrecked railways, disbanded tens of thousands of mobilized conscripts, and recruited a whole brigade of peasant-volunteers. He interrupted the line of communication and food supply of the Reds and created terrible panic in their midst. General Mamontov very nearly made a prisoner of Trotsky, then at Tambov, who fled precipitately to Moscow.

Nevertheless the Red front did not waver. The corps, burdened by an enormous quantity of property which the Cossacks carried away with them, soon lost its efficiency. So that, instead of pushing on to Lisky and then, according to plan, striking at the rear of the Eighth and Ninth Soviet Armies, the corps, avoiding a combat, turned back. Long files of waggons laden with booty trekked to the Don stanitsas, thousands of fighting men trailing behind. Soon only about two thousand men were all that remained in the ranks. Mamontov himself went for a rest to Rostov and Novocherkassk, where he was acclaimed as a national hero.

*

The Volunteer Army continued its offensive. The cavalry had seized Bakhmatch and cut off communication between Kiev and Moscow. One detachment, advancing along both banks of the Dnieper and pushing back the Fourteenth Soviet Army, was nearing Kiev and Bielaia Tserkov. On 30th August the Dnieper was forced and our troops entered Kiev simultaneously with a band of

Petliura's Galicians who had been advancing from the south.

At the same time the former Third Army Corps under the command of General Schilling, after occupying Nicolaev and Kherson, continued to advance westward into the Novorossia territory. Their landing party, assisted by our squadron and British warships, disembarked at Odessa. Parts of the Twelfth Red Army fled across the Dnieper and towards Fastov. General Schilling was subsequently compelled to deal with yet another adversary – Petliura.

In May 1919 the whole of the Ukraine was in the hands of the Soviets. Petliura's Government, with what remained of his Galician and Ukrainian troops, crossed over to Galicia. The Poles by this time had suppressed the revolt in Galicia, and their army had repulsed the Ukrainians and Galicians, and driven them beyond the River Zbrutch, *i.e.* their eastern frontier, thus placing them in a tragic position – between their own rebels and internal disorder and the Bolsheviks.

Any further fighting under Petliura's command did not enter into the Polish plans. Petliura therefore concluded a treaty with the Poles, by which he 'agreed' to the annexation by Poland both of Russian (Eastern) Galicia and of large territories of the Russian south-western region. He also recognized Poland's suzerainty over the future Ukraine. Taking advantage of the fact that the Twelfth Soviet Army was occupied with the Volunteer Armies, Petliura started an easy offensive in the direction of Kiev and Odessa. So that early in September the two forces – those of Petliura and the Volunteers – confronted each other on the line of Kiev-Uman-Birsula.

By that time Petliura's army numbered about forty thousand men of various extraction. The Galicians, who formed more than half, were more or less organized and disciplined, but having lost their native land, became discouraged. They hated their enslavers, the Poles, and refused to fight the Russians – whether White or Red.

The British, French and American representatives urged me to conclude an alliance with Petliura, who claimed as his domain all the territory on the right bank of the Dnieper and the area on the left up to the line of Kremenchug-Novgorod-Sieversk. At the time when our respective fronts came in touch, the greater part of Little Russia (*i.e.* Ukraine) and Novorossia were already liberated and occupied by the Volunteer Army. What, then, would be the prospects of an alliance with Petliura? It would place a vast territory and our own rear in the hand of a government by its very nature hostile to us and one which had once already precipitated the whole of the Ukraine into a state of anarchy, and of an army which had proved its absolute inefficiency in fighting Bolshevism. There could not be the shadow of a doubt but that at the first opportunity Petliura would make peace with the Bolsheviks at our expense, and turn forces against us. Finally, to side with Petliura, who openly worked for seceding Russian territories on behalf of Poland and himself, was contrary to the idea of a One Indivisible Russia, an idea which had taken profound root in the hearts alike of the leaders and men of the White Armies. This would create a most dangerous confusion among them. The true Russia would never forgive our taking such a step.

I therefore entrusted General Schilling and his contingent of eight to ten thousand men to clear the Russian territory of Petliura's bands.

Advancing from three directions – east, south, and south-east – General Schilling's force dealt Petliura several defeats, and on 11th October had already reached Zhmerinka. By the end of the month Petliura's Army was completely routed and General Schilling's contingent occupied the line of Volochisk-Kazatin. The Ukrainian troops were partly taken prisoner, partly dispersed; a small remnant, with the members of Petliura's government and staff escaped to Poland. The Galician units, together with their late government, all came over to us. They were transferred to our rear, as owing to mental shock, fatigue, and an epidemic of spotted typhus, they stood in need of a prolonged rest.

On emerging on to the line of Volochisk-Kazatin, our troops came into contact with the *Poles* stationed on the River Zbrutch, and with the Twelfth Soviet Army. The position of the latter, wedged in from three sides, was becoming extremely critical and a joint attack from us and the Poles would have annihilated it altogether. This, on the other hand, would relieve our troops in the provinces of Kiev and Novorossia and allow them to be transferred to the main theatre for the offensive to the north.

*

The main forces of the Volunteer Armies, strongly protected from the west, were marching on towards Moscow and dealing heavy blows to the Reds.

On 20th September the First Corps, after defeating twelve Soviet regiments, occupied Kursk. On the 30th, Shkuro's corps crossed the Don unexpectedly and seized Voronezh. On 13th October the Volunteers entered Orel and pushed farther on to Tula.

The blow struck at us by the Soviet Armies of the southern front resulted in the latter's own defeat.

By the middle of October the Armed Forces of South Russia occupied a front stretching from Tsaritsyn to Voronezh-Orel-Tchernigov-Kiev-Odessa. This front covered an area of one million square kilometres, divided into eighteen provinces, with fifty million inhabitants – the portion of Russia delivered from the Bolshevist regime.

The position of Soviet Russia was becoming critical, and the Government were preparing the evacuation of all the institutions to Nizhni-Novgorod. In their speeches Soviet authorities, including Lenin, did not conceal their fear of the approaching White Armies. The official Bolshevist Press spoke of the necessity for abandoning the advance into Siberia and of concentrating all available forces 'for the defence of the Soviet Republic's very existence threatened by the armies of Denikine.' . . .

PART IV

CHAPTER 23

The Bolshevist Heritage – The Organization of the
Southern Territory – The Sins of the 'Rear.'

In the process of liberating new territories we were
everywhere confronted with wholesale desolation.

Everywhere a cruel persecution of the Church and her
servitors; the destruction of numerous churches, almost
exclusively orthodox, with sacrilegious desecration of all
holy things; many houses of prayer converted into low
places of amusement or hospitals for venereal Red soldiers.

The schools were administered by 'collegiums' of
teachers, pupils, and servants, presided over by ignorant
whipper-snapper commissars. In places, as in Kharkov,
for instance, all higher colleges had been closed.

All laws and law-courts were abolished.

The economic and social institutions of local self-
government (zemstva), such as hospitals, schools, stock-
breeding farms, horse-studs, etc., were ruined.

Like a horde of Huns the famine-stricken north hurled
itself upon the fertile south. The country was flooded
with worthless paper money, in exchange for which the
Bolsheviks drained it of all its resources – corn, supplies,
raw materials. By a decree dated 23rd December 1918, the
Council of People's Commissars authorized all organizations and citizens of the northern provinces to buy foodstuffs in the Ukraine at 'average market prices.' Another
decree (7th May) ordered the transmigration of the
indigent workers and peasants from the north into the

southern provinces. So an avalanche of outsiders, bagmen, food-collecting and punitive detachments descended on the southern countryside. Wholesale pillage and often fighting ensued. All this led to an exorbitant inflation of prices and the disappearance of foodstuffs from the market, and brought complete ruin to regions hitherto rightly famed as the granaries of the empire.

Works and factories represented huge burial grounds – no credit, no raw materials, enormous liabilities. The monthly output of coal in the Donets basin, which amounted roughly to two million five hundred thousand tons in 1916, now fell to two hundred and sixty thousand tons. The traffic on the southern and Donets railways during the five months of Bolshevist rule fell by ninety-one per cent., with a hundred and eight per cent. increase in the quantity of coal used, and a total deficit of a hundred and ten million roubles as compared to corresponding figures in 1916.

Destitution and ruin stalked the land.

And lastly – there were those graves for both dead and living – the overflowing prisons, those torture-chambers of the Tcheka, the concentration camps, where thousands of victims perished amid unutterable sufferings; where the executioners, those beasts in human form, tortured and murdered both the so-called 'enemies of the people,' and the actual 'people' themselves. The Special Judiciary Commission of Inquiry into the Bolshevist atrocities reckoned the number of victims of the Bolshevist Terror in 1918–19 at one million seven hundred thousand. But their actual number is known to God alone.

The Ukraine and Novorossia suffered most.

The Crimea, where the second Bolshevist invasion lasted only two months, was let off more easily.

Appalling and most terrible of all, however, were the conditions in the district of Tsaritsyn, where the Bolshevist upheaval took place long before the 'October Revolution,' namely in April 1917. The situation is thus described in the report of the Special Commission: 'The entire population, with the exception of Soviet employees and their associates, looked like moving corpses. Not only was there no smile to be seen on their faces, but their whole being reflected nervousness and abject fear. The two and a half years of Bolshevist rule had destroyed everything in Tsaritsyn: family life, industry, trade, civilization, life itself! When at last the town was delivered by the Volunteers, it seemed as though it were dead and deserted, and only after a few days had elapsed did it begin to revive, like an ant-heap.'

*

The Bolshevist system of government gave fresh impetus to the guerilla movement in the Ukraine, which had started in the days of the Hetman and Austro-German occupation. It soon became widespread. Within the strip of land between the River Dnieper and Goryn alone, twenty-two 'atamans' (chiefs) were operating at the head of strong guerilla bands. Sometimes they 'worked' independently of each other, at times they banded together into detachments several thousand strong, with artillery and machine guns. They swooped down with lightning-like rapidity and as quickly dispersed again. The most notorious atamans were: Zeleny, operating between Kiev and Poltava; Grigoriev, on the Lower Dnieper and in the neighbourhood of Odessa; and 'Batko' (little father) Makno, in the province of Ekaterinoslav.

The stimulus to the guerilla movement was the agrarian question. The country-side rose 'for the land' against the landowners and their patrons – the Hetman Government. But even after, when all the land had been seized from the owners and the land-hunger of the peasants been satisfied,

the guerilla movement did not abate, stimulated by other
and still more primitive instincts.

Anti-Semitism was general and also elemental. It was
nourished by the prominent part played by Jews in the
Soviet Government, particularly within the territories of
the former Jewish pale. This led to anti-Jewish pogroms
which were widespread throughout the Ukraine. Equally
fierce was the hatred towards the Bolsheviks, who had
wrought such havoc and misery in the country-side. The
mainspring of the guerilla movement, however, was
banditism pure and simple. The partisans plundered
towns and villages, the bourgeoisie and the 'toilers,' each
other and their neighbours. Between the atamans there
existed a silent and perfectly amicable understanding as
to the 'zone of action' of each. And when armed bands
raided a town hundreds of carts, driven by *peaceful*
peasants with women and children could be seen in the
streets collecting booty.

The political and nationalist (Ukrainian) elements
counted for little in the guerilla movement. It was this
movement which brought the Directory and Petliura to
Kiev, but it also overthrew them when Petliura attempted
to check the licentiousness of the lawless bands. Grigoriev,
with his partisans, turned traitor to Petliura in 1919 and
went over to the Bolsheviks, but in April betrayed the
Bolsheviks also. Makhno accepted Petliura's assistance,
but did not acknowledge Ukrainian separatism: twice
he entered Bolshevist service against the Whites, and
twice turned traitor. In current legends this bold and
highly popular bandit and guerilla chieftain figured as
an 'anarchist on principle,' although according to his
biographer and admirer, 'penal servitude was the sole
school at which Makno imbibed all the historical and
political knowledge he ever possessed.' The Russian
anarchist party, whose part in the Russian Revolution

was in the nature of tragic farce, harnessed themselves to Makno's movement only *post factum*. The movement was purely popular and robber, but in no way political.

Previous to that, six governments had succeeded each other in the Ukraine, and their weakness had engendered in the people a contempt for all authority as such. Absence of authority and impunity were most alluring: all authority, however weak, exercised some restraint and claimed corn and recruits. Consequently the struggle against *every kind of authority* soon became the chief stimulus to the guerilla movement. It interfered seriously with the strategy of all the warring factions, and that is why the three regimes – Volunteers, Petliura, and the Soviets, all actively fought against it.

We shall see later, when the White Armies were nearing Orel, how Makhno's bands, sometimes numbering as many as thirty thousand men, roved far behind in the vast territory between the Dnieper and the Sea of Azov, disorganising our rear and on one occasion even threatening Taganrog, the seat of G.H.Q.

*

For us the Bolshevist inheritance opened up wide vistas of great possible achievements, and at the same time was a source of enormous difficulties. The first lay in the universal hatred towards the overthrown Communist rule and sympathies inspired towards the liberators. The second, in the terrible disorganisation of all branches of the national life.

*

The 'Special Conference,' *i.e.* the Government of South Russia, represented a coalition of which Conservatives constituted the majority and Liberals a minority. Its president was General Dragomirov until the autumn of 1919, when he was appointed Administrative Head and

Military Commander of the Kiev territory. He was succeeded by General Lukomsky, who was also Minister for War. Both were non-party Conservatives. Neither the Extreme Right – the supporters of complete restoration and reaction – nor the Socialists were represented in the Government. The two principal parties – the Social-Revolutionaries and Social-Democrats were hostile to the White Armies and the White regime, being primarily concerned not with the fight against Bolshevism, but with the carrying-out of their own party programme. The Ninth Social-Revolutionary Conference held in Moscow in the summer of 1919 endorsed the resolution to: 'cease the armed struggle against the Bolshevist Government and revert to political warfare instead. To transfer the centre of the struggle into the territories under Kolchak, Denikine, and others, and set about undermining their rule by all the methods employed by the party under Tsardom.' As a matter of fact the Social-Revolutionaries did endeavour to resort to terrorist acts against leaders of the White movement. Incidentally an attempt on my life was for a long time and unsuccessfully being engineered by one Kakhovskaia, a woman leader of the 'fighting squad' who had assassinated the German resident representative in Kiev, General Eichorn. The Social-Democrats were opposed to terror; but having acquired some influence among the factory workers and seized the management of the co-operatives, they endeavoured to undermine the White regime by propaganda.

Particularly difficult were our mutual relations with the Cossack Governments. The semi-independence of the Don Cossack Army reacted most unfavourably on the strategic arrangements, as did the complete independence of the Don, Kuban, and Terek Governments on state administration. Neither were we able to achieve the economic unity of South Russia. The Cossack Governments set up customs barriers along their borders, introduced trade exchange regulations and embargo, thereby hampering the normal economic turn-over of the south.

The import tariffs we established were useless, because the Don and Kuban ports of Taganrog and Eisk were open to export, and the Cossacks exported everything – not only their own goods, but even those belonging to the Volunteer Army – provided they were paid in francs or sterling. For instance, the Don Cossack Government exported anthracite to Constantinople at a time when Odessa had neither water nor light. The Kuban Cossacks made a contract for the export of corn to Georgia, which was hostile to us, when our own adjoining Black Sea province was stricken with famine. And so on. I was obliged to establish a maritime customs frontier and a surveillance over the export, and this measure roused the resentment of Cossack Governments, which accused us of 'blockading the Don and Kuban territories.'

Thus the question remained unsettled to the very end.

The complications which arose with regard to communications are best illustrated by the tragi-comic example of the Vladikavkaz railway, which had the misfortune to cross the territories of 'sovereign' or 'autonomous' states *eleven times*.

All our endeavours to create a provisional united government by means of annexing to ourselves the Cossack regions on the principle of autonomy were equally stalemate. For six months my representatives sat in conference with those of the Cossacks, who were loath to part with their independence. Only at the beginning of 1920, just before the 'end,' the Don Cossack and Terek Governments, deciding to ignore the recalcitrant Kuban Government, came to an agreement with me over the organization of supreme authority in the south. But it was too late.

In opposing the authority of the High Command, the Don and Terek Cossacks did not, however, overstep legal bounds. Not so the Kuban. There the Government, which was virtually in the hands of pro-Bolshevist extremists, left no stone unturned to undermine the Armed Forces of the South. Ekaterinodar became the centre of the most pernicious propaganda, circulated throughout the stanitsas and in the regiments, which lowered the morale of the men and led to desertion. For instance, in one of the proclamations sent out by the official propaganda bureau of the Kuban Government, there was a passage to the effect that 'the Cossacks who have gone into the depths of Russia will never be allowed to return to their native land.'

To save the Kuban forces from complete disruption I resolved on extreme measures. In November 1919, General Wrangel, who numbered under his command the majority of the Kuban Cossack contingents, dispatched loyal units under General Pokrovsky to Ekaterinodar. By his order the headquarters of the Kuban 'Rada' were surrounded by troops, who demanded the surrender of twelve of the most rabid extremists. The Rada capitulated. Amendments were made in the constitution providing for an increase in the authority of the elected ataman and for uniting with the High Command. One of the arrested members of the Rada, who took part in a delegation which had entered into a military agreement with rebel North-Caucasian tribes directed against the Armed Forces of the South, was tried and hung; the rest were deported abroad.

Matters, however, did not improve. The Kuban Cossack force, strong in its anti-Bolshevist principles and brave in battle, was lost through the fault of its leaders; and the will to fight died within them.

A 'coalition' government was absolutely necessary; yet

its component political elements were alien to one another. Herein lay the inherent tragedy of that government's position. Within the Special Conference itself the conflict raged between Conservatives and Liberals. The 'medium' course into which I endeavoured to steer our internal policy was maintained by means of insincere compromise, frequently distorted in its execution. Our civil administration was unsatisfactory. Liberals and local zemstvo or municipal workers avoided administrative posts, which in those days of turmoil were not an honour but a heavy burden. Therefore the administrative bodies were filled by men of the old regime with all its former mentality, who were so alien to the new order of things that they neither could nor would approach it with any sense of fairness.

The solution of the *agrarian* problem – the pivot of all others, was hedged in with insurmountable obstacles. It was opposed by the landed gentry, whose influence predominated both in the civil government and in military headquarters. A compromise was arrived at: the issue of a fundamental agrarian law was deferred to the Constituent Assembly; while by a provisional law, reinstating the right of private ownership, those who had seized the land became the leaseholders of the former landowners. This, coupled with various abuses on the part of certain officials and landowners, excited the discontent of the peasants. All the more so, as the Bolsheviks in their proclamations were lavish in alluring, if deceitful, promises.

The eyes of the landowners and their supporters were only opened by the catastrophe of Novorossisk, which made them realize, too late, their irremediable mistake.

Finally, the behaviour of certain units in our heterogeneous army was not above reproach. The troops experienced a serious lack of equipment and money. Thus came a primitive hankering for 'self-equipment' by means of war booty. 'War booty' was interpreted in a very wide sense, and for those below became a mainspring, and for others above one of the demagogic methods for setting the wavering mass in motion. 'War booty' and 'requisition,' however necessary for satisfying the needs of the army, transgressed all legal limits and became bald plunder and violence.

It is with profound sorrow that one feels obliged to recall these black pages of the army's history, which cast a dark shadow on the picture of its heroic struggle, demoralized the troops, and aggravated the peaceful population.

*

The process of *disruption* which affected our rear was by no means limited to the above causes. The Russian Revolution, like every other, together with examples of noble self-sacrifice, had roused all the worst human passions lying dormant in normal times.

Class egotism flourished everywhere, opposed not only to sacrifice but even to compromise. Employers and workers, landowners and peasants, bourgeois and proletariat—all alike were dominated by it. All claimed government defence of *their own* particular rights, but very few were willing to render the authorities active support. There was also great slackness in the discharge of fiscal duties.

*

Desertion was practised on a large scale, not only among the lower classes but even by the intelligentsia and bourgeoisie. Profiteering became appalling, and involved people of all categories – members of co-operatives, social-democrats, officers, society ladies, political leaders, representatives of foreign missions. Embezzlement and bribery were the order of the day. Whole organizations were tainted by this canker. The attitude of 'eat and drink, for to-morrow we die' adopted in the rear, crippled our strategic efficiency and undermined authority.

Nevertheless, in spite of our many shortcomings, the contrast between the White regime and that of the departing Soviets was striking and patent to all. The system of terror was first abolished and people were freed of its intolerable oppression. All manner of public societies, unions, professional organizations, and political parties, except the Communist and Anarchist, came to life again. With the revival of free trade and public initiative, numbers of co-operative associations sprang up. Peasant claims with regard to losses inflicted by passing troops or abuses of government authorities were rectified by repayments for damages, subsidies were allowed for the cultivation of their fields, exemption of one-man families from conscription, etc. In all territories newly occupied by the Armed Forces, there followed an immediate drop in the price of bread and other essential commodities. And last of all, the White regime brought freedom to the Church, the Press, a tribunal equal for all, and a normal type of school.

The people, while detesting the Bolsheviks, had from fear of them bowed far too patiently to their yoke. Yet those same people refused to realize that the White regime was powerless to pacify and regulate within a short space of time the seething turmoil caused by this upheaval in national life.

The troops continued to advance; while in the rear a feeling grew which, as a matter of fact, was shared by the people, society, practically all the non-fighting population, that demoralization and disruption were gaining ground. This feature, less conspicuous in moments of success, proved fatal in the time of our military reverses.

Great social upheavals cannot fail to leave their impress on the moral outlook of the nation concerned.

CHAPTER 24

The British in Transcaucasia

DEVELOPMENTS in the Caucasus and Trans-Caspian region were largely dependent on British policy.

General Poole, the British representative attached to the Volunteer Army, had resided in Ekaterinodar since December 1918. The British Expeditionary Force in Tiflis, consisting of some fifteen to twenty thousand men, was under the command of General Forestier-Walker. Subordinate to him were Generals Malleson, Thomson, and Collis in command of contingents stationed in the Trans-Caspian region, Baku, and Batum. Above both General Poole and General Walker was General Milne, Commander-in-Chief of the British Forces in the East, whose residence was in Constantinople. When, later, General Briggs succeeded General Poole, the latter became directly subordinate to the Secretary of State for War.

We ignored the moving of this complex scheme, but saw clearly the two divergent lines of British policy; *Ekaterinodar and Tiflis*, the one pro- the other anti-Russian. All three British representatives who followed one another at Ekaterinodar – Generals Poole, Briggs, and Holman – men of great nobility of character and soldierly rectitude, gave us every possible assistance, moved by sincere good-will towards Russia and correct understanding of the true interests of their own country. Such, too, was General Milne's attitude, after closer acquaintance

302

with the situation in South Russia. On the other hand, the generals in command in Transcaucasia supported the chauvinist aims of the newly seceded states.

Russia's restoration versus her dismemberment!

The primary object of the British military occupation of the Caucasus, as stated in the Note to the Ekaterinodar Mission, dated 1st August, No. 1293, was 'to compel the enemy (Germans and Turks) to evacuate Transcaucasia,' while at the same time safeguarding the principle of self-determination of the small nations and supporting the governments in authority. The northern demarcation line of the occupied zone ran through Kizyl-Burun, Zakataly, the Caucasian range, and Tuapse, thus arbitrarily cutting in half our Black Sea province.

The interests of the newly formed Caucasian States being opposed to ours, their governments manifested not the slightest inclination to fight the Bolsheviks. The British representatives in Transcaucasia, on the other hand, frequently abused of their prerogatives. Both these facts led to a series of conflicts.

The first occurred in Northern Caucasia. On our advance towards the Caspian we were confronted with the so-called 'mountaineer government,' under a man named Kotsiev,[1] organized partly under the auspices of General Thomson, who sent a British battalion to Petrovsk and rendered every assistance to Kotsiev. The 'mountaineer government' settled in Dagestan, and General Thomson, contrary to the earlier-established demarcation line of the occupied zone, declared in the name of the British Government Dagestan to be included within the sphere of British influence. We were therefore cut off from the Caspian

---

[1] The 'mountaineer government' laid claim to authority over the territories inhabited by the Tcherkess, Kabarda, Ingush, Ossetins, Tchechen and various Dagestan tribes. Only the latter and part of the Tchechen actually temporarily submitted to it.

Sea, while in Dagestan a centre of agitation was created which infected the whole of Northern Caucasia: the 'mountaineer government' stirred the Caucasian tribes to rebellion against Russian authority, and mustered and organized armed bands of Red soldiers scattered over the territory. General Thomson, by his attitude, instead of quenching the conflagration merely added fuel to the fire.

Particularly trying was the situation created in the Tchechen region. There the 'mountaineer government' resorted to bribery, propaganda, secret smuggling of arms, etc. A serious revolt broke out. Persuasion was of no avail. Then early in April a strong detachment of Volunteers inflicted a severe blow on the mountaineers and the Tchechen surrendered. An assembly of delegates was held, at which General Briggs and myself were present. General Briggs urged the Tchechen to 'cease internecine strife and help General Denikine to fight the Bolsheviks.'

Meantime our advance towards the Caspian continued in spite of the obstacles created. By the middle of May the greater part of Dagestan was in favour of the Volunteer Army's entry into the territory; the Kotsiev 'government' was deposed and the 'Council of the Republic' (Medjlis) dissolved. Our column entered Petrovsk without fighting, welcomed by the Russian population of the town. On 23rd May, Derbent was likewise peacefully occupied.

These developments resulted in a prolonged and serious diplomatic friction between ourselves and the British Government, who demanded that we should evacuate Dagestan. However, my protest, supported by General Briggs, carried weight; and in July Dagestan was included in the Russian zone.

This episode closed the series of manifold collisions with England on the question of Northern Caucasia. From that date onwards British policy towards us in that region became either neutral or pro-Russian.

The members of the 'mountaineer government' and the Medjlis fled to Baku, whence, till the very end, they led a frenzied propaganda against the Armed Forces of the South. These comic-opera 'governments,' without territory or nation, for a long time yet went on concluding 'alliances,' signing 'treaties,' etc. Even now, ten years after their emigration, they still succeed in mystifying credulous persons in London or Warsaw.

The rebellions in Northern Caucasia did not cease. They were fostered by repercussions of Pan-Islamism, Bolshevist propaganda, the agents of the Medjlis in the pay of Georgia and Azerbeijan, inter-tribal strife, the dense ignorance of the masses. A wave of risings swept Dagestan, Tchechnia, and Ingushetia during July, August, and September. Although invariably suppressed, they nevertheless diverted both men and means from our main objective.

*

With regard to Azerbeijan and Georgia we reconciled ourselves to the fact of their independent existence pending the restoration of Russia as a Power, and had not the slightest intention of laying any claims to their territories. The attitude of their rulers towards us, however, was invariably one of antagonism and suspicion. As the Azerbeijan Government was incapable of organizing any serious armed forces, we felt fairly safe from that quarter and merely maintained a small cover along their frontier. Consequently no armed encounter took place, in spite of Baku's extremely aggressive policy.

Georgia, on the other hand, possessed an army of eight thousand men, and in addition a 'national guard' of about ten thousand, strongly tainted with Bolshevism. These forces had to be reckoned with, all the more so that Georgia refused to withdraw from the southern part of the Black

Sea province occupied by Georgian troops. Encouraged by the favourable attitude of General Poole and his Mission, I more than once appealed to the British Government on this subject, begging them to intervene on our behalf, but received no reply. Constant appeals for help were meantime reaching us from the local population suffering under the oppression of the invaders.

To round up their frontiers the Georgians started a war against the Armenians. Its issue would have been disastrous to the former were it not for General Walker's intervention, who put a stop to hostilities and settled the dispute to the obvious disadvantage of the Armenians. Immediately on the outbreak of the war, on 22nd December, the Georgian troops began to evacuate the district of Sotchi (on the Black Sea coast). My troops, following in their wake, reoccupied the liberated territory. But soon the Georgians again came to a halt. Armenian settlers all along the coast rose against their Georgian enslavers, and Georgian punitive detachments were occupied in quelling the revolt.

To put an end to this bloodshed I ordered a Volunteer detachment to occupy the district of Sotchi. Within four days our troops reached the River Bzyb, the southern limit of the province, whereupon the Russian commanding officer, his task being accomplished, informed the Georgians of the cessation of hostilities.

As it proved, the Georgians had consented to the evacuation on the strength of a pledge given them by General Walker to the effect, presumably, that 'General Denikine would abstain from any hostile action,' and that by an agreement between him and the Georgian Government, the district of Sotchi 'was declared neutral.' Neither I nor the British Mission at Ekaterinodar knew of any such statement having been made by General Walker.

Its effect was a demand addressed to me from the

British War Office that I should evacuate the district of Sotchi, threatening to withdraw supplies in the event of non-compliance. This demand, derogatory to Russian prestige, was not complied with, and on the suggestion of the British Mission at Ekaterinodar, London withdrew it. But our well-wisher, General Poole, was recalled, and General Walker also left his post. A company of British troops arrived in Gagry and occupied the line of the River Bzyb. Both sides were pledged not to cross it.

In the spring of 1919 the Georgians, in sight of the British, laid a new bridge across the Bzyb, and having by a surprise attack inflicted severe casualties on our small advance guard, seized Gagry – a narrow strip of coast-line, easily defended. A protest from the Ekaterinodar Mission and General Milne's threats failed to impress the Georgians. They remained in Gagry until the end. Equally, until the end, the contingents of both armies 'stood by,' facing each other and ready for action. The Georgians abstained from further aggression, but supported bands of guerilla rebels called the 'greens,' who assembled on their territory and later harassed our rear at the most inopportune moment.

*

I will not dwell on our various other conflicts in Batum, Kars, Baku, and the Trans-Caspian regions, but would like to point out the general effects of the British intervention.

The only object actually attained was the evacuation of the Caucasus by the Turks. The second object, that of 'safeguarding General Denikine's rear by a British military occupation of Transcaucasia,' was not carried out.[1] The newly formed Transcaucasian states were too feeble to

---

[1] Telegram from the British War Office to the British Military Mission at Ekaterinodar, 23rd March 1919, No. 154. (Not verbatim text.)

constitute a menace of themselves, with the support of the Allies. In the second place, bloodshed in the Caucasus never ceased. War broke out between the Armenians and Georgians, and armed skirmishes continued between Russians and Georgians. Armenians were being massacred by Turks and Tartars in Karabakh and Nakhichevan. The Russian district of Mugan was forcibly annexed by Azerbeijan. The whole country was in a welter of inter-tribal warfare and strife.

The new state formations, needless to say, though protected by the Armed Forces of the South did not in the slightest degree contribute to the fight against Bolshevism. Neither did the British force of occupation actively do so, except on the unique occasion of General Malleson's encounter with the Bolsheviks in the Trans-Caspian region in 1918.

Russian society clearly saw 'two Britains' – 'two hands,' – of which, according to the statement of the British Ambassador in Petersburg, Sir George Buchanan, the one rendered every support to the White movement, while the other wrested the western border states and Trans-caucasian republics, thereby alienating from Britain all patriotic Russians.

General Briggs, who succeeded General Poole in February 1919, also showed himself a staunch and noble friend of Russia. While giving proof of great efficiency and energy in the task of supplying the Russian armies, he took all our needs and successes closely to heart and at the same time invariably offered great moral support both to the High Command and the Russian cause. On all occasions we heard from him a steady and dignified appeal for harmony and loyalty in maintaining the unity of the Russian State. He addressed the Georgian Conference at Tiflis (21st and 23rd May 1919) and urged on them the necessity of preserving peace with the Armed Forces of the South. When he said: 'The British will go away, but Russia will always remain, and friendship with her is essential. . . . General Denikine does not consider himself empowered to alter Russia's frontiers before an All-Russian National Assembly meets, which alone will have the right to settle this question' . . . the reply was: 'Is this the private opinion of General Briggs or that of the British Government? We are informed that the question of frontiers will be settled by the Paris Conference and that the British Government will be in favour of our independence from Russia.'

Colonel Rawlinson, sent by the Ekaterinodar Mission to Dagestan, issued a proclamation in which he said: 'The revolt of the mountaineers is not a national movement. . . . Any resistance to General Denikine will be treated as an act of hostility towards the Allies.' There immediately appeared in the Caucasian newspapers a letter from the British High Commissioner in Transcaucasia, Mr. Wardrop, assuring the Georgian Minister for Foreign Affairs that Colonel Rawlinson's statement did not reflect the views of the British Government.

On his return from the Tiflis Conference General Briggs was recalled to England. With heartfelt regret we parted with this true friend of Russia. The object of his removal was not clear to us, since his successor, General Holman, from the very outset carried on a policy similar to his.

The part played by General Briggs in Russian affairs did not end here. He defended the cause of South Russia in London; with Mr. Churchill's approval he undertook a mission to Warsaw to persuade Marshal Pilsudsky to take part in a common campaign against the world menace of Russian Bolshevism. He also came once more to Russia to find out the best ways and means of rendering effective aid to the Russian armies.

In the autumn of 1919 the British evacuated Trans-caucasia, thereby eliminating numerous causes' for acute dissension. Only a small detachment still remained in Batum. At the time when Mr. Lloyd George was making open advances to Moscow, Mr. Churchill and the War Office continued to render us valuable assistance,. both material and diplomatic.

I do not presume to determine the line of demarcation between the 'two Britains,' so intricately interwoven in the Russian question, and which had given rise to such conflicting emotions among the Russian people. I am merely profoundly convinced that with the England so nobly represented by Mr. Churchill, Generals Briggs, Holman, and others, the new Russia will find language and interests in common.

CHAPTER 25

The Struggle and Fall of the Northern, Eastern, and South-western Fronts at the End of 1919 and Beginning of 1920 – Death of Admiral Kolchak.

In the autumn of 1919 the position on the anti-Bolshevist fronts was as follows:

On the *eastern front* Admiral Kolchak's armies were in full retreat.[1]

Ekaterinburg fell on 16th July, and the Siberian Army, completely demoralized, not so much by fighting as by revolutionary propaganda, was withdrawn far into the rear. The Western Army's attempt to hold Tcheliabinsk, that important railway centre from which ran the only line connecting the Southern Army with the Siberian main line, ended in failure. The Southern Army, which was retreating from Orenburg, was now, by the fall of Tcheliabinsk (25th July) cut off. Straggling fragments of it succeeded, amid enormous difficulty and after a two months' march, in making their way to Petropavlovsk (west of Omsk).

The rest of the armies were stopped between the Rivers Tobol and Tiumen. Here the forces of the eastern front were partly reorganized, and at the end of August started a counter-offensive at first successful: the Bolsheviks were repulsed beyond the Tobol. During September and October hope revived again. But by the middle of October

[1] They numbered at that time one hundred and three thousand men. The Bolshevist forces opposed to them were approximately equal.

the front was once more irrevocably rolling back eastwards.

Admiral Kolchak handed over the High Command to General Dieterichs. As the latter deemed it impossible to hold Omsk, he was superseded by General Sakharov. He, too, owing to circumstances, failed to stem the retreat. On 14th November the Bolsheviks captured Omsk. What remained of the Siberian Armies set out on their march across Siberia to Trans-Baikalia (three thousand three hundred kilometres), the like of which had never been known in history. They plodded on along the heavy Siberian roads or without them, through dense forests and over snow-covered plains, in the bitter cold, through territories aflame with rebellion, surrounded on all sides by antagonism and treachery.

How tragic was the fate of the Ural Cossacks, trekking across the empty and waterless Caspian steppes to Persia.

The causes of the collapse of the eastern front were manifold and profound, and many of them repeat themselves with tragic similarity in the history of all the anti-Bolshevist fronts. I will cite here only a few episodes illustrating how deep was the process of disruption of Siberia's state organism which led to its inevitable final collapse.

Since November the whole Siberian main line from Tomsk to the Pacific was in the hands of the retreating Czecho-Slovak contingents. In their impetus towards the east they seized all the available rolling-stock and carried away enormous 'booty' – gold, copper, silver, machinery, etc., etc. They paralysed all the traffic, cut off the Siberian armies from their supply base and source of reinforcements, and condemned the sick and wounded soldiers and hosts of refugees to starvation and death.

A wave of peasant risings provoked by the abuses of

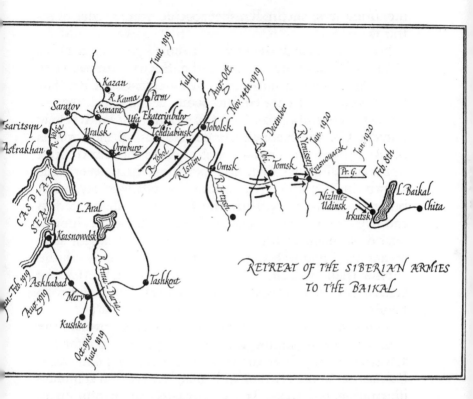

Retreat of the Siberian Armies to the Baikal

government authorities and still more by Soviet and Social-Revolutionary propaganda, swept over Siberia. These risings alternated with the cruel repressions exercised by the punitive expeditions. An armed revolt was raised by the Social-Revolutionaries in Vladivostok, Irkutsk, and other towns, under the slogan: 'Cessation of war, and peace with the Bolsheviks.'

The army was rapidly deteriorating, beginning with the higher ranks. The new head of the Government, Pepeliaev and his brother, a general in command of an army, raised a mutiny and arrested the commander-in-chief, General Sakharov. Another commander, a General Zinevitch, organized a revolt in Krasnoyarsk demanding the overthrow of Admiral Kolchak and that power should be delegated to men 'chosen by the people.'

In the beginning of 1920 the Soviet Armies were advancing from Achinsk. Between Achinsk and Krasnoyarsk were concentrated the remnants of the Siberian Armies under command of the gallant and universally popular General Kappel. At Krasnoyarsk their way was blocked by the mutinous army corps under General Zinevitch. Further east, near Nizhne-Udinsk, the trains carrying the Supreme Ruler and his staff were stranded, cut off both from the army and from Irkutsk, isolated in the midst of a hostile mass of Czech marching columns. Ahead of them, at Irkutsk, a Socialist organization, self-styled the 'Political Centre,' had proclaimed itself the supreme government. With the approval of the Czechs and of the French representative, General Janin, and with no opposition from the other foreign representatives, who with the exception of the Japanese remained passive, the 'Centre' was bargaining with the Czecho-Slovaks for the surrender of the Supreme Ruler and Russian gold. Some Russian units under Ataman Semenov were also stationed in Trans-Baikalia, but their movements were handicapped by the opposition of the Allies.

The sanguinary epilogue was enacted in Irkutsk. Forsaken by his followers, betrayed by Janin, a captive of the Czecho-Slovaks who detested him, Admiral Kolchak was delivered by them into the hands of the Socialists of the 'Political Centre.' He was proclaimed 'an enemy of the people,' thrown into prison and subjected to an interrogation on the charge of 'high treason to the Fatherland.' Before the judiciary proceedings were concluded, and when the Government was under the menace of the army, which was nearing Irkutsk under the command of General Voitsekhovsky, successor to General Kappel, who had died from frost-bite, Admiral Kolchak was shot on 7th February 1920.

Having accomplished this crime – an act of political vengeance – the Irkutsk 'Government' handed over the power to the Bolsheviks, itself retiring once more into the underworld.

*

The assassination of Admiral Kolchak, that great patriot and ill-fated ruler, who had taken up the immeasurably heavy burden of power at a time of severe trial, filled me with deep sorrow.

By decrees of the Supreme Ruler, dated 24th June and 15th December 1919, 'in the event of (his) illness or death,' I was appointed by the first, Supreme Commander-in-Chief, and by the second, Supreme Ruler. The circumstances, however, in which the ruler, the Government, the armies, and the territories of the south were placed in January and February 1920, demanded great circumspection in the application of these decrees. An 'All-Russian' standard would have been out of place.

I therefore left this question open.

*

The *northern front*, owing to its remoteness, the difficulties of communication and peculiarities of character and climate, had never raised any high hopes among other anti-Bolshevist camps, nor excited Moscow's particular apprehension, except in the first few months, when the Soviet Government had overestimated the intentions of the British.

The reinforcements which arrived from England in May failed to raise the activities of this front.

While pressing Admiral Kolchak to give preference to operations in a northerly direction (towards Kotlas) the British pursued the execution of an identical idea on the northern front. So at least it was stated in the Note, in which on 4th July General Holman acquainted me with a *communiqué* received by him from the British General Staff. It ran: 'Notwithstanding the retreat on the Siberian front, the General Staff expresses the hope that . . . it will be possible to accomplish the juncture of Admiral Kolchak's Army with the Archangel Army, for which purpose General Ironside, succeeding General Poole as commander of the northern front, has received the order to commence an offensive.'[1]

Both from the standpoint of its strategical possibilities and line of direction, this operation was bound to fail. Moreover, in conformity with the new trend of British policy on the Russian question, the evacuation of the Army of Occupation was decided upon as early as July 1919. The command of the front was then taken over by General Miller, a Russian, who refused General Ironside's offer, simultaneously to evacuate the Russian troops. By the middle of October the British evacuation was over.

The close of 1919 and beginning of 1920 were marked by encounters which, though successful for the troops of the northern front, were of purely local importance. The front line fluctuated somewhat, but on the whole the Sixth Soviet Army, about ten to fifteen thousand strong, remained passive. When, after the Soviet Command had disposed of the western and eastern fronts and repulsed the southern beyond the Don, the Sixth Army was reinforced and launched an offensive, the success of the Reds was swift and sure.

The Bolshevist offensive opened on 17th February and on 2nd March the last ships flying the Russian flag of St. Andrew sailed from Archangel.

*

[1] Translation from the Russian version.

At the end of June 1919 the *North-western Army*, under the command of General Rodzianko, flushed with success, had reached a line at one hundred kilometres from Petrograd and forty kilometres in advance of Pskov. It numbered thirteen thousand fighting men. It was flanked on either side, on the Baltic coast and in the direction of Pskov, by an Esthonian division, whose fighting activities were limited to the defence of the approaches to ethnographic Esthonia.

Confronting these forces was the Seventh Soviet Army, about fifteen to twenty-three thousand strong, and further south – the Fifteenth Army, with its right wing turned towards Pskov and the front facing the Esthonian and Lettish divisions.

General Yudenitch, summoned both by Admiral Kolchak and the Allies, and bearing the title 'Commander-in-Chief of the North-western Front,' had also taken up his residence in Esthonia since July. As the Russian Army alone was subordinate to him, such a conglomeration of authorities only led to friction.

The army, whose 'Russian' territory was exceedingly small, continued to experience an acute shortage of everything. Practically its only source of supplies lay in the trophies captured from the Bolsheviks, and for food it depended on the Hoover organization. Whereas at the same time the army of the 'Esthonian Republic' was being lavishly provided for by British transports. It was not till the middle of August that British assistance was also extended to the Russians.

During the summer the Seventh Soviet Army having started an offensive, the north-western front was forced to recede considerably to the west beyond the River Luga and Lake Pskov. Only a tiny strip of territory now remained to the Russian Army, limited in front by the Bolshevist trenches, and behind by the thick barbed-wire fence of the Esthonian frontier. This latter fact was all the more menacing as our relations with the Esthonians were of a most indefinite character.

All the endeavours of Russian public men to persuade the Esthonians into active co-operation in an anti-Bolshevist campaign on a large scale led to nothing. In certain political circles, including the British representatives in Esthonia, the opinion prevailed that this was due to the fact that neither Admiral Kolchak, I, nor at first General Yudenitch in the early stages, recognized Esthonia's independence. On these grounds, on 10th August, General March, Assistant British Military Representative in Esthonia, invited members of General Yudenitch's Political Council and several other persons to his residence in Reval, and addressing them in a particularly rude and insolent manner, alluded to the disastrous conditon of the front and proposed that within forty minutes they should 'form a government of the north-west region from among those present, according to a list drawn up by him,' which government should pledge itself to recognize the independence of Esthonia.

Next day, in the absence of General Yudenitch, this extraordinarily constructed 'government' simultaneously proclaimed its existence and the recognition of Esthonia.

Unrecognized itself, and merely tolerated by the army, it resorted mainly to verbal activities and exercised no influence on current events.

A week after this 'recognition' the Esthonian Government started peace negotiations with the Bolsheviks.

Such were the events which preceded the North-west Army's offensive. Although British supplies had arrived, the army was still inadequately provided for and unorganized. Esthonian aid was uncertain. Bermont's Army (of which more later) did not recognize General Yudenitch's authority. General March, however, insisted on an immediate advance, promising the assistance of the British Fleet to occupy Kronstadt. The Esthonian Government announced that should the offensive not take place before the winter, it would become impossible any longer to restrain the people's desire for peace with the Bolsheviks.

The general situation appearing to be favourable at the time (the Southern Armies were nearing Orel), General Yudenitch decided to advance.

The forces of the North-western Army then amounted to seventeen thousand men. The Seventh Soviet Army numbered twenty-four thousand, with the possibility of considerable reinforcements. General Yudenitch's plan consisted in first striking a preliminary blow in the direction of Pskov and Luga, and after protecting himself from that quarter, to advance with his main forces on Petrograd.

The offensive of the southern group opened on 28th September and was crowned with complete success: the rout of two Soviet divisions, and advance on Pskov and the capture of Luga. The offensive of the main forces, which occupied Gatchina on 15th October and approached Krasnoe Selo, was no less successful. Intense excitement reigned in Petrograd. It manifested itself in the suppressed joy of the population, in fear among the Red Army, and was reflected in the hysterical harangues of Zinoviev and Trotsky. The world Press foretold events and expected a near solution of the Russian tragedy.

On 23rd to 25th October, however, the tide suddenly turned. Why? The causes alleged were multiple: disproportion of strength, the refusal of the British Fleet's collaboration, the passive attitude of the Esthonians, rivalry among the High Command, mistakes in strategy, lack of proper administration, the impatience of the leaders to be the first to enter Petrograd, and so forth.

By withdrawing troops from the inactive Esthonian and Lettish fronts, the Bolsheviks, acting with great energy, concentrated two strong groups near Petrograd (at Kolpino) and Pskov. Launching a concentric attack from the north-east and south against the White North-western Army, they compelled the latter to retreat as far as Narova, which it reached on 14th November.

Its subsequent fate was shameful disarmament, concentration camps, physical hardship and moral humiliations inflicted within the territory of the Esthonian Republic, the government of which, on 3rd January 1920, concluded first an armistice and subsequently a peace with the Bolsheviks.

This latter event was preceded by two official statements made by the governments of the Entente Powers. The first, from France, made by General Berthelot, was to the effect that the Supreme Council would take steps with regard to Esthonia, should that country make peace with Soviet Russia; the second, from Britain, made by Mr. Lloyd George, was to the effect that the British Government saw no objection to the conclusion of the above peace. . . .

*

By one of those frequent ironies of fate, at the time of General Yudenitch's greatest success, other armed forces, led by a hitherto completely unknown officer named Bermont, were making an attack on Riga, with dire consequences to the Petrograd operation.

As stated before, a German army corps under the command of General von der Goltz was formed with the approval of the Entente in Courland early in 1919. It subsequently cleared the greater part of Latvia of the Bolsheviks and on 4th June occupied Riga. Its further progress north was stopped by the Entente, whose policy, fearing German influence in the Baltic States, had again undergone a radical change. Under pressure from the British representative, General Gough, and in view of the menace from the British Fleet and an Esthonian and Latvian offensive, von der Goltz was obliged to withdraw into the district of Mitau. In Riga the Socialist pro-Entente Government under the premiership of Ulmanis was restored.

In August the Allies demanded the evacuation of German troops from the Baltic States. An order to that effect was issued by the German Government, and a partial evacuation, purposely protracted, began. The German soldiers, deceived in the promise of a grant of land made to them by the Ulamnis Government, mutinied. During September and October the Entente Governments addressed stern Notes to Berlin threatening a blockade, while Herr Noske pleaded the soldiers' insubordination as an excuse – genuine or otherwise – for the delay. Finally, the German Government 'repudiated' its own troops. They then enlisted as volunteers into the newly organized 'Western Volunteer Army,' in which were also included the Russian detachments under Bermont and Vyrgolitch, assembled in Mitau and Shavly. This army, thirty to thirty-five thousand strong, splendidly equipped by the Germans, was commanded by the man calling himself Colonel Bermont. The army's actual leaders, however, were the Germans, represented on the staff by Major Bischof.

A 'government,' consisting of Russian and Balt Conservatives, was attached to Bermont's headquarters.

Bermont flatly refused to submit to General Yudenitch in spite of Admiral Kolchak's and my own categorical instructions. His isolated position and inactivity in Latvia excited the apprehension of the local governments and grave doubts among the anti-Bolshevist Russians. At last Bermont opened his campaign – but not to the front whither he was summoned by an order of General

Yudenitch. On 21st October Bermont launched a surprise attack against the Latvian contingents which were covering Riga, defeated and flung them beyond the Dvina. He failed, however, to capture the city. The Latvian Government refused overtures of peace. For six weeks Bermont

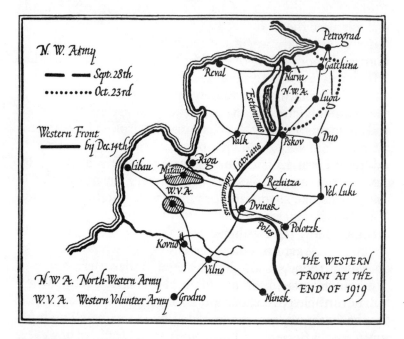

continued to bombard Riga and made attempts at crossing the Dvina.

The Allies, meantime, considering Germany responsible for these developments, carried out their threat of a blockade. Esthonian and Latvian troops were removed from the Bolshevist front and commenced an offensive, and with the powerful support by heavy fire from the British Fleet, so passive against the Bolsheviks, inflicted on Bermont a series of defeats.

Mitau fell on 4th December. Part of the Russian

soldiers of the Western Army dispersed, and others together with the Germans were evacuated to Germany.

In settling their historical reckonings the European Powers had thus dealt a severe blow to the Russian White movement.

*

Such was the external military and political situation during the final period of the struggle of the Armed Forces of the South.

The resolute offensive on the north-western front begun on 28th September reached its culminating point on 21st October, ended in the middle of November in a defeat, and in January 1920 the troops were finally disarmed and interned.

The eastern front, after temporarily arresting its precipitous retreat in mid-August, from the middle of October rolled back like an avalanche irretrievably to the east.

Deprived since the withdrawal of the British of its main support, the northern front passed through a phase of protracted agony, which finally ended in the beginning of March 1920.

These events, seemingly irrelevant and disconnected but nevertheless abounding in profound tragedy, formed the background for the no less tragic destinies of the south.

CHAPTER 26

Retreat of the Southern White Armies beyond the Don

By the middle of October the front of the warring White and Red Armies extended over one thousand seven hundred kilometres, and lay roughly along the line of Zhytomir-Kiev-Tchernigov-Voronezh-Tsaritsyn-Astrakhan.

The Soviet Armies of the southern and south-eastern fronts, reorganized and brought up to strength, numbered one hundred and forty thousand fighting men, which increased to one hundred and sixty thousand by the end of the month. Two powerful 'shock' groups of Reds were concentrated, one to the west of Orel (Fourteenth Army), the other facing Voronezh (Budenny).

The Armed Forces of the South amounted to ninety-eight thousand. Their fighting value varied greatly, so that its numerical strength could not be accepted as a criterion. The Volunteer Army, strongest of all in spirit, was advancing on Orel and Tula, jointly with the advance of the Don Cossack Army, thereby determining our main point of attack. Meanwhile, all our reserves were diverted to 'internal fronts,' *i.e.* suppressing revolts which had broken out everywhere in the Ukraine and Novorossia.

The plan of the Red Command consisted in striking a double blow (from Orel and Voronezh) at the Volunteer Army nearing Orel.

The object of this move was twofold: strategically to drive a wedge between the Volunteer and Don Armies, and politically to alienate the Cossacks from the Volunteers.

THE WHITE ARMY

*

After repulsing the Don Cossacks in a southerly direction, Budenny's cavalry group, reinforced by infantry, started an offensive against Voronezh, which was defended by cavalry under General Shkuro. After nine days of fighting Budenny occupied Voronezh, crossed the River Don, and in the middle of November seized the station of Kastornaia, thus enveloping the right flank of the Volunteer Army. Heavy fighting was now going on simultaneously along the whole front against enemy forces three times superior to our own (twenty thousand against sixty thousand). General Mai-Maevsky having concentrated his main forces in the direction of Briansk succeeded on several occasions in beating the Fourteenth Soviet Army, but owing to the position of his right flank was obliged to retreat. As a result of thirty days of continuous fighting, smarting under the blows dealt to its right wing by Budenny and the Thirteenth Army, which endeavoured to cut off its retreat, the Volunteer Army, almost entirely bled, was slowly retreating. By the end of November Kursk and Bakhmach were abandoned.

The Don Cossack Army under General Sidorin, confronted by an enemy of equal numerical strength, abandoned Lisky and withdrew beyond the River Khoper.

Infinitely worse, however, was the situation in the rear. Bands of rebels swarming in the provinces of Kharkov, Poltava and Ekaterinoslav were daily becoming bolder, and necessitated an increasing number of troops to keep them in check. The revolt raised by the bandit chief Makhno was particularly threatening.

Makhno, after being routed by our forces in the previous spring, fled to the Ukraine with a small band of followers. Pursued by General Schilling's troops, he reached Uman and was there completely wedged in between the Volunteers and Petliurites. Makhno and Petliura, however, soon came to terms. The former handed his wounded over to Petliura's care and replenished his ammunition. Then on 26th September he suddenly raised his men, broke through our lines and pushed on in an easterly direction towards the Dnieper. Covering six hundred and sixty kilometres in eleven days he reappeared in his native village, Guliay-Pole, the centre of the revolt.

During the next few weeks the wide territory between the lower Dnieper and the Sea of Azov was aflame with revolt. By the middle of October the rebels had captured the towns of Melitopol, Berdiansk where they blew up an artillery depot, and Mariupol. Makhno himself, recrossing the Dnieper at the head of a large force, by a daring raid seized Ekaterinoslav. Three times within a fortnight the unfortunate town changed hands, being finally retained by Makhno.

How numerous Makhno's forces were no one exactly knew, not even himself. They were estimated both at ten thousand and at forty thousand. Separate bands would gather, then disperse, obey his orders or act independently. To deal with them we were obliged to withdraw from the Volunteer and Don Army fronts one and a half cavalry divisions, and from the Petliura front a corps under General Slastchev. For a whole month our troops dealt Makhno's bands one blow after another. They would be disseminated, and reassemble again, scatter, and disappear, only to reappear again in numbers, but nevertheless were being steadily pushed back towards the Dnieper wherein thousands perished. By the end of November the whole of the left bank of the Dnieper was cleared of these bands and Ekaterinoslav liberated. But desultory fighting with Makno, who more than once approached Ekaterinoslav from the right bank of the river, went on until the close of the military operations.

This revolt had the effect of disorganizing our rear and weakening the front at the most critical period of its existence.

*

The Kiev Army under General Dragomirov, operating in the west, carried off important successes on the River Desna and round Tchernigov, until after the armistice concluded between Poland and the Bolsheviks, it found itself pitted against the whole of the Twelfth Soviet Army. The Bolsheviks even seized Kiev, making the most of their opportunity during the three days that they were masters of that city. But although they were evicted and the front re-formed, the situation remained full of menace.

On 26th September, Polish Military and Economic Missions arrived in Taganrog, whither my G.H.Q. had been transferred. The Missions were given a cordial and ceremonial welcome. In the course of our conversations with General Karnitsky, the head of the Polish Mission, I insisted on the maintenance of the temporary frontier between the two countries as established by the Allied Supreme Council – pending the settlement of the destinies of the border territories jointly by the Polish and future All-Russian supreme legal authority. I equally pointed out to Karnitsky the necessity, in our mutual interests, for the Eastern Polish Army to open an immediate offensive along the line of the Upper Dnieper.

Months passed. General Karnitsky assured me that both Marshal Pilsudsky and M. Paderewsky recognized the danger of Poland's position between Russia and Germany, and that an understanding with us for the Poles was 'a matter of life or death.' Still no answer came from Poland.

Meantime military operations on the Polish Bolshevist front were suspended. To our query as to the meaning of this, General Karnitsky replied that it was but a brief armistice 'for purely military considerations.' Activities on the Polish front were suspended for nearly three months. . . . During that time the Bolsheviks transferred forty-three thousand fighting men from the Polish front to mine. So absolute was their certainty in the passive attitude of the Poles, that in the direction of Kiev and Tchernigov the Bolsheviks calmly advanced against us – turning their backs on the Poles!

I dispatched a letter to Marshal Pilsudsky on 9th December, pointing out the dangers resulting from the Polish Army's inactivity, adding that 'with the collapse of the Armed Forces of South Russia, Poland might be confronted with a force which, no longer diverted, would become a menace to Poland's culture and very existence.'

It was only some years later that the secret motives of Marshal Pilsudsky's policy came to light.

The Council of People's Commissars, rightly gauging that a combined Polish and White Army offensive against the Soviets would mean their ruin, sent an old friend and a former revolutionary associate of Marshal Pilsudsky's, named Markhlevsky, now a member of the Bolshevist Central Executive Committee, on a mission to the marshal. Markhlevsky persuaded the latter of the identity of Polish and Bolshevist interest in the face of the 'menace' represented by the Volunteer Armies, and succeeded in arresting the Polish offensive in order to obtain the chance of working our ruin.

A secret agreement was concluded between the Polish and Soviet High Command, on the strength of which the Bolsheviks pledged themselves to cease military operations on the Dvina front, and the Poles to undertake no advance for my support in the direction of Kiev. A demarcation line was traced between these new 'allies,' light skirmishes between mounted patrols being still carried on in order to simulate hostilities. The fact of the agreement, moreover, had to be kept secret both from our G.H.Q. at Taganrog, to which a Polish Mission had been sent to carry on *fictitious* negotiations, and from the Allies who supplied Poland with funds and war material, though not as an abettor of the Bolsheviks and Bolshevism.

From that time onwards the Bolsheviks denuded their western front, and all their troops therefrom were transferred to the south.

It was only in December, after the fall of Kiev and the retreat of the White Army to Odessa, when the collapse of the south was beyond doubt, that the Polish Army resumed its activities.

From the Russian point of view this act of Poland's ruler, Marshal Pilsudsky, cannot but fail to arouse the deepest indignation. Yet, perhaps, it served the interests of the Polish nation? History has already given an answer to that question: six months later the Bolshevist hordes, spreading terror and desolation, were approaching Warsaw and bringing the regenerated Poland to the brink of destruction.

Was this disaster the final Nemesis for the acts of the leaders of an innocent people, or was it merely the first clap of thunder heralding the approaching storm?

*

The centre of gravity of the entire operation lay in the Voronezh-Kharkov area. Only by smashing the enemy's 'shock' group concentrated there, could we regain the initiative and once more develop our general offensive. The endeavours to create our own 'shock' cavalry group in the region of Voronezh, in an atmosphere in which strategy, politics, psychology, and personal relations were interlocked, testified to the difficulties which on every side beset the G.H.Q.

Under existing conditions and in the absence of reserves,

such a group could only be assembled by drawing upon the man-power of the Don and Caucasian Armies. The Don Army Command, however, entirely subordinate to Cossack mentality, was anxious not so much to carry out the general plan as to retain and safeguard their own territory. The greater and best part of the Don Army was, therefore, stationed on the River Khoper, and to move these reserves in a 'non-Cossack' direction was extremely difficult and invariably encountered psychological obstacles and passive resistance. Whenever units were summoned from the Caucasus there immediately followed protestations from local authorities over the inevitable destruction of the Terek Cossack force, surrounded on all sides by hostile mountaineers. After dealing the enemy a crushing blow at Tsaritsyn in the middle of October, General Wrangel reported that this success was attained 'at the price of bleeding the Caucasian Army and with the final effort of will power in those commanders who yet remained in the ranks.'

He agreed to detail two corps, *i.e.* the best half of his army, for the 'shock group,' but on condition of no longer remaining himself in its command. The state of the Caucasian Army, judging by his report, was deplorable, so that I resolved to take only one corps.

Finally, as a result of strenuous efforts a contingent of ten thousand Don and Kuban Cossacks was concentrated by December in the district of Valuyiki, equipped with tanks, armoured trains, and aeroplanes. General Mamontov, as senior officer, took over the command.

Great hopes were vested in this contingent.

By this time the unsuitablity of General Mai-Maevsky for the post of Commander of the Volunteer Army became definitely apparent. This brave soldier and skilful leader, who had rendered signal service to the cause and carried off many victories in the Donets basin and on the routes to Kiev and Orel, suffered from a serious complaint – an inveterate passion for alcohol, which at times had a disastrous effect on his activities as a commander. In his stead I appointed General Wrangel, under whom as a brilliant cavalry officer I also placed General Mamontov's cavalry group.

The general plan of the forthcoming operation consisted in placing the whole southern front on the defensive, while the right wing of the Volunteer and the left of the Don Cossack Armies were to strike at the group of Reds endeavouring to break through from Voronezh in the direction of Rostov.

*

The hopes we centred on the 'shock' cavalry group were not justified.

General Wrangel's first step, in spite of my warning to the contrary, was to remove General Mamontov and appoint the gallant Kuban General Ulagai in his stead. This greatly offended the Don Cossacks, particularly General Mamontov himself. Without leave he left the corps, reported his offence by wire to his superiors, and circulated copies of the telegram to all his regiments.

At their first encounter with the enemy, Mamontov's Don Cossacks fled in panic. The Kuban Cossacks followed suit, being completely demoralized by the propaganda of their extremist political leaders. Soon the detachment melted away.

For such an unprecedented breach of discipline I deprived Mamontov of the command, but the Ataman and Commander of the Don Army – the persons controlling the autonomous Don Cossack territory—took his side ; they dared not lay their hands on the general, who enjoyed the immunity due to a 'popular hero.' Moreover they were of opinion that Mamontov was the only man capable of rallying the fugitive Cossacks. When eventually the corps was reincorporated in the Don Army and Mamontov reinstated as commander, they dealt several smart though unfortunately belated blows at Budenny's cavalry.

General Wrangel, instead of making an effort to rally the Kuban Cossacks somewhere in the army rear, on his own initiative ordered the cadres of the Kuban divisions to return home. Once there, they sank into complete torpor and refused to fight any more.

The strategic position on the whole front became extremely menacing.

Having lost touch with the Volunteer Army, the Kiev contingents abandoned the city and retired beyond the Dnieper, where they became enrolled in General Schilling's detachment. The Caucasian Army, cut off from the Don Cossack Army and completely isolated, still remained in the vicinity of Tsaritsyn. Budenny's 'shock' Red group had driven a deep wedge between the Don and Volunteer Armies. The latter, hard-pressed by an enemy of treble its own strength, was for the past two months retreating from Orel to Kharkov (four hundred and fifty kilometres) and beyond, all the while parrying heavy blows, manœuvring and counter-attacking, losing fifty per cent. of its man-power in the process.

In view of the situation obtaining at the beginning of January, our forces were withdrawn: the Volunteers and Don Cossack Armies beyond the rivers Miuss and Donets, and the Caucasian across the River Sal. This retreat towards Rostov created another strategic difference of opinion between our G.H.Q. and General Wrangel, who insisted on his army being withdrawn to the Crimea. This move could certainly have been easily carried out but would have created a disaster. The Volunteer Army's withdrawal to the Crimea would have resulted in an immediate collapse of the Don and whole Cossack front. We should have been accused of 'treason,' while tens of thousands of sick and wounded fighting men,[1] as well as the families of the Volunteers scattered throughout the Don territory and Northern Caucasia, would have been doomed to untold hardships and perhaps to cruel death. Evacuation under such conditions would have been unthinkable.

General Schilling's troops received the order to act as cover for Novorossia and especially the Crimea.

I concentrated my reserve – approximately two and a half divisions—at Novocherkassk as the nearest jumping-off ground to Rostov, and there, if need be, I determined to fight the decisive battle.

Our centre group was unable to hold the line allotted to them. By the force of inertia, due to moral causes, the troops were drawn into retreating to some natural barrier, which in this instance was the River Don. In the battle which raged for two days in front of Rostov and Novocherkassk the troops gave proofs alternately of marvellous valour and panic, of a stern sense of duty and loss of discipline. We suffered a reverse, and on 9th January the Don Cossack and Volunteer Armies both withdrew beyond the River Don. A thaw set in, crossing on the ice became dangerous. The Soviet Armies made several attempts to force the river, but were repulsed with heavy loss.

The Caucasian Army had retreated across the River Sal.

General Schilling, having withdrawn Slastchev's corps from Ekaterinoslav and stationed it on the line of Melitopol to screen the Crimea, deployed the rest of his troops along the Birsula-Nikopol line. Within this region for several weeks our troops carried on incessant fighting against the Twelfth, Thirteenth, and Fourteenth Soviet Armies, Makhno and various other guerilla bands swarming all over Novorossia.

---

[1] By 15th December 1919 there were 42,733 sick and wounded in the military hospitals of the Armies of the South.

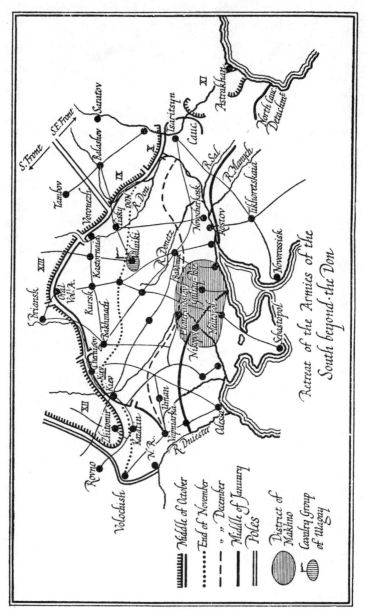

Retreat of the Armies of the South beyond the Don

This task proved beyond General Schilling's strength. It would have been more expedient to abandon Odessa, having previously evacuated the town, and concentrate in the Crimea. The British and French representatives, however, urged G.H.Q. to hold the Odessa region at any cost, as its loss would have created the impression in London and Paris that all was over and might lead to withdrawal of the supplies to the south. They guaranteed the evacuation of the sick and wounded and of officers' families on transports, and a free passage to Bessarabia on the part of the Rumanian authorities for troops and refugees. General Schilling remained in the vicinity of Odessa.

Another of our corps, stationed on the Lower Dnieper, after sustaining a defeat at the end of January, began hastily to retreat westward with scarcely any resistance. The Bolsheviks in pursuit, pushing nearer the coast-line, were emerging far in our rear.

The whole front rolled back without resistance towards Odessa.

Once again – for the third time – Odessa lived through the terrible tragedy of evacuation.

The Allied transports failed to arrive. All who could were evacuated by our own shipping. Many found no room. Heartrending scenes were witnessed on the piers, particularly on 7th February, when the Bolsheviks had already invaded the town. Families were torn asunder, their last belongings perished, and fierce resentment swelled in the breasts of all.

When our troops, under the command of General Bredov, approached the Dniester they were met by machine-gun fire from the Rumanians. The same fate awaited the refugees – women and children. Bredov veered to the north along the Dniester, and parrying the attacks of the Bolsheviks, broke through their lines and joined the Poles.

In Poland our forces found disarmament, concentration camps, days of sorrowing, and national humiliation!

*

The year 1919 had come and gone.

A year which brought us brilliant victories and the greatest trials. Brave deeds, self-sacrifice, blood shed both by the dead and the living, the fame of the army's war laurels – all the bright side of the armed struggle will fade beneath the deadening stamp of failure.

The three months' retreat, extreme fatigue, the spectacle of chaotic evacuations – all these produced an overwhelming effect on the public and the army, and created a soil in which pessimism and panic-stricken rumours grew and flourished. Like an insidious poison the decline of the will to fight penetrated into all circles – political, governmental, and the military command.

In spite of all past vicissitudes the Volunteer Corps, which had emerged out of the Volunteer Army,[1] still preserved its discipline, energy, and readiness to carry on the struggle. On the other hand, in the Don Cossack Army, not only the rank-and-file Cossacks but part of the commanding staff had lost their morale – such periods of depression had already repeated themselves three times among the Don Cossacks, and each time the force had revived again.

It was the same now. The withdrawal to the Don Cossack territory and the respite from fighting calmed shattered nerves and restored self-control. On losing their native stanitsas the laggards pulled themselves together, and deserters returned to the ranks. The army redoubled its numerical strength. The Cossack upper stratum – the Ataman, the Army Commander, and others – stood firm in their resolve to carry on.

[1] General Wrangel had gone to the Kuban region to organize Cossack cavalry corps.

Matters were far worse in the Kuban region. With the return of the extremists to power in January 1920 the process of demoralization among the Kuban Cossacks developed more rapidly than before. Only about five to eight thousand fighting men remained at the front. The rest were 'in process of formation,' or rather of desertion. Those at the front, too, were nearing complete disintegration.

I strained every nerve to overcome the inert force of the retreat, because in my opinion a prolongation of the operation might be an effective means of undermining the enemy's strength and of turning the wheel of fortune in our favour. To me the position appeared far from hopeless, as a march of several hundred kilometres accompanied by fighting and bloodshed could not but affect the enemy's moral and physical endurance. This was confirmed by various reliable data. Now it is not only confirmed, but the commentaries of Soviet recorders draw a picture, which to many comes as a surprise:

Never before had the Soviet Army been in such dire straits, and never were the Whites so close to complete victory as at the beginning of 1920. . . .

Our main Trans-Don group was faced by an enemy depleted by the departure of the Thirteenth and Fourteenth Armies, now operating against the Ukraine and Crimea. The guerilla rebels, formerly hostile to us, had now turned against the Bolsheviks. Makhno himself with his followers had driven a wedge within the disposition of the Fourteenth Soviet Army, and by harassing it until October prevented the Bolsheviks' offensive against the Crimea. The new Red 'Caucasian front,' viz. the Eighth, Ninth, Tenth, Eleventh, and First Cavalry Soviet Armies, stretching from Rostov to Astrakhan, numbered fifty to fifty-five thousand men, *i.e.* were equal to our own. A terrible typhus epidemic, heavy casualties, and desertion had depleted their ranks. The Red forces, left to shift for themselves, lived exclusively on the local population, *i.e.* by plunder. For if chaos reigned in our rear, the Reds *had no rear at all*. An official Soviet recorder writes: 'The railways being completely destroyed by the Whites, traffic ceased. A chasm four hundred kilometres wide yawned between the Red Armies and the centre, across which it was impossible either to send reinforcements or to carry out an evacuation.' When the question arose of renewing the offensive, the present Commissar for War, Voroshilov, then Army Commander on the Rostov front, reported to his superiors that it was impossible, and added that he expected 'some very painful surprises in the near future.'

As matters stood, the material conditions on either side were identical. Victory depended on the *spirit*.

I therefore commanded the troops to prepare themselves for the offensive.

CHAPTER 27

Retreat of the White Armies to the Black Sea

In those days of trial for the army, political passions became particularly unbridled. Pretenders to the rank of commander-in-chief were working secretly; while the United Cossack Parliament, formed of Don, Kuban, and Terek Cossacks, in which the Kuban extremists, numerically weaker but more active, had gained the upper hand, was openly striving to seize power. As a result of this latter contest I was obliged to agree to a certain compromise in the sense of limiting the so-far autocratic civil powers of the commander-in-chief. By agreement with the 'supreme Cossack Krug' (Assembly), I formed a new 'Southern Government,' in which a certain number of Cossacks were included. These changes were not called for by any actual necessity. Still, in my opinion, no sacrifice in the way of a diminution of the ruler's powers should be spared if conducive to the moral recovery of the Cossack force and the annihilation of the Bolsheviks. Moreover, the agreement would cease to have any significance in the event of the loss of the Cossack territory.

It became apparent during the ensuing few weeks that the Supreme Krug had become the centre of manifold political intrigues and had no influence over the Cossack masses. The new Government also held no authority. The Supreme Krug knew how to demoralize the Cossacks but was powerless to make them fight.

Nor was there any improvement in foreign affairs. In

the beginning of January, Sir Halford Mackinder, M.P., an influential member of the British Parliament, after visiting Warsaw, arrived in the south on a Mission from the British Government. Sir H. Mackinder came to investigate the situation in South Russia and discuss ways and means for extending political and moral assistance. From Warsaw he brought Marshal Pilsudsky's consent 'to open the offensive on Moscow in spring,' the details of which were to be jointly worked out at a conference between him and me. This was in January, at a time when the south was passing through an acute crisis, and the promise of aid in *spring* sounded cruelly ironical.

Sir H. Mackinder made me a proposal that I should recognize the border state formations as a means to the removal of the main obstacle to establishing a wide anti-Bolshevist front. Although, for the past two years, events had flatly contradicted this fallacy, I did not object. A statement was drawn up by the Government, which I ratified, and which contained: (1) recognition of the independence of Poland, the Eastern frontiers to be determined on the ethnographical principle by treaty between the All-Russian and Polish Governments[1]; (2) recognition of the independent status of *de facto* border state Governments carrying on war against the Bolsheviks. The British Government, on the other hand, assumed certain liabilities, such as, for instance, the continuation of the assistance in kind to the south, while Bulgaria, Serbia, and others were to be responsible for man-power. Moreover, Sir H. Mackinder assured me on behalf of his Government that for the peace of mind of those on active service, their families would be evacuated abroad.

Events unrolled themselves independently of this belated though undoubtedly amicable intervention of the British Government. Fortunately, the illusory Mackinder agree-

[1] A point of view we held from the outset.

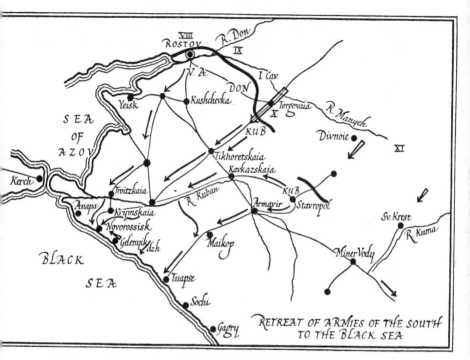

RETREAT OF ARMIES OF THE SOUTH TO THE BLACK SEA

ment brought one positive result: the pledge concerning the evacuation of families was honourably carried out by the British with the assistance of the other Allies. And although Prinkipo, Salonika, Cyprus, and other places[1] stand out as so many tragic stages in the history of the Russian refugees, nevertheless many thousands were saved by this timely aid – some from living as pariahs under the Soviet regime, and others from a cruel death at the hands of the Bolsheviks.

Such were the external conditions under which we carried on military operations.

The Volunteer Corps, under General Kutepov, took its stand on the route to Rostov; the Caucasian (Kuban

[1] The number of registered refugees, evacuated by the Allies, alone amount to over forty thousand.

Cossacks) Army, under General Pokrovsky, on the approaches to Tikhoretskaia, across the River Manytch; and the centre was occupied by the Don Cossack Army, commanded by General Sidorin. Facing them were the Eighth, Ninth, and Tenth Soviet Armies, while Budenny's First Cavalry Army, stationed between Rostov and Novocherkassk, acted as reserve.

The Bolshevist offensive opened on 18th January, but was everywhere repulsed all along the line. It was resumed again at the end of the month. A mass of Red cavalry, having crossed the Manytch, was already emerging on to the rear of our northern group. Six cavalry Don Cossack divisions, however, counter-attacked, and after several days' fighting (29th January–2nd February) defeated Budenny, captured many prisoners and almost the whole of the First Cavalry Army artillery. The Reds in panic fled beyond the Don and Manytch. Equally unsuccessful for the Bolsheviks were their repeated attacks on the Volunteers. The Kuban Cossacks were still holding out more or less on the middle Manytch, and only their right wing was retiring towards Stavropol.

It seemed as though all was not lost, since the 'routed' White Army was still capable of dealing such blows to the best Soviet Armies.

Our general offensive was timed for the middle of February, the main objective being the region of Novocherkassk. At this very moment the Soviet Command, despairing of the possibility of breaking our front from the north-east, altered their plan of operation and diverted their main attack (the First Cavalry and Tenth Armies) to a point between Velikokniazheskaia and Tikhoretskaia. This was all the more dangerous as the Kuban Cossacks, who were holding that particular section, were easily routed and inclined to retreat westward.

To avert this impending blow I dispatched a particularly

staunch cavalry group, twelve thousand strong, consisting mainly of Don Cossacks under the command of General Pavlov, with instructions to proceed up river along the Manytch and strike at Budenny's flank and rear. On 16th February, Pavlov routed Dumenko's Red cavalry corps on the Lower Manytch and pushed towards Torgovaia, already abandoned by the Kuban Cossacks.

This forced march was one of the causes which worked the ruin of the cavalry group. Pavlov decided to advance along the unpopulated left bank of the Manytch. This, from the point of view of secrecy, was correct, but other conditions were averse. The cold was intense, with severe blizzards in addition. The large body of men could not find shelter and warmth in the small hamlets scattered far distances apart. Utterly worn out, both physically and morally, having without fighting lost almost one-half of their contingent from frost-bite, sickness, and laggards, Pavlov's cavalry group, after a three days' march, reached Torgovaia. Unable to capture it, they halted in the district of Lezhanka.

Budenny and Pavlov stood facing each other at a distance of twelve kilometres – neither trusting their forces and afraid of tempting fortune in a decisive encounter.

Meantime we started our general offensive on the northern front.

The Volunteer corps, after defeating the Eighth Soviet Army, by a series of tempestuous attacks seized the towns of Rostov and Nakhichevan. Equally successful was the action of the left wing of the Don Cossack Army, which having crossed the Don, cut off communication between Rostov and Novocherkassk. Our troops captured many prisoners and guns, also enemy staffs including the staff of Voroshilov's Eighth Army.

These were the last bright gleams to pierce the general gloom of the military situation. The advance to the north could no longer be developed, because the enemy had already penetrated far into our rear at Tikhoretskaia. The Kuban Cossacks fled; Pavlov's cavalry group, after dallying for six days, attacked Budenny on 25th February, and after heavy fighting, retired north, abandoning most of its artillery.

The enemy were nearing Tikhoretskaia and Kavkazskaia.

From that time onwards our massed cavalry, sometimes doubly superior in numbers to the enemy, hovered round their flank but avoided an encounter. A prey to demoralization, it was finally merged in the common human avalanche of military detachments, unarmed crowds, and huge multitudes of refugees uncontrollably rolling westward.

Whither?

Strategically, the answer to the query was obvious: the armies must halt on the River Kuban, which presented a splendid natural line of defence. If, however, the Cossack spirit failed to revive once more, then two ways were open to us. One led to the wild Caucasian mountain range and hostile Transcaucasian newly formed republics. The other lay to the Crimea – the last strip of Russian land still in our hands. It was imperative to place some unsurmountable barrier between ourselves and the enemy, where we could sit 'tight' till this horrible torpor, the outcome of overwrought nerves, could be shaken off.

That, in the event of defeat, we were to retreat to the Crimea was known to the Volunteers, who looked upon the decision as natural and correct. The Cossack commanders were aware of it too, but were afraid of telling the men. Would they follow?

And so tens of thousands of armed men, led they knew not whither, tramped blindly and submissively on, with no breach of military discipline – merely refusing to fight.

Meanwhile, fostered by Kuban separatism and the

general disintegration of the Cossack fronts, there sub-
consciously arose and steadily grew a hostile alienation
between Volunteers and Cossacks.

*

The retreat continued. All plans and calculations were
shattered by the elemental factor. The psychology of
masses ruled over men and events.

The Don and Kuban Cossack contingents crossed the
Kuban on 16th and 17th February. Two days later they
were followed by the Volunteers after stubborn fighting
against a Red cavalry detachment reinforced by a unit
of mutinied Kuban Cossacks. The regiments hacked
their way through dense masses of horsemen. The
Drozdovsky regiment, for instance, under the command
of Colonel Turkul, in a march of many kilometres,
repeatedly formed into a square, and striking up the
band, counter-attacked and pushed forward, inflicting
heavy losses on the enemy.

The line of the Kuban River was lost.

The remnants of the Kuban Cossack force, utterly
demoralized, were in full retreat, pushing on towards
the sea across mountain paths to Tuapse. The Bolsheviks,
though numerically weak, easily forced the river at
Ekaterinodar, thus cutting the front of the Don Cossack
Army in two. One corps, separated from the rest, followed
the Kuban forces ; the other two, disorganized and
dishevelled, took the road to Novorossisk, while Novorossisk itself was being threatened from the south.

Since the end of January a committee, consisting mainly
of Social Revolutionaries, taking advantage of Georgian
hospitality, had organized on the coast an armed revolt
of peasants settled round Sotchi and deserters fleeing
from mobilization, known as the 'Zelenyi' (*i.e.* 'Greens,'
from hiding in the woods), who, led by Voronovitch, a

former captain of the Imperial Guard, fell upon our feeble and wavering advance post at Adler. Our detachment offered no resistance; some fled, others joined the 'Greens,' thereby involving the officers and artillerymen loyal to their colours in a tragic situation. The avalanche of rebels, deserters, and 'Greens' soon rolled up as far as Gelendzhik, where it was checked by newly arrived Volunteer units. Once there, these heterogeneous bands deposed the committee and Voronovitch, and styling themselves as 'the Black Sea Soviet Army,' became a continual menace to Novorossisk.

Concurrently with the armies' retreat to the Kuban, G.H.Q. had worked out a plan of action. A new base was being organized in the Crimea (at Theodosia), and supply bases equipped along the coast, including floating ones for the ports whither the forces also might retreat. Novorossisk was being hurriedly emptied of refugees – the sick and non-combatants – who were evacuated abroad.

Owing to conditions of shipping and their own morale, a simultaneous and well-planned evacuation of the troops via the port of Novorossisk alone was unthinkable. It was impossible to ship all the men, not to mention artillery, baggage, horses, and supplies which we should have had to abandon. Therefore, in order to save the army, I mapped out another route via the Taman peninsula to the narrow straits of Kertch, whither transports were being rushed. To gain time, instructions were issued confirming the order for the armies to hold the line of the Kuban River and cover the Taman peninsula.

Not one of the armies carried out the instruction. Within the Don Cossack Army all was chaos and confusion.

Numbers of Cossacks threw down their arms, or whole regiments deserted to the 'Greens.' The link between staffs and troops was severed. The train carrying the Don Cossack Army Commander, who had lost all control over his men, was running serious risk of being made prisoner and was slowly crawling towards the sea through a seething mass of humanity. The mistrust and hostility which by force of circumstances had arisen between the Volunteers and Cossacks now flared up with particular vehemence. The Volunteers were greatly perturbed by the Cossack avalanche which threatened to submerge the rear of the Volunteer corps and cut it off from Novorossisk. To establish any firm plan of action for the corps was psychologically difficult. The projected march to Taman across a restricted area in conjunction with the wavering Cossack mass had the appearance of a trap. The port of Novorossisk was an irresistible attraction, and to counteract it became impossible.

General Kutepov greatly weakened his left flank by concentrating all his attention on the approaches to Novorossisk. The Bolsheviks took advantage of this, and on 24th March, overthrowing the feeble unit which was covering the crossing at Varenikovskaia, crossed the River Kuban and pushed forward to Anapa.

The route to Taman was thus cut off.

That same day the Volunteer corps, two Don Cossack corps and a newly joined Kuban Cossack division, without instructions from their superiors and under slight pressure from the enemy, assembled in the vicinity of the station Krymskaia, from which the whole mass moved off to Novorossisk.

Catastrophe loomed ahead, inevitable and unavoidable.

*

Stunned by the shock of the defeat and unable clearly to discriminate between its complex causes, officers of all ranks were loudly denouncing the *chief culprit*. His name had long been branded thus. A man of a high sense of duty and moral character, whom certain public circles, and following their lead, those of the army, some out of practical considerations, others from ignorance, held responsible for the *errors of all*.

This man was General Romanovsky, the commander-in-chief's chief of staff, who had held this post under General Kornilov and subsequently under myself during the campaign in the south.

I have seldom mentioned his name in the course of my narrative. So great was our mutual intimacy and understanding of each other's every thought that I find it hard to separate his share from mine in our combined work which directed the life and action of the army.

General Romanovsky was an energetic and capable counsellor to the commander-in-chief, a straightforward executor of his plans, and a loyal friend. He was a friend to whom I confided those personal experiences which are not divulged to outsiders or at conferences. He paid me back in the same coin.

From the outset calumny had spun its dark web round his name. This calumny – always anonymous and absurd – had its source in circles of the extreme right, where an intrigue was being set afoot for bringing the army under their control by methods habitual alike to both the 'Left' and 'Right' Bolsheviks. These efforts were resisted by the command, which consequently incurred their hatred. One of the means towards attaining their object lay in tarnishing General Romanovsky's reputation in the eyes of the army and my own, in obtaining his dismissal and supplanting him by a man after their own taste. This they failed to do.

Now that the catastrophe was upon us, hatred and calumny broke out with particular fierceness against General Romanovsky. Persons favourably inclined to the general approached me urging that he should be temporarily relieved of his post until the agitation and anger subsided, as otherwise he might very likely be assassinated. The British representative, General Holman, also called with the request that I should persuade Romanovsky to board a British ship.

Romanovsky said to me:

'This I will not do. If matters have come to this pass, relieve me of my duties, Your Excellency. I will shoulder a rifle and join a regiment as a private. Let them then do their worst.'

We both decided that it behoved us to drink the bitter cup of evacuation to the dregs, and that after we reached the Crimea he would resign.

*

The attitude of the British was dualistic. While General Keyes, the British diplomatic representative, was occupied in inventing new forms of government for the south and kept in touch with the opposition, General Holman, the chief of the Military Mission, was heart and soul engrossed in the task of helping us. He personally supervised the activities of British technical units on the Donets front; urged with the greatest energy the necessity for increasing the delivery of supplies; assisted in organizing the Theodosia base; allowed the weight of British authority to bear in favour of the South Command in our disputes with the Cossack Government and made attempts to raise the morale of the Cossacks. He made our interests his own, took all our misfortunes closely to heart, and never losing hope, worked to the very last, presenting a striking contrast to many Russians, whose courage had completely evaporated.

A great tragedy had befallen the south. The position seemed hopeless and the end was at hand.

London's policy veered accordingly. General Holman still remained at his post, but rumour had already named his successor. It was decided in London to speed up 'the liquidation.' Evidently such a proposal was morally unacceptable to General Holman, for on one of the days immediately preceding the evacuation, not he, but General Bridge, called on me and conveyed the British Government's proposal that I should act as mediator *for the conclusion of an armistice with the Bolsheviks.*

My answer was: *never.*

And in August 1920 I was amazed to learn that a Note from Lord Curzon to Tchicherin had been published in *The Times.* After considerations concerning the futility of a further struggle, which 'constitutes a menace to the peace and prosperity of Russia,' there came the following passage:

'I have exerted my utmost influence with General Denikine to induce him to abandon the contest, and have promised him that if he did so, I would use my best efforts to make peace between his forces and yours and assure the safety of the rank and file of his followers and the population of the Crimea. General Denikine finally decided to act upon this advice and has left Russia, resigning his command to General Wrangel. . . .'

Besides extending moral support to the Bolsheviks by condemning the White Movement, the Note contained a weighty insult to myself. I immediately published in *The Times* the following denial:

'I am deeply indignant at this statement and affirm:

'(1) That Lord Curzon could have exerted no influence upon me, since I have never had any dealings with him.

'(2) That the only occasion on which, during my command of the army, the question of mediation arose, was at Novorossisk, when the British military representative judging the situation critical and evacuation to the Crimea impossible, offered his intervention in order to bring about an armistice with the Bolsheviks. I did not accept his offer, and transported the troops to the Crimea, where the struggle was immediately renewed.

'(3) That the Note of the British Government concerning peace negotiations with the Bolsheviks was handed, as is well known, not to me but to my successor, General Wrangel, and his negative answer was published at the time in the Press.

'(4) That my decision to leave the post of commander-in-chief was due to reasons wholly unconnected with the policy of Lord Curzon.'

CHAPTER 28

The Evacuation of Novorossisk – Concentration of the
Remnants of 'The Armed Forces of South Russia' in the
Crimea – The Transference of the Command to General
Wrangel – The Constantinople Tragedy

THE army was rolling back to Novorossisk too rapidly,
and the number of ships available in the bay was
insufficient.

The transports which evacuated the refugees were
detained in foreign ports by quarantine regulations and
were long in returning. The G.H.Q. were making every
effort to collect shipping, but were impeded at every
turn: both Constantinople and Sevastopol were slow to
bestir themselves on the plea of coal shortage, broken-
down engines and other insurmountable obstacles. Taking
advantage of the arrival in Novorossisk of the British
Commander-in-Chief in the East, General Milne, and of
Admiral Seymour, I begged them to assist in the evacuation with the British Fleet. I was met with absolute
sympathy and goodwill. Admiral Seymour declared that
for technical reasons he was unable to carry more than
five or six thousand people on board his ships. But as a
matter of fact this fine and kindly man transported that
number many times over.

Shipping, meanwhile, was coming into port. Hope
revived that within the next four to eight days we might
succeed in loading all the troops willing to continue the
struggle in the Crimea. The Volunteers, with a very few

exceptions were, of course, willing. But what of the Don Cossacks?

General Sidorin called on me on 25th March. He envisaged the state of the Don Cossack Army as absolutely hopeless: everything had gone to pieces, the men were deserting, no one wished to fight, and assuredly none would go to the Crimea. Sidorin was greatly concerned with the fate of the Cossack officers, and I promised him that all those who were able to reach Novorossisk would be put on board ship.

When, however, the Don Cossack avalanche rolled into port, matters took quite an unexpected turn for the officers' staff: the whole mass of Cossacks hurled themselves on to the ships – why, they were probably unable to realize themselves.

Novorossisk, overrun by troops and refugees far beyond its capacity, its streets one seething mass of humanity, was buzzing and swarming like an agitated hive. A fierce struggle was going on for places on board – a struggle for life. Many were the human tragedies enacted in the town during those terrible days. Many bestial instincts were brought to light at this moment of supreme danger, when the voice of conscience was stifled and man became the enemy of his fellow-man.

On 26th March General Kutepov, Commander of the Volunteer Corps, appointed Chief of the Defence of Novorossisk, reported that the morale and nervous strain of the troops were such that it was no longer possible for them to remain in the town, which must be abandoned during the night.

It was, however, imperative to gain another two or three days until the return of the transports which had carried troops to the Crimea. I proposed that General Sidorin should occupy the nearest approaches to Novorossisk with Don troops still available and hold out at least two days longer. Or that he should lead the troops along the coast route to Tuapse,[1] whither the returning shipping would be diverted. Sidorin either would or could not do so. Any organized evacuation of troops which refused to fight, led by officers refusing to obey, was becoming impossible. There remained but to trust to fate in the shape of the transports due to arrive at night and of British aid.

The loading of the troops went on all night. A section of Volunteers and several Don Cossack regiments who found no room on board, marched off along the coast in the direction of Gelendzhik.

*

Another sleepless night went by. Dawn broke. It was a fearsome sight. In the bay only a single destroyer remained, with myself and several members of my staff on board. In the outer bay the receding silhouettes of the transports could still be discerned, bearing the remnants of the Russian Army away to the last strip of Russian land. Crowds were assembled on the quay. People squatted on their belongings, warming themselves round improvised bonfires. They were those who had thrown down their arms, who despaired of everything. At times one could hear cries for help from persons imploring to be taken on board. An officer threw himself into the sea and swam alongside the destroyer. He was safely picked up. Suddenly we saw a column in perfect marching formation arriving on the pier. How to save them? The crowds would submerge the destroyer. We drew alongside.

'Only armed units allowed on board!'

We took on as many as we could and sailed out of the

[1] The road was blocked by a band of three to four thousand deserters only.

bay. Out in the open we came across a barge rocking on the choppy sea, towed out by some steamer and abandoned. She was literally packed to overflowing with refugees. We took her in tow and brought her alongside the flagship.

Admiral Seymour had nobly kept his word.

The outlines of Novorossisk were still clearly visible. A destroyer turned and sailed full speed back into the bay. A gun boomed, machine guns started barking: the destroyer which had gone to pick up the rear-guard was engaged in a skirmish with the advance guard of the Reds who were entering the town.

Then silence fell. The outlines of the coast, the Caucasian range, became shrouded in mist and receded into the distance – into the past.

A past full of suffering and humiliation.

*

The Armed Forces of the South, once so mighty, were no more.

At the first encounter with the bands of deserters, the units which had taken the road along the coast gave way, began to hold meetings, and dispersed. A small number of them were picked up by our ships, the rest took to the mountains or sold themselves to the Bolsheviks.

Contingents of the Kuban Army and of one Don Cossack corps, which, crossing the mountains, emerged on to the Black Sea coast, stationed themselves between Tuapse and Sotchi, a region with no food or fodder supply, where they endured great hardship. The hopes of the Kuban extremists of help from their friends, the 'Greens' and Georgians, were not realized. The Kuban 'Rada,' the Government, and Ataman Bukretov inclined to peace with the Soviets; the military commanders vehemently opposed it; the rank-and-file were completely bewildered. Finally, Ataman Bukretov, after surrendering the greater portion of his troops (fifteen thousand) to the Bolsheviks, himself disappeared; a smaller force (twelve thousand) succeeded in crossing over to the Crimea.

The troops and refugees from Northern Caucasia trekked to Vladikavkaz, then to Georgia, where they were interned in a camp at Poti. Krasnovodsk fell earlier still, in the middle of February, and the evacuation of the Trans-Caspian region was accomplished under exceptionally tragic conditions.

The Astrakhan contingent and the Caspian flotilla retreated along the Caspian to Baku. To avoid being seized by Azerbeijan the flotilla sailed to Enzeli and placed itself under British protection. When subsequently the Bolsheviks landed at Enzeli and the British contingent withdrew into Persia, the Russian crews followed suit.

The state structure of the south had collapsed, and its fragments were tossed between the Caspian and the Black Sea, drawing countless human lives within the vortex. Gone was the bulwark which had shielded from the north the ephemeral new 'states.' These had incessantly sapped the strength of the south, and now that it had collapsed, their own flimsiness and still-born qualities were revealed to the full. The 'Black Sea Republic' of the 'Greens' fell within a few days; the 'Union of Mountaineer Peoples' did not live more than a week, and Azerbeijan soon ceased to exist. The Georgian Republic was the next on the list, but owing to considerations of a general policy its existence as a separate entity was tolerated by the Soviet Government for a while longer.

*

Within the restricted area of the Crimean peninsula was concentrated all that remained of the Armed Forces of South Russia.

After reorganization the army was formed into three corps, one cavalry division and one Caucasian brigade, a total of thirty-five to forty thousand men, one hundred guns, and five hundred machine guns. But it had suffered a severe moral shock, and the troops arriving from Novorossisk had neither horses, baggage, nor artillery.

The Crimean corps under the command of General Slastchev, a man with little self-control, absolutely unmoral but of great courage (he later went over to the Bolsheviks), was still firmly entrenched on the isthmuses and barred the entrance to the Crimea. The Bolshevist forces opposing us were small – only about five or six thousand. The rest were engaged against Makhno and other rebels. The Soviet Command were certain that the White Armies at Novorossisk, with their backs to the sea, were done for, and that the transference of large forces to the Crimea was impossible. The Crimea, therefore, did not receive much attention – an omission for which the Soviet Government later paid a heavy price.

Comparative calm and a period of assured rest soon had a beneficent effect on the troops. From the outset work was started to reorganize, reinforce, and equip the troops, and reorganize and simplify the civil administration.

Preparations were set afoot for the *continuation of the war against the Bolsheviks.*

*

General Holman, our army's staunch and ever-loyal friend, resigned from his post. In his farewell address he said: 'It is with the greatest regret that I am leaving Russia. Do not think that I am forsaking a friend in need. I hope I shall be able to be of some use to you in England. I am leaving with a feeling of profound respect and sincere friendship towards your commander-in-chief and with a strengthened resolve to remain loyal to that band of brave and honest men who, during two hard years, carried on a hard fight for their native country.'[1]

I also parted with my faithful friend, General Romanovsky. In the order relieving him of his post as chief of staff I wrote: 'Unbiassed history will render justice to the loyal service of this brave soldier, a champion of duty and honour, a soldier and citizen of boundless love for his mother country. History will brand with contempt all those who out of selfish motives spun the web of base calumny round his unsullied and honest name.'

One by one the threads that bound one to the past were snapped, and all around seemed empty.

*

The Crimea meantime was seething with political passions. A number of politicians and senior generals of the opposition were conducting active propaganda and conspiring against the commander-in-chief. Treason was all around. The environment in which I was obliged to work during those last months was most trying.

These as well as other circumstances of our inner life of which I gave a detailed account in my Russian book, prompted me to the irrevocable decision to resign from my post.

On 1st April I issued an order summoning all the senior commanders to Sevastopol on 3rd April to attend a Council of War under the chairmanship of General Dragomirov – 'for the election of a successor to the Commander-in-Chief of the Armed Forces of South Russia.'

I included among the members of the Council several men who, though not on active service, I knew claimed to be candidates for the post, and also the most active members of the opposition.

The next two days were spent in conversations with persons devoted to me, who tried to prevent my resigna-

[1] From the Russian version.

tion. Their entreaties were torture but could not make me alter my decision.

The deliberations of the Council of War in Sevastopol were extremely stormy. In the morning of 4th April I received a telegram from General Dragomirov informing me that 'The Council deemed it impossible to decide the question of a successor to the Commander-in-Chief, as this would create a precedent for elected commanders in the future. . . .' Simultaneously General Dragomirov wrote : '. . . Notwithstanding my categorical statements that your decision to resign is unalterable, all the army appeals to you to retain the Supreme Command, for you are the only person they trust, and fear the army's disruption in the event of your departure.'

I considered it impossible to alter my decision and unconditionally confirmed my order to General Dragomirov.

His reply arrived on the same day, announcing that the senior officers had elected General Wrangel as my successor, but requesting that this appointment should be made as if direct from me.

I therefore published an order appointing General Baron Wrangel Commander-in-Chief of the Armed Forces of South Russia.

*

Then followed the melancholy parting with my intimate fellow-workers, and with the officers, all of them disabled veteran Volunteers who had fought since the earliest days of the campaign. Together with Generals Holman and Romanovsky we arrived on the pier. . . . There a guard of honour was lined up, as were also the representatives of foreign missions come to see us off. I boarded a British destroyer. Our aides-de-camp went on board a French one, which arrived off Constantinople six hours later – a chance delay which had fatal consequences.

Night had already come on when we put out to sea. Only the bright specks of light on the horizon indicated the shores of the Russian land we were leaving. Soon they too became dim and disappeared.

Russia, my motherland ! Country of mine. . . .

*

We were met on the pier at Constantinople by General Agapeiev, the Russian Military Attaché, and a British officer. The Englishman, obviously perturbed, said something to General Holman. The latter turned to me, saying:

'Your Excellency, let us go straight on board a British warship.'

The British seemed to be suspicious of something. Were our people aware of it? I turned to General Agapeiev. He replied that all was well. Taking leave of General Holman, we proceeded to the Russian Embassy, partly converted into a hostel for refugees. There I found my family. As no motor-cars were in readiness, Romanovsky went out to see about one. A moment later an excited officer rushed into my room:

'Your Excellency, General Romanovsky has been assassinated!'

The assassin, wearing the uniform of a Russian officer, had disappeared.

*

A small room. Within it a coffin containing the remains of my dear friend. The face is calm and sad. 'Unto him be Eternal Memory.' . . .

*

That evening my family and I went on board a British hospital ship and next day were transferred to the dreadnought *Marlborough*.

We were abandoning the shores of the Bosphorus. In our hearts we carried away abiding sorrow.

CHAPTER 29

Epilogue

THE Crimea, that last strip of Russian land not submerged by Bolshevism, still held out.

On 2nd April, when General Wrangel was leaving Constantinople for the Crimea he was handed a Note, in the form of ultimatum, from the British Government, proposing that he should 'abandon the unequal struggle,' and offering mediation for negotiations with the Soviet Government. The British, moreover, promised to obtain 'an amnesty' for the troops and Crimean civil population and to accord refuge outside Russia to the commander-in-chief and his senior collaborators. In the event of refusal, the British Government 'declined all responsibility' for the consequences and threatened to withdraw all further assistance.

To say nothing of the moral impossibility of such an issue to men who were fighting both on principle and by force of arms against the destroyers of their native country, Mr. Lloyd George's and Lord Curzon's idea of 'reconcilement and amnesty' was absolutely without any practical foundation. These gentlemen probably ignored what was well known to Russians – that the dishonest and deceitful Soviet Government would not scruple to violate their own pledges, and that as a sequel to the polished and correctly worded diplomatic protocols torrents of innocent blood would be shed.

The Russian Command, after commenting bitterly on

these proposals, refused to participate in negotiations with the Bolsheviks, leaving them entirely to the British Government, and expressed the hope that the British would take steps to evacuate *all* those 'who would prefer exile to surrender to the mercy of the enemy.'

Two circumstances meantime played an important part in further developments. On the one hand, the successful Polish offensive towards the Dnieper and Western Dvina had drawn off all the available Bolshevist forces in that direction. On the other hand, famine set in in the Crimea, which lacked sufficient food supplies for the army and enormously increased population. These two factors prompted General Wrangel to open an offensive with the object of taking possession of the fertile territory lying between the Dnieper and the Sea of Azov.

This episode produced a final rupture with England, the recall of the Military Mission and a new Note from the British High Commissioner, Admiral de Roebeck, who informed General Wrangel of the order received from London to intercept all war supplies intended for the Crimea and carried under the British flag. Although, owing to the insistence of White Russian diplomacy, this order was soon repealed, nevertheless several deplorable incidents did take place, such as, for instance, the scrapping by the British Mission of war planes purchased in Bulgaria for the White Army.

The French Government, on the other hand, being mainly concerned with Poland, eyed the projected White offensive favourably, and the Ministry for War stated officially that 'until General Wrangel receives adequate guarantees for the safety of his troops, the French Government will do their utmost to provide him with supplies and war material for defence against attacks by the Bolsheviks.' Although the French Government subsequently did recognize General Wrangel's Government *de facto*, French assistance was in a great measure moral rather than material.

*

The total strength of the Crimean White Army amounted approximately to forty thousand fighting men, of whom twenty-five thousand were properly armed. The exits from the Crimean isthmuses were defended by the Thirteenth Red Army, which in May was thirteen thousand strong.

The offensive of the White Armies was launched in the beginning of June simultaneously from the front and by striking in the rear of the Bolshevist positions with a corps landed previously at Genichesk. The Bolsheviks were defeated in a series of encounters. The Soviet Command strained every nerve to strengthen their southern front by weakening that of the Polish, diverting to the Crimea Caucasian divisions which were being transported to the west and rushing their last reserves to the south. By this means the Thirteenth Army was brought up to forty-one thousand men.

The destinies of the White Movement, Soviet Russia and Poland were interwoven in a fantastic design both with one another and with French politics. The wheel of fortune had turned. Poland – erstwhile victorious – now suffered disaster. Her army had abandoned Kiev, and hard pressed by the Bolsheviks was retreating westward. The White Army came to Poland's rescue at the price of its blood, only to perish in the end.

At the end of June the Thirteenth Soviet Army, reorganized and brought up to strength, with a cavalry army under Zhloba, started a counter-offensive against Melitopol, directing its main blow from the north-east in order to cut off the White Army from the Crimea.

The projected Bolshevist operation ended in complete failure. The cavalry army, routed and dispersed, not only lost all its equipment and baggage, but very few of its contingents escaped. The territory between the Dnieper and the Sea of Azov was cleared of the Bolsheviks.

Buoyed up by these successes and entertaining the illusory hope of creating an united political and combative front with the Poles with the aid and under control of the French Command, General Wrangel adopted the plan of a simultaneous offensive to north and east: one to the line of Ekaterinoslav-Rostov with the object of raising a revolt in the Don Cossack territory, whither a special partisan detachment had been sent; and the other by transferring a landing party to the Taman peninsula with a subsequent march into the Kuban region.

The disproportion between the scale of the plan and the actual strength of the army to carry it out, the scattering of forces and the passivity of the Cossacks still not recovered from shock, led to the failure of the operation. The partisan unit dispatched to the Don Cossack territory met with no support and the majority of them perished. The group under General Ulagai, which crossed to the Kuban region, sustained defeat and with difficulty crossed back to the Crimea. It suffered heavy losses but was joined, it is true, by a certain number of Kuban Cossacks. The main offensive to the north, commenced at the end of July and ended in the beginning of September, was at first successful. It encountered the stubborn resistance of considerably superior enemy forces and entailed severe bloodshed, particularly in the combats for the crossings of the Dnieper. The White regiments again exhibited great gallantry, seized many trophies, and advanced as far as Alexandrovsk, Sinelnikovo and Mariupol, but the crossings were retained by the Bolsheviks, who were thus able constantly to threaten the rear of the White Army and more particularly Perekop.

The fortunes of war had meantime veered again. At

the end of August, thanks to the diversion of the Bolshevist forces to the Crimean front and to French aid, the Poles routed the Bolsheviks. The Red Armies fled in panic. Rumours were already current of a peace soon to be concluded between the Poles and Bolsheviks, which would place the Crimea in a tragic state of isolation.

No sooner were the outlines of a possible peace with the Poles discerned by the Bolsheviks, than they commenced to transfer large forces from west to south. By the middle of September they had an army of fifty-eight thousand against thirty-three thousand Whites, the Red forces daily growing in number.

Notwithstanding these circumstances and the obvious avoidance by the Poles of any close co-operation with the White Army, General Wrangel persisted in advancing into the Ukraine to join the Polish and Petliura's forces. In the middle of September he started a fresh operation for the capture of the lower reaches of the Dnieper from Alexandrovsk (Kichkass) to the estuary, with the object of crossing to the right bank of the river. These sanguinary but fruitless battles for the crossings broke the army's power of resistance and undermined its morale.

On 9th October the news of an armistice between the Polish and Soviet Commands reached the Crimea. Henceforth all the Bolshevist forces were to be launched against it. By the end of October they amounted to one hundred and thirty-three thousand against thirty-seven thousand of the Whites!

A council of war was held at General Wrangel's headquarters on 14th October, at which the question was put: To accept a battle on the northern position, or to retire beyond the isthmuses? The first alternative carried the day. The decisive offensive of the Reds began on the 25th, and the White Armies, crushed by an enemy numerically four times their superior, were overthrown and severely depleted by casualties. At times completely surrounded they fought their way back into the Crimea.

Political isolation and moral shock excluded any further hopes of success. Forsaken by all, confronted by the advancing masses of the enemy, the troops rushed blindly towards the ports. The amazing slowness of the Bolshevist Armies, which instead of a continuous pursuit halted for a day's rest, alleviated the last act in the White Army's tragedy.

Scores of ships bore the Russian forces, their families, and refugees from their motherland away into exile. The future for the White warriors held the Golgotha of Gallipoli, the migration to the Balkans, then – dispersion.

*

The armed struggle was over. The later anti-Bolshevist rebellions, that of Savinkov and Bulak-Balakhovitch in White Russia, Merkulov, and General Dieterichs in the Far East, and the Kronstadt revolt, however serious the two latter, were all mere episodes.

The tragic collapse of all the White fronts, accompanied by countless individual dramas, was followed at various periods by an *exodus*, sometimes organized, elsewhere by inert force, which eventually led to the settlement of the main bulk of military contingents. Some settled in the zone of the Chinese Eastern railway and China; others in the Balkans; others again in the Baltic States and Germany.

Owing to economic and various other causes members of these contingents, some individually, some in organized bodies gradually dispersed to other countries all over the world or created new centres of conglomeration, particularly in Czecho-Slovakia and France.

With the loss of the last strip of Russian territory, disarmament and dispersion, the real substance of the army seemed lost, the appellation itself becoming, as it were, an anachronism. But there exist ideals that cannot die. Ten years after the evacuation the *force* still exists – maybe potentially – as a widespread organization of men bound together by the comradeship of war, the innumerable threads of the past and a common ideal, which led them to battle and has not forsaken them even now.

The ideal of Russia's Liberation.

Their swords have been turned into ploughs and lathes, and the exploits of war have given place to those of toil.

Only a small minority of the Russian *emigrés* succeeded in finding intellectual work or lighter jobs. The greater part work at the plough, the pick-axe, or the lathe. All are united in a common brotherhood of poverty and toil – old and young, the general who once commanded an army, the officer, private, and Cossack. They work sometimes alone, only seeing one another on days of general meetings, or in groups, sometimes in whole army units. They are building roads in the wilds of the Balkans, digging coal at Pernik (Bulgaria), in the mines in France and in Belgium; cultivating coffee in South America, carrying loads in the Paris goods stations; working in factories in all the industrial centres of the world, tilling the fields in France, Canada, Australia, and New Zealand.

There is not a corner in God's earth whither destiny has not cast some Russian refugee, and whither he has not brought his toil, his Russian tongue, Russian song, holy prayer, and – his profound longing for his lost home.

The younger ones are still studying and waging a bitter war against hunger and poverty, those inseparable companions of their youth, earning their daily bread by giving lessons for a pittance, or wielding a cobbler's hammer or a spade on an undergound railway, working *at night* to be able to study *by day*.

And should destiny never allow them sword in hand

to serve their country's liberation, in any case when Russia's doors reopen to them, they will return to her as capable workers in all branches of toil, erudition, science, and art. They will return as men tempered by dangers, hardships, and the struggle for life, who amid untold and exceptional duress kept alive their spirit, energy, and patriotism.

Reader, if ever you come across a Russian White warrior with toil-worn hands and wearing shabby clothes, but with the open gaze of a man who has the right to look you straight in the eyes, remember that in shedding his blood for his own country, he was also saving your *home* from the Red Terror.

Denikin, Anton Ivanovich, 1872 - 1947
    The white army, by General A. Denikine; translated from the
Russian by Catherine Zvegintzov. [Gulf Breeze, Florida]
Academic International Press, 1973

    367 p. illus. (maps.) 23 cm. (The Russian series, vol. 45)
    Reprint of the 1930 ed.

    1. Russia-Hist. —Revolution, 1917 - 1921. 2. Russia (1917 —
R. S. F. S. R.) Armiia. I. Zvegintsova, Ekaterina, tr. II. Title.

DK265.D42 1973   947.084
ISBN: 0-87569-052-1   72-97041